Praise for Her N

It's rare to find a book t
an open heart, but Her I.
has gathered in this volume exquisite stories of how Sikh American women live their spiritual journeys, their loves, their losses, and their triumphs. This is both an important contribution to women's studies and a moving testimony to the power of religious community.

—**Daisy Hernández**, author of
Colonize This! Young Women of Color on Today's Feminism

Groundbreaking. I read *Her Name Is Kaur* in one sitting, heart quickening at each page, tears streaming at one point, as if quenching a centuries-long thirst. The courage coursing through each story is unmistakable—and reveals what it means to be a Kaur: with love as her moral compass, she becomes the one she is waiting for.

—**Valarie Kaur**, National Interfaith Leader and Founder of Groundswell

Written with honesty and courage. *Her Name Is Kaur* is a tapestry of love, friendship, commitment, and acceptance. Meeta Kaur's book is a selection of intriguing, eloquently crafted, and heartfelt personal narratives of Sikh women who share their stories of sacrifices, expectations, and challenges and deal with the complexity of relationships from dating, marriage, and finding true love to exploring one's sexuality to discovering what it means to be a KAUR. A beautiful journey of the human spirit, self-realization, and ultimately . . . having faith."

—**Harpreet Kaur**, filmmaker, Sach Productions

It has been an honor to read the stories of the women in *Her Name Is Kaur*. So sweet and humbling is this process of unshrouding one's self and finding a sort of liberation in a community of human imperfections, shared re-membering, gendered reclamation, and revealing vulnerabilities. The stories are filling a space in my heart that I did not yet know was open to be claimed, bringing deeper meaning to Sikh sisterhood. This collection is a game-changer.

—**Kirpa Kaur**, Director, SAFAR and independent scholar

Her Name Is Kaur is a delightful collection of narratives of second-generation Sikh women living in America. These narratives provide us with a rare window into the lived experiences of different Sikh American who are constantly striving to maintain their Sikh identity in the face of new challenges. My heartiest congratulations go to Meeta Kaur, the editor of this remarkable book, for giving us much hope and inspiration.

—**Pashaura Singh**, professor, Dr. Jasbir Singh Saini Endowed Chair in Sikh and Punjabi Studies, University of California at Riverside

Her Name Is Kaur is a very important volume that uses the power of storytelling to amplify the voices of Kaurs, and to inspire the rest of us to gain strength from their narratives. Their stories teach us that falling in and out of love—with place, with men, with children, with God, with women, and with themselves—is a struggle on the precipice of time and eternality. Highly enjoyable for the casual reader, this book is also an indispensable resource for university classes in women's studies, religion, and immigration studies.

—**Rahuldeep Singh**, Assistant Professor of Religion, Director of the Center for Equality and Justice, Cal Lutheran University

Her Name Is Kaur pushes past the boundaries of romance to illuminate the love at the very heart of faith. In this groundbreaking book, Meeta Kaur has gathered a diverse and fresh group of stories of growing up Sikh and redneck, Sikh and queer, Sikh and daydreaming, Sikh and heartbroken, Sikh and deeply beloved. Whether discussing the everyday (mother-in-law conflicts) or the taboo (mental illness), these women writers share colorful, intense, and engaging adventures that range from Los Altos to Toronto to Chandigarh. This collection deserves a place on the shelf of everyone interested in South Asian cultures, women of America, and just good storytelling.

—**Minal Hajratwala**, author of *Leaving India: My Family's Journey from Five Villages to Five Continents*

Her Name
Is Kaur

Her Name Is Kaur

Sikh American Women Write about Love, Courage, and Faith

Edited by Meeta Kaur

Foreword by Nikky-Guninder Kaur Singh

SHE WRITES PRESS

Published 2014
Printed in the United States of America
ISBN: 978-1-938314-70-4
Library of Congress Control Number: 2014938616

For information, address:
She Writes Press
1563 Solano Ave #546
Berkeley, CA 94707

This book is dedicated to my mother, father, and brother, who taught me to never give up on love, that the struggle for love is worth everything, and to value the priceless nature of Waheguru's love through compassion, courage, and commitment.

This book is also dedicated to Banjot, Benanti, and Sidak, who show me what love is every day.

And finally to all of the Kaurs and Singhs worldwide. May our presence bring love, peace, and compassion to the world.

rang tamasa pooran aasaan kabhi na bi-aapai chintaa.

May love be yours and your hopes fulfilled. May you never be worn by worry.

—Guru Arjan Dev Ji, the fifth Sikh Guru

CONTENTS

Part 3: Sehaj – Graceful Acceptance

Part 4: Sanjog – Written in the Stars

Part 5: Dharam – Our Sacred Work in the World

Introduction

Growing up, I watched my mother, *nani*, and *maasis* gather around our kitchen table like five-star generals preparing for battle. Dressed in eyelet *salwaar kameezes* with their brown-black hair pinned up in buns, they organized family celebrations, *kirtans*, and critical family meetings to determine the future of each child. Each woman exuded self-confidence in her own abilities, seldom questioning her decisions. And when one did, she asked the others and they generously shared their wisdom, forming a strong alliance. They often concluded that the extra *baturas* (fried bread) made for a *kirtan*, the additional money saved and then spent on graduate school for each child, or the extra *Sukhmani Sahib* prayer conducted for my *Mamaji* (maternal uncle) dying of cancer was all worth it. "A little more . . ." they'd say, despite the aching backs and throbbing knees. "We are almost done," was always the way with these women. They filled the kitchen, family room, and bedrooms with loud and passionate planning debates in Punjabi while punctuating the smallest of details in Catholic School English. Our home, like so many others in the Sikh American community, became a busy command central for the important events that bound us together and united us as a family and community. I remember my father, uncles, and brothers standing ready and willing to execute whatever the vision was. I also

1

honor the moments in my home and so many other homes when my mother, nani, and maasis stood steadfast to be understood and treated as respected equals, their God-given right as Sikh women.

With the bar set so high, I was curious to see if I could meet these expectations as an adult. I was also eager to know what gave these women the grace and resolve to stand centered in their autonomy with such assurance and faith. Throughout their struggles and triumphs as immigrants, as professionals breaking new ground in US institutions, and as mothers and wives bridging the social and cultural gaps between Sikhism and America, they have repeatedly demonstrated how Sikh women are primary stakeholders in family, community, professional life.

They are *Kaurs*: Sikh women, daughters of the Sikh Gurus, unfettered by limitations of gender, class, or patriarchy. I believe they derive inspiration from the unconditional love and faith the Sikh Gurus demonstrated throughout Sikh history, and these Kaurs set out to achieve a similar type of love and faith in today's world.

As a young reader, I searched in vain for the Kaur voices I grew up with. I found solace in other women's voices; South Asian, African American, Latina, and American Enlightenment writers resonated with me, but I still yearned to find the voices that shaped me. When I didn't find them, I asked American Kaurs across generations to tell their truest stories of love as Sikh American women living in the United States. This is how *Her Name Is Kaur* came to be.

The beauty of these stories is that they not only tell, they ask: What does it mean to be a Sikh American woman in today's world? The voices are distinct and the experiences on the Sikh spiritual path are varied, but three tenets bind us together: hard work, honesty, and love. In the pages of this collection, we explore what it takes to love fully while also making mistakes, learning how to love ourselves while also loving those around us, and staying resolved to love the world no matter what. These Sikh love stories are expressed through personal journeys, relationships, family, work, and our faith in *Waheguru*. These writers have brilliantly unpacked the traditional "love story" and re-engineered it into Sikh stories of love that reflect back our humanity and the power of our faith.

Introduction

Today, as a community, Sikh women are experiencing a renaissance—a re-envisioning, renewal, and rebirth. There is a growing desire to honor and write about the experiences of Sikh women in the home, community, and in public life. But it takes tremendous courage to write a personal narrative, especially a narrative that depicts a character's transformation from vulnerable to determined—from crying in a corner to gathering herself up to exhibit the internal strength of Sikh heroines like Mai Bhago or Mata Gujri, or in today's world, Malala Yousafzai. This collection does not represent all of the stories Sikh American women are creating in their day-to-day lives, but it is a very strong start towards deeper conversations. I have found that the space to write and share these stories has sparked a deeper trust and respect amongst Sikh American women, and I hope it continues. I believe these stories move us beyond the limitations the world places on Sikh women and all women and ushers us into a place where we understand ourselves as whole, honored, and free to pursue our highest potential as spiritual beings. Please join me in celebrating these Sikh American writers as they celebrate their identities, stories, and capacity for love as Sikh American women. We have the opportunity to share and celebrate the sisterhood that quietly perseveres in so many Sikh homes and take that step toward a larger sisterhood within our community and across spiritual and cultural communities in the world.

There are five sections to this book as there are five rivers in Punjab and five *kakkars* (articles of faith) we live by as Kaurs.

Anakh – Living with Dignity. Kaurs explore the critical development of self-love and dignity.

Himmat – The Courage to Live as a Kaur. Kaurs illustrate the integrity it takes to live fully as Sikh American women devoted to themselves and their faith.

Sehaj – Graceful Acceptance. Kaurs depict the struggles and losses that move us to surrender to Waheguru (God).

Sanjog – Written in the Stars. Kaurs embrace the opportunities that life presents them in their search for true partnership and love.

Dharam – Our Sacred Work in the World. Kaurs exhibit compassionate leadership, working to preserve civil and human rights.

As you read the stories, please use the appendices and glossary to learn more about Sikh culture through the Gurmukhi terms in italics.

Her Name Is Kaur: Sikh American Women Write About Love, Courage, and Faith is a project established by The Sikh Love Stories Project, a larger creative collective.

Foreword:
Beanta

Her Name Is Kaur: Sikh American Women Write about Love, Courage, and Faith is a kaleidoscopic anthology of twenty-five narratives. Written in the lyrical modality of the "I" by Sikh American women, they erupt the mute silence idealized as the "jewel" of women in conventional Indic society. Their stylistic immediacy pulls readers into their multicultural twenty-first-century reality. Although Sikhs have been a major presence in North America for over a century, very little is known about them, and much less so about Sikh women. For the general public this volume illuminates a vibrant segment of the American population and strengthens the "patchwork heritage" evoked by President Obama during his historic inaugural address. Importantly, in a religiously diverse country, these heartfelt narratives intimately familiarize the "foreign." Individual snapshots shatter simplistic stereotypes. They help us understand the complexities and intricacies that shape Sikh American women. This anthology is indeed a timely and significant contribution towards overcoming the corroding xenophobic "fear of ourselves" so accurately diagnosed by Professor Diana Eck (*A New Religious America*, Harper Collins, 2001).

For the Sikhs this work offers a rich reservoir of self-affirmation. They can identify with the joys, anxieties, pain, desires, and

5

dilemmas voiced here by sisters, daughters, friends, lovers, mothers, wives, and daughters-in-law. They can draw upon a wide range of experiences—that of students, scientists, anthropologists, computer-scientists, teachers, lawyers, physicians, writers, filmmakers, social activists, human rights activists . . . Interestingly, the volume includes not only women born in a Sikh household, but also former Hindu and Baptist women who have adopted Sikhism. Nevertheless, Sikh ideals, values, spaces, and identity are woven into each of their textures. The varied authors share the greeting *Sat Sri Akal* and the ubiquitous *Waheguru*; they share the daily routine of the morning *JapJi* and the evening *Rahiras*; they share the ceremonies of *Anand Karaj* (wedding) and *Antim Ardas* (at cremation); they share the feeling of exaltation in Babaji's room (enshrines Sikh sacred scripture) and the mesmerizing beauty of the Harmandar Sahib; they share the heartbreak at the 1984 violence back in India and the tragic 2012 shooting at the Gurudwara Sahib in Milwaukee. How often do we encounter these in mainstream literature? Even an innovative South Asian-American volume on women and gender leaves out the Sikh experience (*Living Our Religions: Hindu and Muslim South Asian-American Women Narrate Their Experiences* (Virginia: Kumarian Press, 2009)). *Her Name Is Kaur* affirms a Sikh person's sense of being and becoming. A reader's habits, lifestyle, sacred spaces, treasured scriptural verses, cultural tensions, vulnerabilities, strengths, inter-generational conflicts, clash between tradition and modernity, pressures of home and work . . . are right on the page! Such recognition raises one's consciousness; it gives self-authenticity. Any tight constricting loneliness opens to a wide inter-subjective feeling. In her introduction editor Meeta Kaur celebrates the deep trust that developed amongst the authors during the writing process. That profound collective togetherness embraces their readers as well. The volume splendidly succeeds in creating a vital communal building block, a *sangat* men and women can meaningfully participate in. For sure, the male protagonists in the lives of the narrators, the male supporters of this project, and all the male readers are equal and essential participants!

These are also inspirational autobiographical portraits. Strongly grounded in their faith and history, the authors *"write the self to write the world."* With the name "Kaur" they assert their agency, for "Kaur" is an expression of radical change in the patrilineal structure. Traced to Guru Gobind Singh, "Kaur" eliminated the family name, caste, and profession that had come down from the father *and his father* through the centuries. As "Kaur", women do not adopt the name of the father at birth nor that of the husband at marriage. Each narrative in *Her Name Is Kaur* reverberates with an ineffable inner power. In their own and different ways the authors remind us of the Sikh Gurus' repudiation of caste-ism, classism, sexism, and bigotry. The Kaur-s here courageously ask: Why dowry? Domestic violence? Privileging of sons? Marriage to be the defining point in a girl's life? Why can't my Sikh sisters and I do *seva* in the inner sanctum of the Harmandar Sahib? Why can't I marry a fellow Sikh from another caste? Why can't I marry a person from another religion? Why can't I be in a same-sex relationship? What do age-old androcentric norms have to do with my Sikh religion? Full of faith they state, "Sikhi does not teach hate or discrimination, but people do." The Sikh Gurus were phenomenally liberal for their day and age. Their aspiration for equality, inclusivity, and gender justice is poignantly concretized in these personalized pleas. While reading *Her Name Is Kaur*, such images of the Gurus spontaneously flash on our mental screen: a non-homophobic Guru Nanak is sitting comfortably as he discusses divine love with a cross-dressed Sufi Sheikh Sharf (*b-40 Janamsakhi* painting #50), Guru Gobind Singh is offering the ambrosial *amrit* to his Five Beloved so they sip from the same bowl and spew out hegemonies of caste and class, the founder Guru is surrounded by men and women reciting ambrosial hymns together by the banks of the river Ravi in Kartarpur . . . The narratives incite us to carry on the liberating momentum generated by the visionary Sikh Gurus and actualize the enormous potential of their teaching.

Our diasporic writers embody the humanity and the inclusivity central to the Sikh religion. They do not view the host country as the *other*. Completely at home in the West, they do their best to subvert oppression in its various guises and make this world a better place for all of us. What is written in one narrative—"Sikhi teaches us to find the light of Waheguru within everyone"—replays throughout this text. A Sikh physician sees her beloved son in every child she takes care of at her hospital in the USA. Another physician and a human rights activist upon returning to a post-1984 Punjab, "felt a granular connection to each and every Punjabi," including *darjis, cha-valas, rickshaw-vallahs,* and *dhobis.* A doctor mother in her aching pain for her lost twins bonds with all the mothers who lost their children in the 1984 genocide in Amritsar and Delhi. For a youngster who grew up in the deep American South, perfect strangers soon become family and friends. The Kaur who practices Sikhism as "the art of battle" challenges norms "by embodying knowledge of those nothing like me." Breaking constricting egoistic boundaries these Kaur-s confidently walk out on the world stage. Their boundless passion and compassion for fellow humans establishes strong inter and intra religious bonds.

And so they open up for us significant new ways of recognizing the past and of being in the present. The Kaur at Guru Gobind Singh's birthplace in Patna writes, "It dawned on me that he was an immigrant like me." Her identification with the Tenth Guru enlivens Sikh collective history and generates important insights into his personality. The first author in this volume sees her Sikh past through the lens of Margaret Mitchell's epic novel *Gone with the Wind.* The concluding author, a filmmaker, hears rhythmic echoes of Guru Nanak in thinkers as distant as Bullhe Shah and Joseph Campbell. With these writers we not only animate our past but also design new arabesques for mutual understanding. With them we get to enjoy our global reality while sipping the typical Punjabi drink of Rooh Afza mingled with the waters of the Savannah River.

Of course the singular force energizing these remarkable bridge-builders and agents of transformation is the Guru Granth Sahib. Love is the leitmotif of Sikh scripture and so it is of this volume: *"love is our most powerful, lasting form of activism."* As they aspire to subvert oppression from their own unique perspectives, the twenty-five writers empower themselves with the sublime verse. In fact the unique way in which the respective authors understand, interpret, and apply the hymns of divine love in their everyday complex transnational lives, exposes us to a rich hermeneutics of the sacred text. Their organic integration disrupts our habitual patterns of perception and creates exciting possibilities to imagine, know, and relate with one another and with the Divine.

The epigraph of this book is itself a verse from Guru Arjan in the measure Gujari (GGS, p. 496). The hymn expresses a mother's desire for her child to enjoy worldly colors and entertainment while immersed in divine love. The material of the clothes adorning our body must be transcendent honor; the ingredient of the food we eat must be constant divine praise. So with love for the singular One within and around us we exist enjoying infinite delights (*anad ananta*)--ripples of love and joy extending to our fellow beings (*sat sang teri preet*). My mother, who is no more, recited this particular hymn for my birthday each year. Personally, from the very outset, this volume hit me at a visceral level, and the more I read it the more deeply it imprints my consciousness with new insights and experience. I want to express my enormous gratitude to the editor and the authors for the precious gift of *Her Name Is Kaur: Sikh American Women Write about Love, Courage, and Faith.*

—Nikky-Guninder Kaur Singh
Professor and head of Religious Studies Department, Colby College

February 1, 2014

Fisherwoman

Preeti Kaur

For the Kaurs Who Share The Responsibility of Word
Kaur derives from Kanvar which means Prince
which is The One With the Responsibility
(And also in remembrance of the girls lost, born and unborn.)

i am looking for love
i am looking for the lost
cave at the lost ocean's
bottom where the abyssopelagic fish
swim i throw my fishing
line at the space of all lost
things the space between
my legs the space which gorges
blood the space within chambers
of heart the space my liver
unlocked like jewelry box
the space where words forbidden
the space between ladder
rungs of loss in a sea
horse's spine tapered like mortality
i braid my seaweed

hair into a nitnemi net
tread churning flow (why call her bad?)
where Queens are born

i am looking for love
my skin salted into bride paddling
the thieves in gulf of khambat my boat carved of five
starfish arms i circumambulate four times round
this Harbor speaking sat santokh daya nimrata
pyaar searching for the Baba
in Bakala
swimming for herself
a Queen being born

Part 1: Anakh

Living with Dignity

Gone with the Pind

Sonam Bhimbra

"Don't you let me catch you not saying 'Yes, ma'am' and 'No, ma'am,' y'hear me?"

"Yes, ma'am."

My mind wandered back to this exchange between an elementary school teacher and our second grade class many years ago as I replied to the scary, heavily made-up, thick, nasally, Bronx-accented drugstore cashier in New Jersey when I was visiting extended family. "What I look like? Who says 'ma'am'?" Thirteen-year-old me apologized and hauled my ass out of there. I thought everyone said that; you were supposed to. And that's when I realized I might be a Southerner.

I didn't realize it when I wore John Deere paraphernalia. ("Ooh, they love tractors in Punjab too." —My parents)

Or when I went to my friend's house and every inch of her wall was covered in taxidermy deer heads.

Or when I used to sing along every time Gretchen Wilson's "Redneck Woman" came on the radio.

Or when I went to the racetrack, where hundreds of impassioned white people watched cars go around in circles.

Or when complete strangers would voice their concern about my salvation, declaring that my heathen self "needed to be saved."

Or when I visited family in New York and California and they tried to imitate my accent. "You have a twang," they assured me. Listening to their politically correct Yankee selves trying to say "y'all" correctly still didn't tip me off to this fact.

We moved to South Carolina when I was just knee-high to a grass-hopper. Though I can't remember, I'd like to think five-year-old me had tried her best to reason with my parents' naiveté. We came here in '95, and it has been my life's goal ever since then to get the hell out. We left Queens, New York, a hub of diversity, for Hardeeville, South Carolina, a hub of rednecks. This has resulted in the unusual upbringing that my younger brothers and I share, a peculiar blend of Southern hospitality and Punjabi traditions. We eat *makkhi di roti* and cornbread. We say "*Sat Sri Akal*" and "Bless your heart."

After seventeen years in Bumfuck, South Carolina, I've learned that small towns are another world. I've learned that I've spent my entire life in a bubble. I've learned that Southerners have a really weird reputation in other parts of this country (usually for good reason). But most of all, I've learned that even though I will probably deny it if you ask me: I truly love this place.

I often wonder what was going on in my father's head when he decided that we needed to leave New York and migrate South, leaving the safety of our diverse Jamaica, Queens, neighborhood for the wide-open white (really white) boonies of the South. His turban must have been tied on too tight. I mean sure, he got a really good job here that led to his having his own private medical practice, and my mom loved the lack of snow and the peace and quiet. They thought it would be a great place to raise kids; New York was just too crazy. But I really wonder if they thought it all the way through.

When we moved here, our parents put us in a small private school. It was not uncommon to attend a private school, mind you. This was not one of those bougie, preppy, squash-playing kinds you're thinking about. It was a small brick building with three hall-ways. One was the elementary school, one was the middle school, and the other was the high school. Roughly five hundred students in the entire school, K–12. I attended this school from kindergar-ten all the way up to twelfth grade. The school's insignia was the Confederate flag, a symbol whose meaning and controversial (read: racist) history I was unaware of until I entered college. The alchemic transmutation of Punjabi-speaking brown baby to Carolina country girl was ineluctable.

My younger brother experienced the transformation right away, too. To be able to attend our school, he was forced to cut his hair in pre-K because hair past the collar was "against the dress code," as were facial hair, tattoos, facial piercings, and untucked shirts. "But we are Sikh; it's part of our religion," my mother explained. Unfortunately, they didn't play when it came to the dress code. My pigtailed brother's beautiful *kesh* was shorn. It broke my father's heart, but my mother comforted him. "If he decides to grow his hair when he's older, it will be that much more meaningful." The first thing my brother did when he left this school in tenth grade was to grow out his luscious beard.

I was the only non-white in my class for the first two years. Then finally, in second grade, we got our first black kid. His parents were from Zimbabwe, so we were pretty much in the same immigrant boat. I don't think either of us knew exactly what was going on as we screamed our heads off at pep rallies with Confederate flag tempo-rary tattoos on our cheeks, yelling "The South will rise again!" Not really but, you get what I'm saying, actually, I think we really did say that once.

I remember having crushes on the whitest boys ever. Like, i'ma-go-lynch-me-a-nigger-ancestory white. I mean, I didn't have that much of a variety to pick from. Fifty shades of white, we'll call it. Camo jacket wearing, dip chewing, blue-eyed, blonde-haired good ol' boys really did it for me. But I knew we could never be together for the sole reason that I had more hair on my body in sixth grade than they would have in their entire lives.

I didn't really realize how Southern (read: "whitewashed") I was until I came to college and met actual people of color. The unspoken understanding shared between my first Punjabi friend and me was something I had never experienced before. I surrounded myself with brown faces to make up for the lack of color in my earlier years. Yet this contrast emphasized how very much a product of my environment I was. Going to school in Charleston, South Carolina, the blue eye in a red state, was a culture shock for me. I had never seen so much diversity before, mind you, a college that was 90 percent white was diverse to me. Never before had I known Persians, Moroccans, Egyptians, Vietnamese, Jamaicans. Never before had I known people so like me, and so unlike me at the same time.

Another red flag was when my younger brother started learning about American history at his not-so-country school (the public school system he attended in Georgia was much more of this planet—no school-sponsored Confederate flags). I remember him working on his Civil War PowerPoint, and my inner Confederate was awakened. I remember the pride I felt when I learned that South Carolina was the first state to secede from the Union. I was so clueless and brainwashed that I was proud of my state for divorcing the Union largely because of South Carolina's commitment to the institution of slavery (largely because of South Carolina's commitment to the institution of slavery) I also developed an unusually deep distaste for William Tecumseh Sherman. My little brother would say, "What are you talking about, you weirdo? He was a Union military hero," and I'd respond, "No, Robert E. Lee was a hero. Show some respect."

Yet the fact that the cemetery down the road from our house is segregated to this day never felt quite right. Though I was too young to put a finger on the feeling quite then, the gravestones I made crayon rubbings on not only elucidated the name and dates of these peoples' lives, but also the racism, classism, and fear that is so profoundly embedded in the collective psychosis of our nation. How some people could adhere to some illusory division even after death befuddled me.

We lived right on the Savannah River. The only non-whites in our neighborhood. The South had quite the influence on our brownness, but we brought our Indian flavor to this tiny little town, too. We went to church a few times with family friends, and occasionally friends came to the *gurudwara* with us. We tailgated at football games, and they learned how to *pao* the *bhangra*. Moments like these I relish most as they serve as a reminder that it was once almost okay to be brown in America, Sikh in the South. Remembering that five-year-old me was given the honor of being the flower girl for our closest family friend's wedding (and the most Southern people I have ever met) at their Baptist Church to the many times my best friend in second grade would come over pretty much just to run to "*Babaji's* room," as we called it, put on a *chunni*, light incense, and recite the *Japji Sahib* because she thought that was the coolest thing ever. Needless to say, she was my parents' favorite. I knew these two cultures could come together in harmony, and it was up to me to prove it. In our post-9/11, Islamo, brown-phobic society, it has become my mission to promote Sikh awareness more so than ever.

They say Sikhs who wear the *dastaar* are born to stand out and have a far greater responsibility than those of us who can pass inconspicuously. My dad was definitely not afraid to stand out. And not just because of his turban.

It was not unusual for him to bike to the clinic. "Ay doc, your car break down? You need a ride?" concerned patients would often pull over to ask. Nope, he was just biking five miles to work because he enjoyed the exercise. He also liked to coerce chubby middle-school-aged me to bike the long arduous journey to the boat ramp with our dogs almost daily. Now, let me tell you, we lived in the boonies. Biking through this thickly wooded area, I often saw snakes and once even a baby alligator on the side of the road, but did this possible threat to our safety worry my dad? Nope. Neither did the armadillos or the probably-rabid-disease-infested possum, which I was sure the dogs were going to provoke, resulting in my being viciously attacked if I didn't pedal like hell. In the meantime, my dad was already out of sight because my lardass was too slow to keep up. That wasn't even the worst part. Once we got to the boat ramp, my dad would take me, and my brother, once he was old enough to come on these fabulous excursions with us, to this cemented area overlooking the water and make me do *Surya Namaskara* with him. The man had no idea what a hippy he was. Sounds kind of nice to some of y'all, but let me tell you: it was not nice. The dogs would slobber all over me every time I got into plank, mosquitoes biting me all over; I could hear strange animal sounds coming from the trees; and we looked like freaks doing downward facing dog as boats passed by—boats filled with perplexed fishermen trying to figure out why their respected and poised Dr. B had his rear end in the air.

"Where'd you get this watermelon?" I asked when he picked us up from the bus stop one day.

"Dasher," he replied.

The barter system was not unusual for patients like Mr. Dasher who weren't insured but who did have a dope little garden going. It also wasn't unusual for us to know the names, addresses, pets, favorite colors, and horoscopes of most of the patients. Other patients used to bring fresh fruits and vegetables for Dr. B too. Something probably unfathomable to the big city doctors. But in these kinds of Southern *pinds*, villages, anything goes.

They loved him. He was even a special guest for our town's annual Ebony Fest once! He was an internist/nephrologist, but he was all about natural cures and Ayurveda and whatnot. It wasn't unusual for my mother to run into patients at the grocery store asking where the nearest Indian grocery store was, so they could get some *haldi* (turmeric).

There's a hardened thug somewhere deep in the projects of Hardeeville who is still doing Baba Ramdev breathing exercises, I'm sure of it.

I know the topic of 9/11 and the effect it had on Sikhs has been written about ad nauseam, but it's indisputable how this event transformed, or at least brought to light, this nation's racial landscape.

Islamaphobia hurts us all. Thirteen years later, my little brother still has to hear things like "son of Osama," by people who have never even seen our father.

"Random security checks" are always fun.

"She beeped and he didn't?!" I'll never forget the TSA officer that expressed his surprise when my metal belt buckle set the detector off while my father passed through without beeping, as if it was out of the realm of possibility that a brown man in a turban could walk through an airport without setting off alarms. I was probably fourteen or so, but I was heated the rest of the flight, while my father acted like he hadn't heard the TSA agent's remarks. Nothing ever got to him. He never lost his composure.

Even when, after thirteen years of being an inherent part of our community, my father was accused of a crime he did not commit. Even when he was arrested publicly and jailed without a lick of evidence. Even when his name was libeled in the local newspapers. Even when the judge, his own patient, took the side of the white family friend who accused him of the crime. Even when it became clear that all it takes is melanin to be considered a felon in this country. Even when he lost his medical license and fled the country so he could keep working. Even as I watched our entire lives turn upside down. He always maintained his composure.

I saw my mother make sacrifices we will never be able to repay her for so we could stay in America and focus on our education. Though my younger brothers were deprived of physical father presence, he called every day. Twice a day. He knew what was going on with our lives from thousands of miles away more than when he had been here. But none of us could ever fully understand what the other went through in the span of those five years. Sometimes we didn't have money for basic things like food. Sometimes we felt alone. Our memories managed to sustain us in times like those.

A favorite is the many beach days we spent at Hilton Head Island, our entire family blissfully hypnotized by the ocean. Watching my brothers skim board, my dad floating serenely in the sea while my mom sunbathed, I sometimes wondered if Guru Arjan Dev Ji experienced a similar enchantment when he wrote, "Just as the waves that break and rise, but then return to water, we too will merge again with the One."

South Carolina will always be my home. Hell, I've lived across the street in Georgia for over a year, and I still haven't had the heart to change my South Carolina driver's license. And I get way too excited upon seeing one of our state's college football mascots, the gamecock, on T-shirts or bumper stickers. It takes a special kind of love to yell, "Go Cocks!" as proudly as we do.

I knew it was inevitable I would leave the South, but I know I will always return. Like the waves that always return to the shore no matter how many times they get pushed away, it's a love that won't quit.

I see the world differently now but often reminisce about the days of my youth. Sitting in the back of my closest friend's dad's pickup truck eating fresh-picked strawberries dipped in powdered sugar. Back when life was dial-up slow. In the land of mossy oaks and ladies with names like "Cookie" and "Tilly" and boys called "Bo," "Bub," and "Cooter."

Nothing takes me back to the balmy summers of my childhood in the boonies of the South quite like the rosy goodness of a frosty glass of Rooh Afza. It might seem odd that an eighteenth-century concoction developed in British India has this effect, but it does. Or sitting on the porch with a cardamom-infused *cha* during a thunderstorm, watching the lightning and listening for thunder to gauge the distance. Smelling the cleansed sky and tasting the sweet, milky cha as my brother sipped his ice-cold sweet tea.

Though firmly ensconced in the depths of the South, the spirit of the motherland somehow still found us. The same Rooh Afza and chai is imbibed thousands of miles away too, but ours is made with water from the United States. The more we drank this paradox, the more discombobulated we became. At home, my brothers and I were considered too "American" and outside "too un-American." We belong to neither, yet we belong to both. Othered in both worlds—yet in retrospect I realize this rejection was a gift. Somehow this ostensible separation gave way to a divine sense of unity, of *Ek Onkar.*

I sometimes fancy the idea of raising my own kids here. There's something about the beauty of the palmetto tree–lined streets, mossy oaks, marshes, wildlife, and ocean air in which the quiddity of the South lives. The deliberate and leisurely slowness, as opposed to the clever and perfunctory fastness of big cities. Despite its history, there is something charming and childlike about the South. Something pure, almost sacred. Here is where I was given room to grow in a way I don't know I would have had I been brought up in New York, or anywhere else for that matter.

Uncrowded by family or any kind of Indian community, it was up to us to branch out and create an identity all our own. My parents were in their early twenties when they moved to America. Settling in America as immigrants, we learn we must adjust and interact with others of every variety. Often we find people that are from the same place as us, who look like us, who speak our language and build our own communities. Oftentimes we try to create our own idyllic bubble as a means to imitate the lands we left behind. But when that's not an option, you're catapulted into a surrounding so out of your element and comfort zone that you have no choice but to adapt and grow. I honestly believe my ability to relate to people stems from this. As a woman, I feel like I've already been given the gift of empathy, but the environment I found myself in helped foster and utilize this gift.

Girls are often expected to carry out traditional domestic duties as prescribed by our Punjabi culture, but Sikh women are a force to be reckoned with. With ancestry like Mai Bhago and Maharani Jindan Kaur, their spirits live on within us.

I've realized I am, without a doubt, a Kaur.

I didn't realize it when I made it a point to raise awareness about Sikhs with every person I met, whether through English presentations or through my unwavering belief that we are all manifestations of the One and deserve to be treated as such.

I didn't realize it when I fell in love with martial arts at a young age, oblivious to the fact that I was carrying on a legacy of the Gurus.

I didn't realize it when I learned to trust my intuition and voice and stand by my beliefs, even when I was the only one on my side.

I didn't realize it when my desire to cultivate the land and learn how to grow fresh food could be contained no more and finally came to fruition with my work on a local organic farm. This was not only an homage to the farmers of Punjab but also an expression of a nurturing feminine spirit promoting support and sustainability versus subordination.

I didn't realize it when teachers, acquaintances, lunch ladies, crackheads, you name it turned into family wherever I went. The nurturing feminine spirit and Sikh teachings that God is in everyone have always served me well. I don't know what it is, but perfect strangers and even the most seemingly depraved souls reveal their Oneness and soon become friends and family.

Might be a Sikh thing. Or maybe it's a Southern thing. Sometimes I can't even tell the difference.

Moonlit Jogs, Yoga, and Faith

Anu Kaur

I left fuming. I had never run a long distance before but was so pissed off I dug out my relatively unused sneakers and ran out the door before anyone could stop me. I turned left at the stop sign and felt the downward slope of the hill give me momentum and carry me faster and farther than I had ever gone before. Until that moment I did not know I could run and was surprised that my feet continued to pound the pavement. Before I knew it, I had reached the end of our development. I had arrived at a crossroad and had to make a decision. Did I turn back or move forward onto the main road and continue this new movement? I could still feel frustration and anger pulsing through me like a freight train and, in that split second, decided to continue onward.

I hardly ever went outside the neighborhood onto the main street and was a bit worried as I left the sanctuary of my neighborhood but felt shielded from the sun under the shade of hundred-year-old trees. I kind of liked this solitary run. I ran and ran, stopping only to catch my breath. It felt so good. I could feel the tension dissipate as my thoughts and memories fell into place.

I began to think back to the parks where we held our rendezvous, and to the memories cloaked in shady old trees and nature's flowing streams over the last few years. Our connection seemed immediate from the first time I made eye contact with him as a young teenager at a party. Over the years we became close. We did *kirtan* together, and he became my *sangat.*

Parks were our favorite places to retreat to and hide from the wondering eyes of others. We had frequented many public parks in the car his father had invested in as he started college; he was trusted as the next man of the house. The smell of leather and the way he shifted gears, making his *simran* beads jingle lightly as they hit his steel *kara,* made the hair on my skin stand. I glanced over and admired his profile, with its curly beard and sculpted turban. We would drive down winding roads away from the world of the *gurudwaras,* and his commitment to me felt unwavering. And yet, in a corner of my mind I felt a small tug every now and again that something was not quite right.

As we hung out more frequently, I often waited patiently for him in a parking lot at the mall and watched people. They would park, do their shopping, come back, and drive off while I continued to wait. I would occasionally glance up from doing my *paath,* trusting he was delayed for a legitimate reason. I had traveled an hour, crossing over state lines, over the river, in my old station wagon that shook dangerously as I pushed it to sixty miles per hour. I rushed to our designated meeting point, fearful he'd miss me or mistakenly think I had not shown up.

Years later, in that same car, he agreed to meet me in the parking lot, but this time on my side of the state line. I leaned back against the glove compartment, facing him to look into his eyes and squinting to get a better look as the closest lamppost cast its dim light. He had purposefully chosen a dark spot among a few cars, walking distance from the mall. I had gotten used to these dimly lit places. It felt familiar to us.

I couldn't understand why it had taken him a few weeks to meet me after he returned from his college graduation trip to India—a gift from his parents. I had been anxiously awaiting him. He owed me a call and a visit. It was the first time I had felt close to indignant, that I had a right to something, some sort of decency. He had said this trip "would make or break us," and I had done due diligence, fervently praying that this would keep us together. Yet I kept having vivid dreams of his leaving.

We were parked and quiet. We had just had our usual Popeyes chicken with Cajun magic sparkles, as I called them. I could feel the remnants of the Cajun chaat masala on my fingers. I licked them to clean the stickiness. I should have cleaned my hands better, I thought mindlessly, as I sat in silence not wanting to be the one to break it. As I looked down, I noticed a ring. It made no sense that he was wearing it on his ring finger.

He never did start the conversation. I finally asked, *What's up with the ring? Why are you wearing that?* It looked just like my *Mamaji's* engagement ring. Nine diamonds neatly lined to create a box. But it couldn't be true. He was trying to be funny, I thought, as my stomach tightened and offered me true awareness of the situation. It was a blur of a conversation. A lot of choppy and short answers. Yes, he had gotten engaged. It had felt right, he said. It was expected of him. I asked how she looked. She is okay, he said. She had some acne, but it would get better, he assured me. I did what I could to not vomit in the car.

A year later, destiny left me devastated and lonely . . . destiny left me stranded on the side of the highway with a flat tire in the middle of nowhere in southern Virginia as the universe provided me a bread crumb trail to find my calling.

I got out of the car to survey the damage to my tire on the side of the highway. I had never had a flat before and was hours away from home. As I attempted to stand my ground, the wind from big rigs pushed me back, and I felt the real danger of being run over or stranded on the highway. I decided to raise my thumb and hitch a ride, feeling aimless, as I thought about all my efforts in the last year to pick myself up by my bootstraps and start over—from my grades to friends to the possibility of graduate school.

My hitchhiking attempts led to an older gentleman and, as I discovered, a born-again Christian who explained why he felt it was his duty to stop. We had a conversation about divine intervention across cultures, but he still left me with information on how I could be "saved." A mere hour and a half later I was on my way with a donut spare, headed back to northern Virginia, when I noticed that I had passed by a college. On a whim, I veered to the right lane to take the exit for the school as something in my mind and body told me, "*Do this.*" The serendipitous meeting with the director of the nutrition program in her office led me to start my nutrition graduate program. It became an important stepping-stone for me in learning how to nourish myself physically and, more importantly, mentally.

Between classes one day I sat down to do *Rehras Sahib*, the evening prayer. I gazed at the Blue Ridge Mountains in the distance and contemplated valleys. A feeling of being alone and yet okay crept over my entire body as I sat down on the cold grass in front of the brown, low townhouse complex on the easement side. I was the solitary figure as the occasional car drove by. The breeze blew my *chunni* as if announcing the sun was retiring for the day and sent a chill through me as I rhythmically began to utter my evening prayer. The words "*dukh daro sukh rog bahai*" ("pain is the medicine and happiness the disease") resonated with my very being as I recognized my pain had a noble purpose and was the catalyst for growth. Pain had offered me the willingness to move away from home and change my professional aspirations. Pain offered me the ability to let go of him. I had this deep feeling that the pain the universe had dished to me was challenging me to rise up every morning and get comfortable with not knowing what I'd accomplish or where I would go.

As I recited my evening prayer, my chanting gradually became more balanced as I surrendered myself to something deep within me and anchored myself to the feeling of the unknown. A fleeting thought, "After all, I am here," began to gain voice. A feeling of being strong and fully present in the here and now despite how painful it was began to materialize. I had survived the worst. I lost the most important thing to me—my future—and life continued. Although something had broken, it was not my foundation, as I had initially feared. Rather, my shell cracked and a glimmer of light had crept into my being. I soaked myself in gratitude that I was away from all that was familiar and embraced being alone with nothing. My future was a fantasy that was wide open as I contemplated never getting married. Listening to hours of Leonard Cohen's sorrowful melodies as I witnessed the bareness of the trees on my road excursions on Route 81 in the heart of winter. They showed me a beauty in loss and being alone. Perhaps my heart was numb, and I had only begun to scratch at my loneliness.

Then one day, out of the blue, he called. It felt like I was dreaming, and the fact that I was in my townhouse when he rang up early in the morning was strange. He was calling to see if we could meet up. A flood of thoughts ran through my head. *How did he get my number after two years? Did he know where I was now? Had something changed?*

He said he would drive two hours to come to visit me at my college before he left for India to get married. Stunned, my intuitive self spoke up and practiced the first tool of self-care I had learned over the years. I paused and offered myself space and time.

Let me call you back in a few days and let you know.

I heard the surprise in his voice, given my history of compliance, loyalty, and constant presence. I was someone who showed up at all costs *to myself.*

Okay, I will wait for your call.

I walked around in a stupor about what to do. Yet I knew in my heart exactly what I had to do. I called back three days later days later as planned. Sweating and slightly shaky, I dialed the number in front of me, wondering if it would even be a working number.

Hello?

I have decided that it would not be okay for you to come.

(Stunned) . . . *No?*

No.

(Silence.)

Okay. Bye.

I sank to the ground as I leaned against the wooden desk in my room, my new home, where I was studying to rebuild all that I had lost. Instinctually, I knew I was closing the door. In my bones, I understood the finality of my choice. I never heard from him again. That brief interaction changed my life as I let go completely. I learned that self-care could be lonely and in many ways a simple path. With him gone forever without a full explanation or an apology, I was left to figure out what was my true north as I found the willingness to let go of things that did not serve me and create simplicity in my life with authentic friends and a focus on my studies.

Eventually, my life journey began to open me to the possibilities of healthy relationships as I finished graduate school. In those two years of graduate school I began to understand how to live my life fully. I also realized commitment doesn't guarantee an outcome. I was in deep meditation and in my cocoon of learning how to find the courage to gather my strength to live a life that took me into consideration.

I walked down the stairs as the doorbell rang. Just as my mom opened the door for our guests, my eyes met his. I felt slightly confused. *Did I know him?* I immediately knew we had met before even though I wasn't sure where or how. I felt a strange but familiar sensation flow through my body that there was some connection to my future husband. I remembered the words my mother said to me just before they came. "Don't just make him your friend like you usually do." I chuckled and thought, "We will see about that" as I comfortably began chatting in the dining room where the food was set up for chai.

We stood leaning against the wall, and I knew there was an ease and comfort that automatically flowed between us. *Could this be love?* I thought fleetingly. I also leaned on a distinct feeling of trust as I spoke to him, such a welcomed feeling. I had learned over the years to go with my instinct, and it told me that there was something deeper here that would offer me honesty, sincerity, and integrity. On the other side of the house, our parents were also naturally conversing and laughing. He had come with his mom, who was visiting from India. I liked his mom. She had an air of kindness and sophistication about her that I was drawn to. No one was even eating, it seemed, just talking. Eventually our parents came over and said it had been a couple of hours, much to our surprise. As we parted ways as families, his mom called out, "Well, if the kids don't like each other, let's still stay in touch."

Within weeks I was visiting both him and his mom in Richmond, feeling a cosmic pull toward them. . . . I knew we were kindred spirits.

You are engaged? My friend asked incredulously. *Yes.* One by one I told my closest friends of my decision. They'd never pegged me as one to have an arranged marriage. *Are you sure you are doing the right thing? You've only known him for months, really, weeks.* My Indian friends were in an uproar. I had not felt the need to consult with anyone. I was moving down a fast-flowing river, and things were happening as they needed to. It was my American girlfriend who, after hearing about my feelings and my conundrum of moving forward so quickly, looked me squarely in the eyes and said, "I haven't seen you light up like this before. You should marry him."

Married life offered me the opportunity for growth as I changed from me, to we, to us as a family. The passing years reinforced the lesson that being compassionate—to ourselves and one another—was love made visible.

As I sat on a chair and breast-fed my second beautiful baby boy, the energy drained out of me. My body was spent, not having enough resources to produce the milk and nourishment my child needed. The family's discussion of what to eat swirled around me. I could feel my immune system spiral downward as body aches swelled inside me. I wanted to sink into the ground and cry. We were still reeling from Mama's (my mother-in-law's) sudden death from cancer right as our second son was born. I knew I needed to be capable of making decisions that served my family.

In that moment, a seed was planted as the reality of survival welled up inside me. I swore to be fierce with my self-care so that I could survive wholly and wisely. I promised myself I'd do what it took as a professional, a mom of two, a wife, a daughter-in-law, and still a daughter, sister, and friend to thrive in life. It was at that moment I realized I was the *Ma Shakti* of the house, and I needed to take care of myself mentally, physically, and spiritually if my family was to thrive.

So with determination I took to the road while I had a few hours between breast-feedings. I kept checking the directions I had printed to find the yoga studio. I felt like a madwoman as I left with a stained T-shirt and some yoga pants I had thrown on in seconds. I raced out the door just to barely make it, sitting on my yoga mat just as the class tuned in and I found my breath.

Week after week I went back to this yoga studio for this one and a half hours of quiet time. I noticed I started to feel slightly different as my breath changed the shape of my lungs and my life. I'd walk in on the verge of a cold and walk out a renewed person. It shocked me but kept me coming back for more and more. I never knew what to expect as the yoga teacher seemingly spewed out crazy talk about how the energy flows differently and my chakras would become unblocked. I didn't know what to think about what she was saying, but I did know I was different and lighter.

As I lay down for deep relaxation after vigorous yoga exercises, I felt my heart center tremble and eventually begin to shake uncontrollably. My mind began to race. How was my chest moving when all my exercises were with my legs? My pragmatic mind could make no sense of it, and I was left with a feeling akin to giving birth. It was as if my body had taken over, and I was left to only bear witness to the changes and movement. The tears began to flow uncontrollably and they overwhelmed me and released me at the same time. A sense of self-compassion and forgiveness flowed over me for everything that I had ever experienced in my life. This release strengthened me and gave me a deep sense of light, love, and kindness. I began to realize that self-compassion is a precious tool of survival and has its own sweetness and contagiousness when practiced with pure intention.

Eventual divine blessings brought me full circle to recognize the connection of my body and spirit through the doorway of my breath, and grounded me with meditation and sound. During the past decade of my marriage, my toddlers grew into boys, and simultaneously, my self-awareness grew. I found myself developing deeper roots in community and soaring in so many aspects of my life.

One morning in my family home, we gathered our friends and family to remember Mama and also to acknowledge our blessings. Healthy and balanced individuals of all walks of life expanded our sangat. I embodied the steadiness and the rich sound of the *tanpura* in the background, offering accompaniment to the *tablas* my boys were practicing in preparation for the *kirtan*. Serenity came over my body. I reflected with gratitude on how far I had come as an individual and how far we had come as a family. Over the years, healthy and balanced individuals of all walks of life and communities expanded our sangat.

During the kirtan, I mentally noted how my communities were merging, the energy and power of love vibrating through me. I noticed postures straightening as the guitar was tuned for the "Song of the Khalsa (Pure)"* and the focused intent with which people listened and joined in:

> *Many speak of courage. Speaking cannot give it.*
> *It is in the face of death, we must live it.*
> *When things are down and darkest, that is when we stand*
> *tallest.*
> *Until the last star falls, we won't give an inch at all.*

As we all sang from our hearts, from our different experiences and life interpretations, I felt the spirit of the sangat align, and I reminisced about how my understanding of *love* had changed over the years. My journey had started with my running away from myself, seeking validation from another. I believed I could only be complete with someone else's acceptance—or I was nothing. I now found myself in healthy relationships, clear that I was deserving of mutual respect. Tears pooled in my eyes as I continued to soak in the words:

> *Daughters of the Khalsa, in your strength our future lies.*
> *Give our children fearless minds to see the world through*
> *the Guru's eyes.*
> *Stand as the Khalsa, strong as steel, steady as stone.*
> *Give our lives to God and Guru, mind and soul, breath and*
> *bone.*

Eventually the tears overflowed as we stood and I heard the *Ardas* (humble request) slowly and deliberately spoken from the heart. My friend, who was like a younger sister, had honored our request to do the *Ardas* in Punjabi and in English. Her voice carried the strength of all my brothers and sisters, young and old, and later she shared that she had had tears in her own eyes and didn't know why.

Sitting there, listening to and feeling the power of the singing, I took in how our actions and choices and the respect and commitment we offer every moment in our lives, to one another and ourselves, is *love*. Gratitude flowed through me as I took in the moment of blessings.

The next day, as we recouped, my boys and I decided to go explore the tree house in our new neighborhood. My six-year-old scooted ahead on his Razor scooter as my nine-year-old chose to jog beside me. "Mom, why do you like jogging so much?" he asked as his legs kept up with my steady motion. "Honey," I replied. "It keeps me sane."

I thought back to my twenties and all those moonlit jogs. Over the years my runs have offered me precious moments of contemplation as I felt the wind on my face and eventually became the wind as I gained the strength to be present. It was in those moments that I became ruthlessly honest with myself about my choices and my life, feeling grateful that I found the courage and willingness to take part in the process that awakened in me the capacity for self-love.

As we picked up momentum racing down the hill, I smiled, remembering my first jog and recognizing it was no longer confusion and anger that propelled me forward but self-care. It is compassion, trust, and love that now motivates me to listen to the deep noisy silence of my inner being and ask the question of how I will honor myself with abundance today, so I can offer to others my *love*.

*"Song of the Khalsa" lyrics by MSS Livtar Singh Khalsa.

I Call Her Lovingly, Unyielding

Gurleen Kaur

My legs collapse from underneath me and my hands barely break my fall to the ground.

Breathe in—Wa. *Hold*—and He. *Breathe out*—Gu. *Pause*—Ru.

I make it to the top of the mountain-like peak, the physical space I hope will allow me to escape the fiery turmoil that has invaded every crevice of my mind.

Breathe in—Wa. *Hold*—and He. *Breathe out*—Gu. *Pause*—Ru.

I try to focus on my breath, to concentrate on the Energy within and around me, but to little avail. My mind is like a preteen child, holding selfishness and stubbornness as the only doctrines for her existence. She does what she wants and refuses to let go.

Breathe in—Wa. *Hold*—and He. *Breathe out*—

I try again.

Breathe in—Wa. *Hold*—I don't need him!

I am a strong Sikh woman and I don't need him to satisfy my existence.

Again.

I pull my legs in close to my knees and wrap my arms around them, forming a cocoon to shelter me from the wind. I try to keep breathing, repeating the name of the One.

Dried plants cover the edge of the trail; the wind overtakes them. They look and move like stalks of wheat, vibrate in a synchronized fashion, as if driven by the Same breath, the Same force. Every seed grain moves as one. They prevail together, deep within the hills formed by the rupture of the earth beneath them. And so they'll continue to, until the breeze slowly sweeps away one particle of their being at a time, until there remains no difference between the seeds and their surroundings, until their Union is complete.

I want my body to move with his body, as one. Less our bodies, more our thoughts as one. Less our thoughts, more our beings as one. I want us—him and me—to vibrate on the same frequency, that only of Wa-He-Gu-Ru, to take our breaths in unison, always in remembrance. I want to be wrapped in Oneness, as we erase the lines between him and me, as we erase the lines between Bliss and Us.

Breathe in—Wa. *Hold*—and He. *Breathe out*—Gu. *Pause*—Ru.

But what if he's the one? Patience . . . that's all I need . . . just a little more patience.

I give up.

I awaken each morning, hoping that I won't remember him, that the minutes that follow my mind's return from the mystical world of slumber are reserved only for remembrance of the one they call *Akal*.

Another day, same hope, same fail.

I inch my body from underneath my blue-and-white-striped covers and with both eyes still shut, trip my way down the stairs of my lofted bed. "Today," I tell myself, "I will not wonder if he will text back. Today, I will not await his call as the sun makes its way to the land of my grandmother's birth."

It's a quarter to seven and I am running late for work as usual. I apply some minty goo to the end of my toothbrush, a plastic stick bound to live out its days in a landfill years beyond my own existence.

"Today," I think as I move the brush back and forth in my mouth, staring at myself eye to eye as whitish foam runs down my chin, "I will not fall for him like rain drops to the earth, powerless against the attraction of gravity. I will not fall for him like Rachel's lips toward Noah's in *The Notebook* as he confesses his love for her outside the mansion he rebuilt for her. I will not."

I spit.

I put on my overly casual clothes for a job I believe myself to be too young for, slap both cheeks with a rosy dose of confidence, and walk out the door. I arrive at my office in the city, place my phone facedown on the farthest corner from my desk, take a seat in my entertainingly squeaky chair, and immerse myself in oil spill response coordination, US–Mexico border trash level management, in . . .

> *those eyes, crinkled with laughter*
> *wide and blanketed with concern*
> *dark—*
> *two black holes*
> *my heart and mind powerless against their force!*

"Focus, Gurleen. You are at work. Get back to work," I tell myself.

I close my eyes and try to center myself with *Naam*. I breathe in and try to focus on the light shining through my eyelids, but all I see are flashes of moments of euphoria—the ones that take you by surprise, occasionally take your breath away, and draw you dangerously closer each time.

> *like when I was shivering, and he came up from behind and put his jacket over my shoulders*
> *like when he Snapchatted me a picture of his hair, saying it reminded him of mine*
> *like when he grabbed my arm and told me he cared about me*

And as easily as these memories are vibrantly repainted, injecting chemical doses of bliss into my mind, they fade away. And as they fade, they are replaced with moments of impatience and confusion. My mind is subjective—as she waits for him to take the next step, take *any* step, she begins to filter out the moments that leave me girlishly giggling, leaving only those that leave me distraught and disheartened, that close my heart, begging for my legs to run away from any moment that tries to reopen it. The easel has run out of color; what is left are only black and white.

Hurt. That's all I can remember.

> *how he promised to take me to dinner . . . and skipped to*
> *play video games with his boys instead*
>   *how he said he would call on Tuesday . . . and never did*
>   *how he canceled on our trip to Los Angeles, the night before*
> *our flight*
>   *(how I proceeded to cry at the airport as soon as I arrived)*

It's been almost thirty minutes, and my boss is asking for a progress report on the work she assigned to me earlier this morning. "Almost done!" I scream across the office.

The daily petal plucking of "he likes me" and "he likes me not" has become too much. I like him. I do. But my mind, she is beaten with mental and emotional exhaustion. She is tired. I am tired.

On a kind, blue-skied afternoon, he and I make our way to the *gurudwara*. We enjoy the wondrous devotional songs, the *kirtan,* of our favorite *Bhai Sahib.* His voice enters my ears, and I find myself in Ecstasy, engulfed in energy so sweet I cannot describe.

I want nothing else but to be here with my *sangat*—my community—as well as with him.

I feel complete.

We *matha tayk* and go downstairs to eat *langar.* Some of the kids from a children's camp where I was a counselor come up to me and give me a hug. They sit next to him and ask, "Do you two like each other?" I quickly laugh it off, refusing to make eye contact with him and replying, "What do you mean? We're just friends."

I am thankful for the brown skin covering my blushing cheeks. We finish up, and as we walk away, he smiles. I smile back.

He drives me home. We park outside my apartment and the topic of discussion turns to marriage. He says, "I told my mom that if she sees someone she thinks I would get along with that she can introduce her to me." My heart stops. I don't know how to react.

The words exit my mouth out of panic, "You're getting married?!"

He replies, "Nooo, but it's every mom's right to look for a girl for her son."

My mind begins its never-ending cycle of speculation. Why is he telling me this? We say our good-byes, and I get out of the car.

I walk into my apartment and shut the door behind me. Tears roll down my cheeks. I don't understand. I'm confused. I don't understand our friendship-relationship. I don't understand why I have to hear these things. I'm done. No. This time, it's real. I'm done. I text him something small and pray.

Waheguru. If it is not meant to work out between us, then please do not let him text me before 12 a.m. tonight.

He does not text back for three days.

I believe it, that my *Ardas* has come true. I can move on.

The Beloved Guru Nanak Dev Ji writes, "*Jo Mange Thahkur Apne The Soee Soee Devay.*" *Whatever I ask for, Waheguru gives it to me.* I had an answer. And that is what I wanted—a reason to stop the daydreaming and reminiscing and reliving of every moment I had experienced with him.

I held on to that for about three days. And then the doubts came flooding back. I convinced myself that my Ardas was just superstitious and that for a real answer, I would have to take *Hukam* from the Guru Granth Sahib, an action I refused.

I do not know if the answer I received that night was real or not— my Faith is not yet that strong—but I do know this: my judgment was clouded. I could not tell what my heart was telling me, what voice was Real. After those three days, I took a step back from Truth. I ignored the happenings of that night and continued on for the next half a year as if nothing had changed. We talked late into the night, he bought my meals, and every now and then there would be another moment of questioning endearment, a smile, a glance held too long. The lines of friendship kept smearing. I remained complacent.

We are at my apartment getting ready for an engagement party. He ties his *pagh*, and I finish doing my hair. My friend calls, upset about family and friend conflicts. I calm her down and tell her to join us at the party. I tell her that we will pick her up in fifteen minutes and hang up the phone.

He's lying down on the makeshift bed on my hardwood floor. I sit next to him while we wait. He sees that I look troubled. He grabs my arm and tells me not to worry, that she'll be okay, that we are going to have a good night. I take in a couple of deep breaths. All is good.

"Do you think I am immature?" he asks.

"Sometimes." I laugh. "Why? What do you mean?"

"Well, I'm trying to impress this girl who's two years older than me, but my other friend thinks I am too immature. Do you think I am immature?"

I panic. "What girl? I'm not answering the question until I get more details!"

He gets distracted and asks me to get him something from the other room. We leave for the train station. I walk away and cry in the corner.

The night ends and I am glad to be back. I let him take a nap in my bed that afternoon. I'm scared it will smell like him. It doesn't. I thank Waheguru.

I call my friend and let everything out. "Gurleen, this is your moment," she says. "It's over. You finally have an answer. And he's driving home for the next thirty minutes. Call him and tell him whatever you need to, to finally close this story."

I dial his number, and he doesn't pick up. He calls back ten minutes later. I yell at him about some unrelated things, trying to build up the courage to say something. I tell him he needs to draw boundaries in his life if he's really looking for a girlfriend. He's confused. He says, "I feel like you're trying to say something . . ."

I pause. I hang on to the silence for what seems like years, immobilized to continue my thoughts further.

"When you're ready to talk, I'll be here."

It's 1:45 in the morning and tomorrow I have to see him again. I wait until the clock strikes 2:00 a.m. and dial again.

"Promise not to get mad?"

"I can never be mad at you."

And I say it. That I've liked him for so long now and that I am not asking him to reciprocate or anything like that but that I need him to know that our relationship is ambiguous at times and that isn't okay with me and that he should work on that with his other friends who are girls so that what happens between us doesn't happen again and so he can have a successful relationship with his future girlfriend/wife—whoever that may be.

I breathe in and out. I feel relief.

He thanks me for being straightforward and says this is not something he will forget. Not wanting to put him more on the spot, I say good night. I hang up knowing this will be our last late-night conversation.

I call my friend back and the tears stream out uncontrollably.

I have since questioned every moment of that conversation and of our time together. In the days following, a range of thoughts and feelings poured irrepressibly out of me.

There was an expected, abrupt sense of regret. I almost immediately felt the loss of a friendship from which I had gained so much. I learned that the lessons gained do not disappear with our changed relationship; that I keep them as part of my existence forever; that he is not lost; that there is no returning to normal, but rather a discovering of a new normal that respects both his boundaries and mine.

There was a day of thinking that maybe I just wasn't beautiful enough, but even I laughed at the idea, recognizing my self-worth and that we, as humans, all have different desires and attractions.

I think I had prepared myself for a lot of the emotions I expected to feel, my speculative abilities being one of my greatest attributes. What I did not expect, but feel more strongly than anything, is a feeling of being lost. That day, he told me the truth, Truth I could not see for so long, whether from my own ignorance or inability to see past conflicting behavioral signals. I feel like I failed to trust myself, in my innate guiding sense of *dharma*. And though I do not beat myself up for not following the answer of the Ardas I received months prior, I scold my mind for continuing to look past signs of warning both selfishly and blindly.

This becomes the scariest part of my journey: learning to listen to my Heart and the guiding Oneness within.

And this journey continues never-endingly today.

My mind, she finally yields. For the first time in months, I hear her speak Silence.

Life, Friendship, and the Game of Love
A. Kaur

I

The first time I fell in love, I was seventeen. It was August, just three weeks before my first day of my senior year, and my goal was to have my first kiss before school began. Living in a small suburban town designed for raising families was, to the say the least, the least likely venue to meet a nice, mature Sikh boy. I decided to go to a camp, a Sikh retreat, in Toronto. That's where I met GrayEyes.

Toronto was hot, so hot we sweated at night even with our thin comforters. There was *diwan* every morning at 8 a.m. For a girl who hadn't been to such an early diwan in about seven years, the routine was a little tough to get used to. Classes and workshops and lectures followed, and everyone always wanted me to do a hymn when I hadn't done a *shabad* in god knows how many years. It was intense.

I didn't notice him at first, still trying to get over being in an environment of strangers who were much more versed in their *paath* and *Sikhi* than I. I had come to camp at the urging of my cousins who went every year, thinking it will be a good experience, and maybe different to go as someone a little older. But I was awkward with new people and making small talk was still a work in progress.

Perhaps the third day, when I was a bit more comfortable. I finally saw him. I remember his eyes, a beautiful brownish-gray. The more I looked at them, the more I saw them looking back at me. Me: five foot two; long black hair; my own, light brown eyes. Me: hopeful and scared for a semester filled with college applications (which I'd thankfully started) and some of the hardest classes of my academic career. Me: secretly wishing for someone to lay his eyes on me–someone my age, someone cute, someone caring. Someone I didn't have to chase. I wanted to know I was worth it. It was a time when I thought women were validated by the gaze of men, when I felt validated when someone liked me. Though I was stubborn and ambitious, I hadn't quite found myself; I was still developing my style, my life perspective.

GrayEyes started hanging out with me instead of his other friends during free time. He asked me questions and stared at me with this kind of twinkle in his eyes. Ever since I'd started liking boys in elementary school, my feelings had never been reciprocated. I felt special, wanted. I got goose bumps when he sat next to me on the bus. We talked until sunrise the last night of camp, about nothing and everything. It felt like we'd shared everything we could possibly know about each other. The day camp ended, we hugged for two seconds too long. That was it, I thought.

But then he texted.

"Hey."

"Hey."

Fireworks went off in my head. *I can't believe GrayEyes texted. Oh my god, does he really like me? Where is this going to go? Do I actually like him?* It was the quintessential self-doubt of a hopeless romantic. This time my wear-my-heart-on-my-sleeve syndrome could be cured by a beautiful man I'd met at a camp in Canada, and who conveniently lived only an hour from me in the States?

We decided to meet. I told my mom I was going to hang out with some friends––which I did—but afterward, I went to see him. I was nervous. This was the first time I'd seen him since camp. Would we still relate the same way? Would he still think I was cute? Would he hold my hand? How would I feel if he did?

We walked down a long line of shops and restaurants, the sun accompanying us as we turned corners and wandered. We sat on a bench, and I accidently sat on my purse. Inside was a Ziploc full of blueberries that got squished, and we laughed as we emptied my entire purse and searched for napkins.

Later we walked back to my car and sat inside for a while. We looked at each other, smiling, not knowing what to say. Thoughts were racing through my head. I wanted him to hold me. He made me feel so safe. He took my hand. The butterflies inside me, didn't flutter—they galloped, with part excitement, part nerves, part curiosity. His face came closer. I looked down, not knowing where to look. He tilted my head back up gently with his hand. His face was right in front of mine. He asked if it was okay. I nodded slowly, hesitantly, but with a slightly expectant smile. And then we kissed. The day before the first day of my senior year! Wonderful. Amazing.

For two months it was everything I had ever wanted. Our lives revolved around each other. We hung out every Friday. I finished my homework and college applications by 10 p.m. every day so we could talk for two hours before going to bed. *This is it,* I thought. This could be me for the rest of my life. I imagined marriage. I imagined vacation homes. I imagined happiness. I was seventeen.

Then everything fell apart. Everything.

"We're breaking up."

Suddenly, I felt the weight of an entire bookcase—an entire library—crash onto my shoulders. My tear duct drought since my *Daadi Ji* had passed away years before broke open the dam. I skipped school that day. I couldn't stop crying. I didn't know what I had done wrong. I didn't know why he didn't want me anymore.

GrayEyes and I broke up in December; from then to August, the process of recovery was a struggle. Every single day I thought about him. For the first few months, I cried at least once a week. It was exhausting. I felt like my entire future had collapsed upon itself. Even as my life went on and I was getting accepted into the best schools, the memory of him and our ever-so-short relationship felt fish-hooked into my happiness, making me crawl back into periods of regret and self-doubt. Seventeen was the age of first love and first heartache.

II

Eventually what helped me keep my head up and get over him was the prospect of college. Of a whole new world. New friends. New experiences. New boys. I busied myself with picking out a comforter and wall hangings. With setting up my e-mail account and spending the last few weeks of summer with high school friends. My entire family came to move me into my dorm, but after they left, all I felt was lonely that first night. In fact, my first semester was horrible. I was constantly afraid that I'd never find that mythical group of lifelong friends, college only seemed like "golden years" for others who were more outgoing and interesting than I was. Fortunately, *Waheguru* gave me a little something to ease the disappointment.

Mid-semester, I met FitBody. I didn't fall in love. I liked him. He liked me. We were just getting to know each other. I definitely felt like it could go somewhere. For two weeks I felt like I was on top of the world. Like college wasn't going to be that bad.

Then one night, he took me for a drive. The streets were quiet. It was midterm season. People were probably studying. We drove through neighborhoods lined with beautiful silhouettes of trees streaming down on us beneath the moonlight. The moon peeked out from time to time from behind drifting clouds. It was all very calm—too calm. Something wasn't right. I got a feeling in the pit of my stomach.

FitBody couldn't see himself with me in a serious way, he told me. He tried to hold me, to show me that he still cared, just not in that way. Only a year earlier, I had felt the same kind of rejection. I felt worthless for a while. At that time, I was under the impression that I needed a man to accept me in order to feel valued. My feelings were always amplified: my affection for a boy felt like forever-happiness, and a breakup (even from something that wasn't an actual relationship), seemed like the absolute end of the world.

What got me down was the sense that I might never be wanted by someone else, that relationships weren't for me. The void forced me to get involved in organizations and activities—the *bhangra* team, the Sikh Student Association (SSA), blogging. I was forced to meet people and really connect with them because I didn't have a boy to fall back on. College started becoming college, and I started loving it. I was engaged in my English classes, struggling and hoping to keep up with writing at a university level. I had plans to go to free concerts, try new restaurants, and work on SSA events every weekend. *These are going to be the best years ever.* I finally understood why people said that.

III

Two years later, I planned to attend a Sikh leadership conference on the East Coast. One of my really good girlfriends was also going, and I was looking forward to seeing her. I didn't expect to meet anyone. Things really do happen at the craziest times.

Just like the camp where I met Gray Eyes, I didn't notice Ray-bans at first. I talked with him as I did everyone else, but I didn't think anything of it. He was nice, friendly. On the last night, we sat across from each other at dinner and talked for a bit—it was over in what seemed like a heartbeat.

I ran to the ladies' room before a group of us headed out to do some night sightseeing. When I came back, everyone—and my purse, which I'd left on the table—were gone. When I got downstairs, Ray-bans had it on. I thought it was cute and let him keep it on, thinking it would be funny. He wore it the whole night. It was an icebreaker of sorts and an excuse for us to talk, which we ended up doing through an hour of not really seeing monuments, and then until 5 a.m. back at the hotel. It was instant attraction.

Two weeks later, he told me he liked me. Two weeks after that, he stopped talking to me. I hadn't done anything wrong; I knew that this time. I was halfway through college and a bit older since FitBody. I had seen people drop into and out of relationships. I had seen many of them change to fit the lifestyle of a significant other, while others allowed themselves to see new things and show their partners new perspectives and beauty in this world. With Ray-bans, I refused to change any of myself and thus, after weeks of constant smiling and the excitement of meeting someone new, I was heart-broken and disappointed. I knew in my heart that I had been completely and totally myself. I couldn't help it if someone else did not see that; I would not and should not change myself. Love is the meeting of souls; what is the point of two souls meeting when one isn't telling the truth? The rawness of two people coming together is how they connect at the very core of their beings.

Something was wrong with our connection. If Ray-bans wasn't willing to see in me and in us what I saw as an incredible syncing of gears, I could only push so much. For the first time, I had met someone smart, driven, and honestly, inspiring. It was awesome, and the thought of having to let that go was devastating, and a whirlwind of tears, self-doubt, and misery ensued.

This time, however, we reconnected and began talking again—soon, almost every day. In his mind, it was just as friends; in mine, it was with hope. I became one of his best friends. He needed my support, and I needed him to push me. We worked well together—and still do—but just as friends. Getting over him has been one of the most arduous, painstaking journeys I have undertaken. I have had to bar myself from social media, interacting with other friends from the conference where we met, to not think about him. I don't hope anymore, but I am disappointed. Even through him being involved with someone else, I have slowly, slowly, come to understood a few things about life, friendship, and the games of love and happiness.

I'm in a place now where I can think clearly about myself and my personal goals. Where I am not concerned about my romantic future or any kind of current relationship. I am determined to become the best me I can be.

IV

In the end, this is not a romantic story. These three snippets of my love life are not really about me at all. They are not even about the boys in the stories. These snippets are really about my friends, about falling in love with human nature.

When I broke up with GrayEyes, my best friend from high school sat with me in my car the entire day. She hugged me awkwardly from the passenger seat, automatically replenishing my tissues. She was with me every single day thereafter; she didn't judge, didn't push. At school, she would hug me randomly during the day or steal me away to the dance studio just for fun. I'd protest, but truthfully, dance was a release. As soon as I was there, my confidence took over. I was free to jump and twirl and lunge as I wished.

She reminded me who I was—smart, driven, and destined to be so much more than a girl distraught by a boy. She made me laugh and lectured me when I wallowed too much. I might have had incredible downs, but she and other friends ensured that my senior year of high school had more ups than I could have ever imagined: water balloon fights, dressing up like superheroes, kayaking in Santa Barbara, and making early-morning Starbucks runs before finals. Through the self-pitying and the self-doubt, I realized something beautiful. My friends were selfless, resilient, patient, and supportive. They afforded me their unconditional love, their time, their ears.

The first person I called when FitBody broke up with me was a high school friend who, lucky for me, lived in my dorm. This was three months into freshman year. She had her own adjustment issues to worry about, friends to make and new memories to create, but she made time to be there for me and to continuously check up on me. She made me feel a little less alone in a world that seemed unconquerable to an eighteen-year-old. And I still had my friends from back home as well. I can't imagine the number of phone calls I made during that first dreadful semester. But my friends stuck with me. I couldn't talk to my parents about the hard time I was having; I didn't want them to worry, and I certainly couldn't bring up a boy. Even without my parents' advice and support, I felt surrounded by a safety net of calls and coffee dates and text messages. My friends stayed on the phone with me until I fell asleep, asked me about classes, and encouraged me to realize that this was my freshman year, that there were endless opportunities to get involved on campus.

And I did. I got so involved that I barely had time to relax. My weeks were filled with bhangra practice, SSA events, and blog writing; my weekends were filled with parties, trips to the city, and visiting coffee shops. School itself started to seem like the "extracurricular activity." I fell in love with college life—the independence, the self-sufficiency, the freedom. I was learning about myself, and it was invigorating. And I was lucky enough to be doing this with people I loved as friends. My college fantasy was coming true.

At the beginning of my third year, probably one of the first nights back from summer vacation, my roommate and I had a few friends over. Our apartment, by default of its size, had become the place to hang out over the previous year. I loved it. We'd made food, as usual—pasta with my homemade alfredo and a bit of tomato Ragu sauce thrown in—and were just sitting around, TV on mute, talking.

"Did you hear about that new arts event happening in town?"

"No, but I started taking painting classes this summer. Fantastic stress reliever. I'm down to check it out. When is it?"

"This Friday. It's going to showcase paintings, sculptures, and music, including some bomb female emcees. And food trucks, so bonus right there."

We laughed. I looked around the room and saw the faces of five beautiful individuals, some I had known since my first year, some I had only become close to the last few months of my second. We'd met through classes or mutual friends, and some I don't even remember experiencing that awkward "acquaintance" stage with. We shared stories about everything: our summers, painting, sailing, worries about graduation. The conversations with them taught me to be self-aware, to constantly recognize and check my privilege, to cherish what I have been given, and to always be in pursuit of knowledge and change. They made me think, and think critically. I had changed because of them. That night, I almost wanted to cry, this time not over love lost, but love found. Love found in friendship. Kinship in a modern form.

Waheguru has gifted us with a capacity to love and listen. I have been fortunate enough to experience this firsthand, in situations where I should not have found myself but was able to trudge through anyway. To me, Waheguru's presence is channeled through these friends. The self-awareness that I have gained through the process is that love snuck up on me. I had been urged by others time and time again to embrace my body, to own my thoughts, and to feel beautiful because I am beautiful.

Waheguru is in each of us and if it is in everyone, it is in me. My heart proverbially broke three times because I had given someone else too much control. I wasn't trusting myself or making decisions for myself. Just like my YWCA basketball little league days with the Junior Sparks, I caught the ball and immediately passed it. I don't want to pass on that kind of control anymore. So I don't. I'm still no good at basketball, but next time I catch that ball, I'm going to keep it and I'm going to dribble it down the court the way I want, no matter how much I want to give it away. I want to make the basket myself. If someone else wants to work with me to make that basket, they are welcome. They just can't take my ball away. Not anymore. I've learned too much about myself to let that happen. I've learned that I have too much ambition and too many goals. I have a huge, vivid, amazing, messy, chaotic picture of what I want my life to be like and to get there, I need people who will work with me and support me, not people who take my smile away and drain my tear ducts.

I gave in to the love exuded by friends, so I don't worry about loneliness and I don't think I've felt it in a very long time now. Instead, I focus on myself, on keeping the beautiful individuals Waheguru has surrounded me with close, and on positively impacting my communities, to share the love that I have received. I learned the truth about what Guru Nanak Dev Ji advocated hundreds of years ago—that we are equal. All are equal. That balance should be maintained in every relationship, in every friendship. So in order to love others, I have to love myself. And I came upon this fitting cliché because others loved me.

Friends are the family I have chosen, family that gives me more than any relationship. Although I may still think about my heartbreaks from time to time, they are no longer the focus of my thoughts, no longer worthy of Facebook checks or text messages. With the help of friends, I have been able to contextualize my life trajectory in a bigger picture. I have chosen to work toward goals that not only benefit myself but also perhaps, in some way, those around me, even if that just means being the one person who is always smiling out of true happiness—such a relative term in itself. I want to see the world—and so I travel. I want to describe what I feel and what I see—and so I write. I want to be healthy—and so I dance. I want to be the positive influence in others' lives, as my friends have been in mine—and so I smile.

The love stories became heartbreak stories, which became friendship stories, and now a story of loving myself. I am but twenty-one. I am young. Willing and waiting for the incredible and awesome that lies around each corner, each month, each trip, each disappointment. I have my friends by my side. I keep my mind open and my heart permanently strapped to my sleeve.

My Mama's Hands

Sargun Kaur

Those early years in America, I did very little without the tight grasp of those big, worldly hands of my beautiful Mama. Her hands were the most magical feature about her. Freckle-like marks traced the inner edge of her left hand, a birthmark I often liked to read like tea leaves. They were big hands. Not big like Hagrid big, but big as if they had the strength to hold the entire world in position.

At six, I have a hazy memory of Boston with my Mama, having newly arrived to this land of uniquely tall buildings and strangely pale people my mother affectionately referred to as "foreign." I have a cloudy recollection of my mother then, at twenty-eight. She was a beauty, all around. The first in all our extended family and beyond to travel *foreign*—much less alone with a child—my mother carried herself with the caution and strength of a Chandigarh city girl paralleled with the demure of a Punjabi *kuri*. She had a thin frame yet to be burdened with the birth of twins and slowed by aging, and a shy smile paired with bold, beautiful, and caring eyes. Tracing back to those early faded memories, I recall an image of two best friends, my Mama and me, treading through the streets of Boston, gulping in the newness that surrounded us.

Seeing snow for the first time. Building a snowman in the driveway with my Mama—utterly awestruck by the blanket of snow that had magically appeared overnight. Then, getting lost in an American mall. Crying in desperation because I lost my Mama among the hoard of foreign people. Wiping tears and snot on the clothes hanging on the rotating racks. My memory skips to when I am seven. Taking walks to the local park near our apartment complex in Fremont, California. Just my Mama and me. Mama hospitalized due to pregnancy complications. My dad, his mother, and me alone. My first memory of being apart from my Mama.

Skipping through the aisles of Safeway. The seven-year-old me chirping, "My mom's having twins. My mom's having twins." In repercussion, receiving my first and only *thapar,* slap, from my dad: a rough, unknown hand coming down on me, setting off a geyser of hot tears that I tried hard to keep dammed—only to be released by the unlocking warmth of my Mama the next day. My dad, charismatic and handsome in his four-and-a-half-meter *pagh* and full *dhaari*, complemented my mother aesthetically quite well. When recalling the story of how they were arranged, Mama always smiles, recalling the number of accolades and medals that trailed my father's newspaper bio-data description and her feeling too "simple" to ever end up marrying such a guy. My dad was the lone male of his village to become a computer engineer, much less work abroad. He grew up in a small conservative town outside of Punjab, under a very traditional societal construct that strongly held to the cultures and traditions surrounding patriarchy—unlike Mama. But while my Mama, a lover of food, laughter, and stories often found herself at the center of any crowd during family gatherings, my dad was a rather shy person in public, content to stand aloof with his few friends. He was always a lot more conscious of "image" and of being "proper" and thus constantly pushed for assimilation of our dialect and etiquette.

Looking back, to a soon-to-be father of three daughters born under all the cultural implications of his time, I was so naive then, my chirpy disposition only underscoring the ruins of his institutionally placed hopes of a "complete" family consisting of at least one strong, handsome, intelligent son.

These few, messy childhood memories often shared a common source: my *Mama*.

In April 1998, my twin sisters took their first breaths, born a minute apart. They were small in size, barely two pounds each. But it wasn't long after that I realized there was something even more wrong with them and by transition—me.

They were twins. They were girls. I was a girl. We were girls. That's what was wrong.

A couple months later, I came to acknowledge a quintessential fact: their existence came to influence every part of my life.

Perhaps it was the older child syndrome, where I suddenly and rapidly realized the logarithmic deterioration of singular attention toward me and became aware and conscious of my mannerisms, actions, and comments in correlation to how they were received by others, including my parents.

And from there on my vivid memories activate. With the birth of my sisters and losing the age of innocence, these memories shared very little of my Mama directly. I recall a more passive relationship with her. The strolls through the park, visits to the mall, were all replaced by Mama taking care of my sisters.

I recall leveraging the recent birth of my twin sisters to gain the quick affection of my first-grade peers as well as the particular adoring attention of Mrs. Smith, my first-grade teacher. I also recall a pull towards a higher force, something to grasp onto as I let go of my Mama. A young girl draped in a *chunni* that was constantly slipping off her head, squeezing her eyes shut and clasping her hands together tight, as if the tighter she clasped them, the more powerful the wireless connection to God. I knew very little of God then. Or how the whole request system worked; I just knew that when *mathatayking*—bowing my head down in respect to the Guru Granth Sahib, God's physical eternal presence—I could ask God anything.

Waheguru kicked in heavily in the next few years and well into high school.

Babaji, please please let me get an A on my test.

Oh Babaji, please get me into the honors program. I really want to be good. I'm really trying. Can't you see up there?

Babaji, I just need to get into a good college. That's it. I have to get into Stanford. I'll do anything. Just give me a sign.

Babaji, please keep my Mama happy. Don't let anything happen to my sisters. Oh please, Waheguru, please.

I often had long conversations with Him there. Eventually, as I got older, I became self-conscious of friends in the *sangat* or the women behind me centralizing their focus on me at the *Gurudawara*, and the conversations became short and quick.

Just get me through this. Please. Thank you.

By eight years old, I could single-handedly warm milk and feed my sisters, rock my sisters to sleep, complete my schoolwork, maintain my third-grade 4.0 GPA, and embrace the role of an older sister with such maturity that it was commended by teachers on every report card thereafter. My memories involve very little of my Mama from then on, or anyone else. Childhood evaporated through hairline cracks on sidewalks, never allowing me to fully soak in its dew. While my young peers in elementary school were pushed to embrace the responsibilities of independence, I strived for codependence.

Mama, do you see how much I've improved on my cursive writing? Papa, look, I got an A on my math test.

I tried to seek positive confirmation from a young age, but I was often left unsatisfied. I began to construct my identity from borrowed puzzle pieces, building a rather jagged and unfitting sense of self. In front of friends and classmates, I was Sargun—the one with the adorable twin sisters. Among family friends, uncles, and aunties, I was Rashi (my affectionate family name)—the ever obedient and caring older sister. And in front of my parents, I was their self-sustainable firstborn. But these were all constructions formed from exploiting the cuteness of my twin sisters—images, personas, identities I had pieced together consciously to be seen as the best, or perhaps as a son. Amongst the company of myself, I was lost—lacking the courage and voice to speak out against my grandmother's constant snide undertone or to step in between my quarreling parents on the subject of raising and marrying off three daughters.

"So, beta, what do you want to be when you grow up? What is your favorite subject? Maths or science?"

"I . . ."

Tongue in cheek, I'd think, *What do I want to be? So kickass that every son of every uncle of mine in India regretted that his sperm had ever created a son and not a daughter. I want to defeat every male cousin of mine in India that my grandmother adores like kings and have them do chores for once.*

"I like math a lot, and science too, Aunty. I think I want to be a pediatrician." To a child who knew no more than three or four possible professions at the time, I equated loving my baby sisters to pediatrician potential, arguably the most intelligent choice.

I hesitated to explore myself, my boundaries, my rebellion, my voice, in fear of losing.

By then, I had heard enough arguments through walls and read enough tense body gestures, to become very cognizant of my existence. I tried hard to make sure to excel in all aspects I could control. I was so caught up in this game of "Who's the Best" that I measured love and warmth in direct proportion to achievement, success, and, most importantly, acceptance.

We never spoke about love at home. I always tensed up a little every time friends ended phone calls with "I love you too, Mom." It was just . . . awkward. I loved my parents, but in traditional Punjabi households, no one really threw around the awkward, eyebrow-raising "L" word—at least not in mine. Western, Hallmark-created, capitalist holidays like Valentine's Day and Father's Day were dreadful. Forced to vocalize my love with hugs, cards, candies, breakfast in bed—what was this madness? The societal pressure to express something sugary sweet usually kicked in the night before. I made a quick card sticking the word love in the message to avoid having to say it out loud to my parents. Obligation hung thick in the air on these particular mornings. I held my breath, dove in deep, and resurfaced holding a gold ribbon titled, "Congratulations on completing your Happy [fill in the blank] Day exchange. You may now pass to the next year."

My vocal love for the Guru was also a bit sparse. I often forgot to do *simran* and spent my days in worrisome doubt when Waheguru was not my first word of the day. My mother was very adamant about raising us around a constant voice of the Guru.

"I barely missed two brutal car accidents, and I've been feeling uneasy all day," I remember my mother saying of the days she skipped her morning *nitnem* to attend to the works of daily life.

As a growing teenager entering the eye-opening, life-transforming world of college, Waheguru didn't seem to have an effect on me—I thought with the bitter undertone of a Stanford-rejected UC Berkeley freshmen. My skeptical mind began to view religion methodically. *Mata-tayking*, once my special place to catch that high-speed wireless connection to Waheguru, seemed ritualistic. Sitting in the *Darbar* Hall, listening to *kirtan* I didn't understand or connect with at all, seemed forced and unnecessary.

Disengaged from Waheguru, I found myself even more detached from my Mama. Raising my sisters and me had aged her. Memories began to line her face, and while her eyes gleamed with a lot more wisdom, her hands remained the same. They had washed thousands of dishes and spent countless hours combing through the long tangled hair of her three daughters, but they still remained strong, beautiful, and protective.

The summer before I started college, my dad and I had a talk regarding my major, career, and future. At that point, I was still sticking to the "pediatrician" story, but only half-heartedly. Becoming the editor-in-chief of *TIME* magazine was a dream I had taken up as the editor of my high school newspaper, disclosing to no one but the self that lacked courage and a voice. But the logical side of me knew that easy living and prosperous lifestyles were not sustainable in that career—nor was it considered the "best" to do. During my late years of high school, I took a deep interest in marine biology. I always had a kinship to water—water rides, water sports, water animals, beaches, and plain old H2O too. During my last two high school summers, I interned in a marine biology lab in San Francisco, often bearing a wetsuit and riding the low tides of the SF bay to track the growth of eelgrass. But my father did not echo in either of my interests.

What came as a shocking disappointment was my dad's discouraging outlook on my becoming a doctor, his rationale: the large expense and considerable number of years I would have to be in school—underhandedly insinuating I will be well beyond marriageable age by the time I finished. And while my Mama supported and wished for me to become a doctor, she could not withstand the stubbornness of my father. Neither of my parents supported a track in marine biology, due to lack of job opportunity—a term I, with the developing rational of a young adult, loathed at the time.

Lost, disengaged, and stumbling to find a coherent identity, I spent a large part of my first year in college struggling to choose between my passion for marine biology or medicine and my father's push for engineering, better known as *job secured*. When I approached my father about pursuing civil or mechanical engineering, he suggested they might be too "boyish" as they protracted an image of physical labor. Had I the courage at that time to argue with my father—an action atypical of me then—I strongly believe I would be treading another journey now.

Four semesters in, with my transcript showcasing myriad classes in chemistry, physics, and rhetoric, I was groundless. I translated much of this frustration toward blaming my parents.

In what was a time of desperation to declare a college major, some genuine newfound interest, and logically the most compliant decision with my ego and my father, I declared Computer Science as a major my fifth semester at UC Berkeley. The day-mares I had about having made the wrong decision were assuaged by convincing myself that the major was a solid route to everything and anything else I might want to do in the future. A mantra I repeated often in those years.

While I had temporary solace of mind, my solace of heart came from a rather unusual medium: my sangat comprising of orthodox Sikhs, avant-gardists, partygoers, and activists—they externally shared very little in common. While it was a group of people I admired and enjoyed the company of, it was every bit different from the English translation of "clique" and its connotations. My sangat was discovering Sikhi, identity, and college life in every way I was and wasn't—accessing Sikhi through the academic realm of conferences, the religious realm of kirtan and *gurbani*, and the personal realm of understanding, *seva* (community service), and *rehat* (Sikhi code of conduct). It was refreshing, enlightening, and overwhelming. I ventured into activism, Sikhi, and decisions previously not laid down by my parents. While I was born into Sikhi, for the first time I felt I was becoming a Sikh and understanding the "why" behind it.

Simultaneously, I became more curious about my Mama's blind faith in Sikhi and began to initiate conversations on subjects I had never broached before.

The conversations started innocently:

"Mama, you know we're not supposed to shave—so why do we still do it?"

"You're right, we aren't. We shouldn't. But you and me, we're trying our best to get there. And we have Guru's *rakha* to help us."

The fact that my mom recognized we weren't our best representations of Sikhs and understood the root of my questioning mind was humbling. She didn't expect me to be the best, but rather just to make the best effort.

These conversations grew to discussing equality, superstitions, and culture—bringing with them a newfound connection between my Mama and me.

Meanwhile, my sangat helped me discover a connection with my Guru, unlike that of before. The kirtan I once found incomprehensible was melodious and soothing—and is often what I now prefer to listen to in lieu of mainstream radio pop. More importantly, I was empowered. The conversations with my mother, my sangat, and my Guru settled my internal conflicts of identity and acceptance. I stopped worrying about measuring success and discarding the limitations placed on me for being a girl and began to become more concerned about developing myself. Being one of ten girls in my Computer Science lectures of three hundred students also reconfirmed my empowerment. I pursued a path in a "boyish" career. That was the unique identity I had the opportunity to create.

So I was a girl. A girl with two sisters and no brothers. A girl pursuing a career in a male-dominated field with one too many questions on all things Sikhi. On my visits to the now-developing hometown of my father in India, I was the educated ambitious girl of great potential, rather than just a girl without any brothers. And while my grandmother still showed no outward cheerful recognition to my job offer as she had a few years prior in a chirpy phone call to me relaying my male cousin's great job at Infosys that came with a great compensation package, I had a feeling she was surprised. Amazed not at the job offer that was nearly double the package of my cousin, but surprised I had achieved it as a girl. I fear the recognition from her will only come when I have mastered making *parotheys* or sabzis good enough to impress potential arranged suitors and their mothers.

As for my newfound courage and voice of confidence, though often channeled through passive aggression and thick attitude, has slowly begun changing the family dynamic. While the transformations are slower with my father, I see my sisters—not shy of expressing their thoughts and exploring their liberal interests—stepping away from any reservations of being girls.

As their sister, best friend, teacher, and mother, I still see them as newly born pocket-sized dolls with just a bit longer toes and fingers, similar to my Mama's hands. Having paved their way to a unique sense of self, perhaps their time will come when they are able to share their stories of disengagement, questioning, and empowerment. Until then we are all learning and adapting our identities, born from my Mama, raised by her hands, and growing into mine. From my Mama's hands to mine.

Part 2: Himmat

The Courage to Live as a Kaur

Like a Lotus on Water
by Puneet Kaur Sahota

At the age of 22, after sorting through many ads on Sikhnet, I had found only one that seemed interesting within a four-state radius of Missouri. Three e-mails later, I discovered Gurmukh was pursuing the same set of degrees as me, an MD and a PhD, and was a student living three hours away. Nine months later, we were engaged to be married. I had it made. I met a Sikh American guy who described himself as "gentle and open-minded," and bonus—he was a doctor-in-training too!

Four years after we were married, Gurmukh and I had a son at the end of our PhD training. He was our bliss—our Anand. When Anand turned eight months old, it was time for me to return to clinical rotations to complete my MD, and it also became a time to face the challenges of being a mother in medicine.

On the first day, I rose at 3 a.m. to pump breast milk before leaving for the hospital, where I'd stay from 5 a.m. to 8 p.m. that day. I arrived at the hospital to meet my new supervising physicians. I told them I was a nursing mother and asked for permission to take a brief break in the middle of the day to express milk for my son. They agreed and showed me where the pumping room was. Conscious of my clinical responsibilities, I tried to minimize the time I was away.

I said, "I can pump over a lunch break, if that's okay."

"Oh, we don't always get lunch," my supervisor replied. "Things are pretty busy on this rotation. Before you leave to pump milk, let me know, and I'll tell you if it's an okay time for you to go."

Two weeks later, she tells me that I'm not doing enough procedures because of the time it's taking me to pump, despite my procedure card tally showing I exceeded the course requirement. She says, "I know pumping is important to you. You need to make sure you're able to fulfill your responsibilities to the medical team while also meeting your personal need to pump." One of the other physicians tells me, "I have a baby too. I'm switching to formula because I just don't have time to pump. Maybe you should consider doing the same."

"But the American Academy of Pediatrics recommends breast-feeding up to a year, or as long afterward as mother and baby can. I'm trying to get there," I say. She shrugs. "Babies are fine with formula." A deep sense of shame convinces me I am taking time away from my duties in medicine to provide milk for my son. I am embarrassed that I have a need to breast-feed, and that it takes time away from my work.

I agonize over what to do. At this point in my life, my only connection to Anand is that I provide milk for him. I'm not home to see him wake up or tuck him in at night. This is all I can do for my child—make sure he still has nutrition, as women have been doing since the beginning of humankind.

The next day, I see my supervisor. I tell her, "I'm trying really hard to get in all of my required procedures and to help out the team. I brought extra pump parts so I won't have to wash them. It will take five minutes less this way for me to pump, so fifteen minutes total instead of twenty minutes."

"Fine," she says.

That night, bleary-eyed and exhausted, I try to find my dirty pump parts and empty bottles in my backpack amid textbooks, a stethoscope, and random junk, thinking that I will wash everything at night. Gurmukh finds me sorting through stuff. He puts an arm around my shoulder.

"Dear, I think you should rest. You look really tired. Why don't you let me wash the pump parts, okay?"

I nod and fall into bed. The next morning, when I rise at 3 a.m. and the rest of the family is sleeping, I find my pump parts washed, dried, and packed in a bag ready to go with me to work. When I thank Gurmukh later that day, he says that I am doing something important for Anand by breast-feeding, and he is going to help me do it. With his support, I find courage deep within me and decide to keep pumping. I move through the rotation, just barely keeping my head above water. Gurmukh quietly supports me and our family— washing pump parts, making sure dinner is on the table, and taking Anand to and from day care. I continue breast-feeding and pumping milk until Anand is thirteen months old, at which point he and I are both ready to wean. Soon afterward, Gurmukh finishes his PhD and also returns to medical school. We both fight to get through our training while keeping our family life healthy.

In these tough years of medical school, we are each married first to medicine—rising every day at *Amrit Vela* but without any time to do our *banis* except to listen to what we can in the car on the way to work. The hours are longer than I ever imagined, and the work more taxing than what I ever thought I could handle. But while we are each married to medicine, we remind ourselves every now and then that we are also married to each other. In brief, fleeting moments, we seek one another out for companionship along the way.

Many times, in the middle of a busy day of caring for patients, I receive a page. I check my beeper. It says, "10 minutes for lunch. Want to meet?" If I have those same ten minutes off, I reply. Many days I cannot meet, but when I can, it feels serendipitous. And so Gurmukh and I randomly have spontaneous "dates" in the middle of the hospital cafeteria. We wolf down sandwiches, sitting together at the table, husband and wife, married to each other and connecting briefly before we are swept back in by the never-ending waves of pages, patients, paperwork, and daily demands of medicine.

One day at the hospital, I'm rushing down the hallway when I see a flowing beard and turban out of the corner of my eye. I turn and see a Sikh family with two young boys wearing *patkas* as they all run to a doctor's appointment. I briefly meet the mother's eyes and raise my clasped hands in a silent "*Sat Sri Akal*" before entering my next patient's room. I realize that the boys remind me of Anand, who just started to wear a patka a few weeks ago.

Later that week, I sit quietly in the back of the room as my supervising physician explains to a couple that their newborn baby has a severe genetic disorder that has resulted in multiple problems with his organ systems, including his heart, lungs, and intestines. After listening and a long silence, they both take a deep sigh. The father says, "Well, you know what they say. God gives special children to special parents. We must be special." My eyes fill with tears as I think about the significance of this statement—and the living example before me of accepting *Waheguru*'s will.

Ideally, to be a Sikh is to be like a lotus on water. Floating above worldly attachments, always connected to Waheguru, yet serving others in this world, on Earth. Although I spend my working days in the world of medicine, I'm always swimming in motherhood, holding my head above water. Sometimes I'm floating happily; sometimes I'm barely treading water as the waves of beauty and grief wash over me. And sometimes, when a parent cries in front of me, or I hear a young patient say "Mama!" in a tone that reminds me of Anand, the waves engulf me; all I can see is the blue sea of mothering while the hospital is washed away for a moment. In my journey, I am attempting to mother, heal, love, and work—all while remaining rooted within the undercurrent of *Sikhi* and remembering Waheguru has put me here for a reason. My prayer for Anand is that he will experience the same rootedness in his faith as he steps out into the world. My prayer is that of Sikh mothers throughout generations: "*O son, this is your mother's blessing. May you forget not Lord God even for a moment, and ever remember the Lord of the Universe . . . May joy and playful pleasures be yours. May your hopes be realized and may you never be worn by worry.*" (Guru Granth Sahib, page 496)

Yet, even as I set this Sikh ideal for myself, I wonder if I have made the right life choices. When I am gone from home almost all of Anand's waking hours, and sometimes don't see him awake for days, how can I care for other people's children without being a hypocrite? What is *seva*, really? Who do we serve, when, and how? And how is the concept of seva unique for Sikh-American women? How does Sikhi guide us in balancing family life and seva to others outside our homes?

After another particularly long and difficult month at the hospital, I wonder what job I should take next and how many hours it's okay for me to miss of my child's daily life. Anguished, I go to the hospital chapel to pray and seek guidance. The round, marble ceiling is accented by religious symbols of faiths from all over the world. I gaze at the *khanda*, the Sikh nation's symbol, and feel a gratitude that I, too, am welcome in this sacred space where parents of sick children come for hope. Water flows down a sculpture built into the wall. I sit in a pew in front of the water flowing down, and the sound fills the chapel. Burying my head in my hands and asking Waheguru to help me, I start to remember important values with which I was raised. I remember Guru Gobind Singh's courageous statement after all four of his sons were killed. He declared that the whole *Khalsa*, the Sikh people, were his children. I was told this story as a young child both to inspire courage and to illustrate that worldly attachments were important to avoid as a Sikh. Guru Gobind Singh was the model of *sant-sipahi* (saint-soldier) life: to live for a righteous cause and not be deterred no matter how close to home the pain hit, even if one's own children were taken from them. So, was my journey supposed to be that of service to others, treating all my patients as my own children, equal in importance to Anand?

In every child I care for at the hospital, I see my own son. In every parent's hopes, dreams, and tears, I see my own—which is why I empathize with them and cry with them too. And then, a quiet voice inside me says, "Charity begins at home." I suddenly remember Guru Arjan Dev Ji's joyful poetry about the birth of Guru Hargobind. He thanks God and celebrates the birth of his son. To me, his love for Hargobind fills the page and overflows out of it. It exactly describes how I feel about the day Anand was born.

Asa 5th Guru
The True Satguru has sent the child.
The long-lived child has been born by destiny.
When he came and acquired an abode in the womb, his
mother's heart became very glad.
The son, the saint of the world—Lord is born . . .
The vine has extended and shall last for many generations.
The Lord has firmly established the machinery of devotion
and love.
I have become carefree and have fixed my attention on one
God.

(Guru Granth Sahib, page 396)

Remembering these lines gives me confidence that even the Gurus, who treated all Sikhs like their children, rejoiced and celebrated at the birth of their own offspring. Their biological children were gifts, blessings from Waheguru. While being detached from worldly affairs and serving others is a worthy spiritual Sikh goal and one I will continue to pursue, I can only do so with gusto when I intuively know my own family is well cared for. I gain the strength to do seva and give back to others when I feel my family is strong and happy and that I have given all that I am able for my son. I resolve to put Anand at the center of my life, always prioritizing him and his needs. I find creative ways to mother even while I am not home: I send him video greetings every day from the hospital. I call home whenever I can. And I stop being ashamed that I am a doctor who also is a mother and that I may need time to pump milk or otherwise care for my son. I start wearing my motherhood with pride. And I schedule more research months during medical school so I can be home when Anand wakes up at night to put him to bed for at least some time while he is young.

A few months later, I have a particularly difficult day as a new doctor. The nurse asks me, "Why is the patient on this new medication?

The family is upset about it." This is yet another question I cannot answer today, and it is the final straw. I burst into tears. "I have no idea why. I just don't know." A kind physician comes over to help me sort this out. We figure out the answer, but I realize that there is no way I am going to see Anand today. There are just too many patients, too many questions, too much paperwork to be done before I can leave the hospital. I quickly text Gurmukh to tell him I will be at the hospital very late. Somehow, Gurmukh senses my emotional distress. Ten minutes later, wearing his surgical scrubs, he quietly appears on the floor where I am working. He sits down at a computer behind me and does not say a word. He sits there for five minutes as I work—just literally, physically being there for me, saying through his body language, "I am *behind you*." He says nothing, but I feel support and a deep empathy emanating from my husband. He has been through this same transition into young doctorhood, and he knows exactly how hard this is. Five minutes later, he waves a quiet good-bye as he leaves to go home and care for our son. In the coming weeks, Gurmukh appears spontaneously at random times on the floor where I am. Sometimes, it's just a glance and wave hello, or a hand on my shoulder quietly as I work. Sometimes, it's checking on me before he goes home, and a quick hug, a reminder that my family supports me as I strive to provide excellent care for my patients. When things get hard, I remind myself that no matter how difficult the work is, Gurmukh is always there, not far away, just a few floors down in the hospital. We are colleagues, friends, partners, and co-parents. These multiple enmeshed roles make our relationship strong, like knotted ropes weaved into a strong basket. The lines between family and work blur every day for us. And I am grateful every moment for his support.

In current moments when I am unbalanced and unsure about how to balance mothering and medicine, I think back to the seminal moment when I finished school. Finally, after ten years of hard work, I graduated from medical school and graduate school. I had imagined this moment for many years: Gurmukh and I would graduate together with our two degrees each. We would march across the stage one behind the other, the two Dr. Sahotas who had somehow made it all work and had had a child during training. Because of the extra months I took to do research and be more available to Anand, this is not how it happens. On my graduation day, Gurmukh has already finished—he has graduated one year earlier. He sits in the audience to watch me graduate. And when the time comes for me to march across the stage, my eyes fill with tears. Gurmukh hands me Anand. I proudly hoist my son on my hip, and together, Anand and I cross the stage. I carry Anand with one arm, and accept my diploma with the other hand. With deep pride and gratitude, I publicly honor my son and the central place he has in my life. I will never again be ashamed that I am a mother in medicine. I will proudly acknowledge my family and the emotional foundation of strength they provide that enables me to be a doctor. I am both mother and healer, and these identities are inseparable. My seva to the world is that I will raise a strong son and I will serve others as a doctor. I will carry my child in one hand, and care for my patients with the other.

Y2K Love

Surinder Singh

Summer of 1999,
somewhere in sunny Southern California . . .

Going shopping with girlfriends can sometimes be more of an annoyance than a leisurely activity. I didn't want to sit and twirl my thumbs outside of a fitting room, so I decided to wander off to the mall lobby sitting area and wait for my friend Rodella to get done trying on her clothes at the department store. As I sat there minding my own business, my eyes came in contact with a middle-aged Caucasian woman. I smiled at her and quickly gazed away. I tried to act like I didn't notice her, but in my periphery, I could see her stand up and head toward me. She sat down in the empty seat beside me. She wore a long crinkled brown cotton skirt with a brown cotton tank top. Her curly hair was a bit scraggly with a few strands falling onto her cheeks. I noticed the many wrinkles around her eyes and lips as she smiled at me and said:

"Hello."

I was a bit intimidated but replied back with a cautious smile. "Hi."

I tried not to pay much attention to her as she sat next to me reading a magazine. She turned to me and said, "Would you happen to know where the nearest children's toy store would be in this area?"

Without hesitation, I politely directed her to the closest toy store, situated a few blocks from the mall. She smiled and thanked me for my assistance. I stood up and headed back to the department store. She, yet again, caught my attention.

"Miss, have you ever had a reading done?"

"A reading? You mean like a psychic reading?"

"Yes, a psychic reading. "

Oh great! It was all a scheme of hers. The nerve of her to scam me! I thought I'd give her a taste of her own medicine and just play along.

"Why no, I've never had a psychic reading. I don't think I could financially afford one."

"Really? Well, you should get one sometime. I'd be willing to give you one in exchange for giving me directions."

"Sure, I'll take the offer." I sat back down in anticipation of her predictions.

She didn't ask me for my hands, nor did she pull out any Tarot cards or something of the sort. She merely sat there beside me, staring at my face. A few moments of silence later, she said:

"You're going to get married next year."

I wasn't too surprised by her comment. After all, I figured, I'm twenty-three years old and employed as a professional, and have parents harassing me about marriage nearly every day; it's bound to happen in the near future, although not likely as early as next year.

"I see a man wearing a white coat, and he has dark facial hair."

Duh! I would hope to marry a Sikh man and would expect him to have dark facial hair. Oh and the white coat . . . being a healthcare professional, I would hope to find someone in the healthcare industry as well. Every clinician wears a white coat!

"He will be from the East."

When you live in Southern California, practically every geographical location would be east of you in the United States. Perhaps she meant East Indian. Just as I was starting to lose interest, she shared:

"You'll get married on June 21, 2000. But . . ."

"But what?"

"But your parents won't agree to the marriage. You will have to choose between the man of your dreams and your parents."

I was appalled! Was she kidding me? She had watched way too many Hindi movies and was now pulling this Bollywood line on me. I must've been the only *desi* with "sucker" written on my forehead that she could find that afternoon. I was puzzled. I was a very obedient child of whom my parents were very fond of. I could never possibly be placed in a situation where I'd have to choose between anyone. Besides, my parents were so dear to me that I couldn't ever consider putting anyone on the same pedestal as them.

"You have been with this man in the previous two lifetimes. He died in a war in your last life, and you died shortly after his death."

At this point I was disgusted! Where was this lady pulling this death crap out of? I thanked her for her free reading and shuffled off to attend to my friend.

December 12, 1999

The Internet and home PCs were becoming household names in the late '90s. I spent much of my free time, usually the late hours after work, on the Internet chatting. Sikhnet was a popular chat room at the time for many young Sikhs. I met numerous people from all over the world. Many of the chatters were single and I assume online in search of a marriage prospect. Others were students who fooled around during their spare time. I had met a few other frequent flyers with whom I became chat buddies. A gal with the alias of "Levophed" from Chicago became a good friend. We often looked out for each other and would send private messages warning the other of certain chatters, especially perverted ones.

I found many of the guys in the chat room to be sleazy and just so not my type. However, today was different. I ran into a chatter named "Chicagoan." We chatted for more than two hours, poking fun at other fellow chatters. Although it unfortunately sounded much like a case of Internet bullying, I was actually having fun with this Chicagoan guy. He didn't share too much about himself, nor did I disclose very much about myself. He requested to move our conversations onto the telephone instead. He offered to call me, but

I was not willing to give out my phone number. It was past midnight Pacific time, and I couldn't possibly be caught on the phone at this hour by my parents. Besides, I was leery about talking to a stranger. I had heard stories about identity theft and stalking, and didn't want to be a victim myself. I told him I wasn't willing to disclose my telephone number to someone I had met merely a few hours earlier. He asked for me to call him instead. He was so insistent on my calling that he even instructed me on how to block my caller-ID using "*67"—something I never had tried. After a bit of reluctance, he finally persuaded me to call him.

He had a very pleasant, masculine voice. Even better was his laugh, which was infectious and so attractive. We talked that night about irrelevant stuff, although the question of marriage did come up from his end. I shared with him that my parents would only permit my marriage with a Ramgharia Sikh. He was a gentleman and did not make any judgmental comments about my parents' choices. Nearly three hours had passed, and it was almost dawn. My dad was going to be up any minute to do Guru Sahib's *prakaash,* and I needed to get off the phone before that. We ended our telephone conversation in good spirits. Ironically, neither one of us had shared any personal information with each other. We still didn't know each other's names. All we knew that was that we were both in our twenties, in the healthcare industry, and most importantly, single.

The next day, I daydreamed about his wonderful voice. I was tickled by our conversations. I was eager to get home that night and was hoping to run into him again in the chat room. I rushed home from work and, to my pleasant surprise, there he was . . . waiting for me to log on. We were enjoying each other's company so much that we quickly decided to prefer the telephone as a means of chatting instead of the Internet. It became nearly a daily routine for us to talk on the phone.

Chicagoan had no shame in asking me to make the phone calls most days, as he confessed he was a "starving med student." I was earning a decent salary and living with my parents and didn't mind paying the phone bills. In those days, cell phones weren't common, so I carried a pager as a means of contact. My family and friends paged me when they needed to talk to me. Our conversations became frequent enough that he would page me whenever he was available to talk, and I'd get in touch with him as soon as I could.

After a week of talking, we shared our names and ages with one another. Astoundingly, we didn't know how the other looked but still continued to express mutual interest. Neither one of us was willing to e-mail the photo first. "Levophed" was the only chatter with whom I had shared my picture online. She and I were good buddies and had gained each other's trust over time. Two weeks of chatting with Chicagoan had gone by, and one night, he sounded very playful on the phone. He confessed that he had seen my photo! It turned out that Levophed and Chicagoan were hangout buddies in Chicago who attended med school together. He sided with her and said she was reluctant to share my photo, but after his constant pleading, she gave in. He guiltily offered to share his pic with me that same night. And my, was he attractive! The voice, the personality, and now the face! What I was afraid of was happening . . . I was falling for him.

March 2000

Regardless of my parents' requirements for me for marriage, I continued to chat with Chicagoan on a daily basis. I was hooked! He and I would have many philosophical talks about Sikhism, including those on the so-called caste system that Sikhs followed—a practice that was strongly condemned by our Sikh Gurus. We as Sikhs were equals—irrespective of our socioeconomic status, gender, or any other background. Chicagoan asserted that he was strictly against the thought of segregating people, let alone practicing it. He had dropped his father's surname once he turned sixteen and kept Singh as a last name. He wouldn't claim to be a part of a group within Sikhs, but after much pestering, he finally confessed that his family claimed to be Bhappas. I commended him on keeping Singh as a last name but was disappointed at the same time. He wasn't a Ramgharia. I was almost sure that my parents would never agree to my marrying with this guy.

I didn't understand why my parents were being so difficult about the whole caste thing. This guy was a Sikh with unshorn hair, in his last semester of med school, and he exhibited an awesome personality. He had stayed behind after his parents and younger sister moved back to India when he was sixteen. His parents did not like the hectic lifestyle in the United States and had wanted to move back for a more leisurely standard of living. He had lived independently without any financial support from his parents. With the help of scholarships and grants in addition to large bank loans, he had put himself through med school. He was humble. He worked odd jobs, many that I could never consider holding. He wowed me more and more, and I couldn't help but to grow closer to him the more I got to know him.

It was now approaching the middle of March 2000. My mother had booked a flight to India at the end of the month. After much debate with my parents, they booked my flight to India for May 3, 2000. My mother assumed the extra month she spent in India prior to my arrival would provide her with ample time to filter out the "biodata" for the so-called marriage prospects for me. I wasn't too thrilled about this. I had shared this with Chicagoan, and he wasn't too thrilled either. I was torn. I had finally met a wonderful guy with whom I got along very well, but I knew that there would be no future between us.

Early April 2000

A male friend of mine was getting married on April 22, 2000. I was infatuated with Chicagoan by this point and had the crazy idea of inviting him to attend the wedding with me. I thought I'd at least take the liberty of treating myself to meeting this fabulous guy! He had often made subtle remarks about meeting up, but we had never seriously discussed the idea. This was my chance, so I proposed:

"Would you be up to coming out to LA and chaperoning me to a friend's wedding reception?"

He excitedly took me up on the invitation. "Sure, but you know I'm a starving medical student. I couldn't possibly afford the flight and the hotel. Would you be willing to pay for my room and board?"

My jaw dropped at the sound of his words. "Wow, that was bold. You're going to have a girl pay for you?"

"Yeah, why not? We are equals, aren't we? Why can't a girl be expected to pay for something for a change?"

I chuckled and agreed to cough up the payments. I figured losing a few hundred bucks over this guy would totally be worth my while.

He had booked his ticket for LA for arrival on Friday, April 21, 2000, the day before the wedding reception. I was working that Friday night and couldn't take time off to pick him up. One of our mutual female friends on Sikhnet who lived in LA offered to pick him up from the airport and show him around the city for the day.

April 22, 2000

It was "D-Day." I was finally going to meet Chicagoan live, face-to-face! Indian wedding receptions are quite formal. I knew he would be dressed in a suit and, in hopes of looking my very best that day, I went out and purchased a new *lengha*.

I knew I was going to be out late that night but didn't know how to stall my parents. I covered it up with a white lie, claiming that I had to attend a friend's wedding and would have to go to work thereafter. I was a good kid and my parents were naive; they believed me.

I was all decked out, wearing a designer black *lengha* and black heels, my makeup perfected, an updo held together with a velvet flower hair pick. I had planned to pick him up by 5 p.m. so we would have enough time to get acquainted.

I inquired at the hotel concierge about his room number. Room 221. I headed up the stairs in the direction of his room. My legs trembled as I walked, my hands were sweaty, and my belly was full of butterflies. A number of wild thoughts raced through my head: What if he is a psycho? What if he is smelly? What if he isn't as attractive in real life? What if . . . ? I was terrified and excited all at the same time. It felt like I was on a roller coaster.

I took a few deep breaths and then knocked on his door. He opened the door and with a smile greeted me in a playful voice. "Hello. How are you?" I bashfully greeted him back. He was gorgeous, and he smelled so masculine. He gave me a hug and asked me to have a seat.

He was wearing a crisp ironed white dress shirt and black slacks. His head was crowned with a perfectly tied black turban, and his dark facial hair was tidied up without a loose strand in sight. He excused himself and asked me to make myself comfortable only to step away to grab a couple of his ties. With a grand smile, he held up two ties, one in each hand, and asked me which looked best on him. I blushed and could feel the warmth of blood rushing to my face. I bashfully pointed to the one I liked, and he quickly started to knot it up. He grabbed his suit coat and was ready to get off to the party. I excused myself to the restroom prior to leaving his hotel room. I touched up my lipstick, dabbed off the excess with a tissue, and tossed it into his hotel wastebasket.

We talked on our way to the reception. He asked me about my parents, questioning if they were aware of my going out with a guy. I confessed to him that I was meeting him secretively. No one but my coworkers were aware of what was going on. If someone from home called my workplace, my coworkers knew to page me to notify me. I had switched my workdays with a few colleagues to allow me to spend four days with Chicagoan.

We arrived at the party, and it was pretty uneventful. We ate a bit and chatted at the table. We did a bit of people-watching and chuckled a bit. At about 10 p.m., we decided to leave. We arrived at his hotel, and he asked me to come up to the room to "hang out for a little bit." Up to this point in the evening he had been a gentleman, so I figured it would be safe for me to go to his room. We had a few conversations, and all the while he was quite flirtatious. I sat down on the edge of his bed and relieved my aching feet of my heels. He had taken off his suit jacket and tie. He made himself comfortable and sat down next to me. He looked me in the eyes and compli-mented me on how nice I looked that evening. My heart raced, and I recall seeing his lips moving, muttering something I couldn't make out. I had gone deaf and was feeling euphoric sitting beside him. The next thing I recall was kissing and embracing him.

It was nearly midnight. I was supposedly working the night shift, as I had told my parents. I hung out with Chicagoan until 1 a.m. and left to sleep at Rodella's place. In the morning, I changed into my scrubs and met Chicagoan for an early-morning breakfast before I headed back home. Each one of the four days he was in town was planned schematically. I would show up in scrubs with the intent to go to work but instead would take off, showing Chicagoan the town. I would've never accomplished this without the aid of my colleagues and the gullible nature of my parents.

I feared running into someone I knew, an Aunty or an Uncle from the community, but figured I'd come up with another white lie of some sort to cover up. The only thing that worried me was the possibility of getting into an accident. I would be caught red-handed hanging out with a guy. Then my parents would catch on to all my lies and lose all faith in me. On Chicagoan's last day, as we were going to the airport, I shared this fear with him. His response was, "Well, if we get into an accident and survive, it could pose a problem, but if we die, it'd be okay. I wouldn't mind dying with you." That overall feeling of euphoria crept up on me again. I felt myself falling inside . . . on that thrill ride again.

Chicagoan was on the verge of finishing med school in a few weeks and had planned to move in with his aunt in the northwest suburbs of Chicago. I asked him for his new contact information, so we could keep in touch. I couldn't locate any scrap paper in my car, so he offered to write it on a receipt he had in his pocket. While I was driving, I turned my head and watched him reach into his right front pants pocket. He pulled out a handful of receipts and, to my surprise, that same tissue with my lipstick imprint that I had tossed in his hotel room wastebasket and a flower that had broken off the black velvet hair pick I had worn to the reception. My eyes lit up, and I was speechless. He quickly shoved everything but a receipt back into his pocket, wrote down his contact info, and handed it to me.

I was in love and didn't know what to do about it. I was leaving for India in less than two weeks to meet some marriage prospects I didn't have any feelings for! I was bewildered. Should I elope with this guy and defy my parents, or should I be the obedient daughter and marry the husband they approved of for me?

We were running late and racing to make it in time for his flight. I dropped him off at the terminal and asked him to meet me at the gate. I requested that he not board the plane without saying good-bye to me. I rushed and parked my car and ran up moving escalators to get to his gate. I arrived at his gate and looked around frantically among the crowded sitting areas. My heart raced and I feared he had left before I could see him off. He was sitting in the far back, looking straight at me. He stood up and we walked quickly toward each other. I hugged him tightly and said, "I was so worried. I thought you had left." He rubbed my back and said, "I would not have left without saying good-bye."

I watched him as he was about to board the plane. I ran up and gave him yet another tight hug and shared that I would miss him dearly and thanked him for coming out to LA. He sighed and said he would miss me too. I turned around and promised myself not to look back at him. It would be too painful. This was, perhaps, the last time I would see him. Tears ran down my cheeks as I walked away from the gate and out of the terminal. Flashbacks of our time spent together on the phone and in person ran through my head. I was shattered. This was it. It was over. I would never feel so mesmerized and in love again.

April, 26, 2000

The next day I was back to work—this time for real. I was unable to concentrate all evening. I had a heartfelt dilemma and felt helpless. The day to take my flight to India was approaching. After work that night, I was unsure about logging on to the chat room. Why was I leading myself on when I knew it wasn't going to happen? My heart kept winning the battle over my mind. I logged on to chat only to find Chicagoan waiting for me. He instantly sent me a private message asking to speak on the phone. I was reluctant, but so desired to hear his voice. I called him. He was his usual cheerful self. He asked, "So what do we do from here on?" I was perplexed and told him that I wasn't willing to hurt my parents in any way. He asked, "But you are willing to hurt yourself?"

I didn't have any answers, for him or for myself. After much debate and pondering, he suggested I talk to someone in the family I felt comfortable discussing such the topic with. I was afraid. Growing up, we never talked about love or even sexuality for that matter. Talking to boys or dating was pretty much a no-no. And now for me to go off and tell my family that I was out with a guy for four days when I should've been at work or college would definitely throw my family into complete disbelief. Chicagoan and I talked about any and every possible solution to our very complicated mess.

There was no doubt he wanted to be with me. He had spoken to his aunt and uncle in Chicago and his parents and discussed the next steps with them. They offered to talk to my parents, but I declined their offer in fear of rejection from my parents. I finally built up enough courage to have a talk with my eldest brother, Veer. Often, what Veer said influenced my parents greatly. I was pampered by Veer, and he was always nonjudgmental and calm with me. Perhaps he would be receptive to my feelings and help me out.

On Thursday, April 27, I called Veer and told him I needed to talk to him alone. He came by that evening to see me. I bawled and pleaded for his help. He listened very attentively and questioned why I had not told him about Chicagoan when I had started chatting with him? He was frazzled, especially since I was leaving for India in merely a week. He hugged me and assured me that he would talk to Daddy.

Veer's thirty-third birthday was approaching on April 30. My parents always held *langar seva* at the *gurudwara* on the Sunday falling closest to our birthdays. So this time the langar seva was to take place without my mother, who was already in India. We all spent the Saturday prior to that day prepping for the langar. That evening I questioned Veer about talking to Daddy, and he mentioned that he planned to do it that night. I was worried. Inevitable thoughts raced through my head.

It was Sunday, April 30. I was entering the langar hall and could see Veer in the kitchen cooking away. I softly asked him:

"Did you talk to him?"

He nodded. "He said no. There is no way this marriage can take place."

I was badly heartbroken. I didn't have the heart to argue or question Veer further. My eyes filled with tears. I didn't know what to do but to leave the gurudwara immediately. I sobbed the entire route home.

I reached home and called Chicagoan to share the horrible news. He was silent on the phone for some time. He asked for me to speak to the aunt he was staying with for a few minutes. She came on the phone and very pleasantly tried to console me and advised me to be optimistic about the future. She said, "*Waheguru* (the Almighty Lord) will make things right. It will work out. Just keep faith in him." She tried to reassure me that parents always eventually give in to their children's wishes.

Chicagoan asked me if I was serious about him and to what extent would I go to be with him. I wasn't sure. I did not want to hurt my parents. He said he was willing to leave everything behind for me only if I was willing to do the same. All I knew was that he had nothing to lose; I had my parents and my entire family at stake.

I spent the remainder of the day and night and much of the next morning hiding out in my room. I avoided coming in contact with any family. I spoke with Chicagoan that Monday morning. He attested his love for me again and stated that he wanted to spend the rest of his life with me. He proposed leaving Chicago that same day and driving out to California to pick me up within twenty-four hours. The ball was in my court. I had to make the final call.

I struggled with my thoughts and, after much debate, I reached a verdict. I was going to elope and was ready to put everything at stake. My parents had lived most of their lives. I had my entire life yet to live. Chicagoan would arrive on May 2, a day before my planned flight to India. I called Veer and informed him of my decision. He said he wanted to talk to Daddy one last time before I left.

Later that evening, I was in my room packing my belongings and Veer stopped by to see me. He mentioned that Daddy wanted to talk to me. I was terrified. I had never raised my voice or had arguments with my father. We all had this sense of fear around him, not of his hurting us physically in any way, but of us disappointing him.

Daddy Ji loved me dearly. As a child, he always wiped off my tears when I was hurt and reassured me that everything was going to be all right. I was praying for the same this time. I entered his room. My parents slept in separate beds. He was sitting on his bed. He very softly asked me to sit down, designating me to sit in front of him on my mother's bed. I had never had a serious discussion such as this one. I didn't have the courage to look him in the eyes. The hurt in his voice could be sensed as he said:

"You know we love you very much, right?"

With tears flowing down my face, I nodded. "Yes."

"Would you be willing to change your decision and step back from the whole scene?"

I sniffled a bit and shook my head. "No, I can't." I somehow had the courage to speak up. My father was a baptized Sikh. I asked him, "Did Guru Gobind Singh put his Sikhs into groups, categorizing them by castes, and expected them to take *amrit* in a segregated fashion?"

He stayed quiet, still looking down. After a long pause he asked: "Is this what you want?"

I sobbed and nodded. "Yes, I'm sorry, and I love you very much."

He raised his left hand toward the door, indicating the conversation was now over, asking me to leave.

I rethought my decision but planned to stick with it. Chicagoan was leaving that night and was to arrive by the following night to take me away. I resumed with my packing. Less than an hour later, Veer walked back into my room. He said Daddy Ji had had a discussion with him and had agreed to my marriage with Chicagoan. I was astounded with their decision. I hugged Veer tightly and sobbed with relief and appreciation. He asked me for Chicagoan's number and said he was going to call and talk to him and his family. I quickly called Chicagoan and informed him of the good news and gave him a heads up on receiving a phone call from Veer. He was ecstatic.

I had stopped packing my stuff and was now just waiting impatiently for Veer to get back to me after his phone chat with Chicagoan. I later received a call from Chicagoan. He sounded relieved and very happy. He informed me of the plans Veer had made with him on the phone. I was to catch my flight to India as planned the following day, on May 3, and he had booked a flight to leave for India shortly after mine, on May 5. As Chicagoan's parents resided in India, the plan was for us to get married while visiting India. I followed as directed and did nothing more. I didn't want to ruin it for myself.

I took the flight to India the next day as intended. I was afraid that once I had arrived in India, I wouldn't know how to break the news to my mother. She was there at the gate to receive my arrival in Delhi. She gave me a hug with an incomplete smile. I presumed she already knew what was going on. My mother didn't make much conversation with me the first few days I was there. She spoke to me only on a "need to know" basis.

A week had passed and she finally let it out. In an angry voice, she accused me. All in one breath she cried: "Why are you doing this to us? We raised you with so much love and affection. You were pampered by all of us." She pulled out a few photos and shoved them in my face and said, "You want an educated guy?" She threw an opened duffle bag filled with male photos and biodata at my feet. "You want an engineer? Here. You want a doctor? Here . . . here's a doctor!"

I stood there sobbing, helpless and speechless. She held her head and walked off to her room. I lay back down in my bed and cried myself to sleep.

May 15, 2000

My mother picked up Veer and Daddy Ji from the airport that night. I was already asleep by the time they came home. I woke up the next morning to discover that Daddy Ji and Veer had already left the house to meet Chicagoan and his family. The wedding was fixed. I was to get married in four days on May 21, 2000.

I was excited that it was finally happening for me but upset that it wasn't happening on good terms with my family. My mother had picked out an outfit on her own. I didn't protest. I was just pleased that things were working in my favor.

Chicagoan, my knight in shining armor, arrived on a white horse to the gurudwara and swept me away. We received blessings from both parents and took on our own path as husband and wife. I moved to the Midwest with him, and we carried on with establishing our careers. Relationships with each other's families were a bit awkward initially but steadily worked out their wrinkles.

Chicagoan and I moved to Michigan a year after marriage. He completed his residency, and I completed graduate school and became a nurse practitioner with his ongoing encouragement. We practiced medicine together in the same clinic and cherished each other's company.

We have sustained the many changing seasons in our lives. It has now been thirteen years since our marriage, and we've moved back to my home state of California. Life could not be any better. Our love has been triumphant. Our marriage between so-called castes conquered the beliefs of my family. They have come to the conclusion that a Sikh is simply a Sikh, with no divisional sects.

Looking back at the timeline, perhaps the dates were merely coincidental with the psychic's marriage prediction. I got married exactly a month before her predicted date. Or perhaps she was a godsend who had come to forewarn me of what the future was to hold. Maybe her predictions even aided my own psyche into subconsciously following through with my actions in order to fulfill my destiny. Whatever the case, it was a happy ending.

LoveSikh:
My Journeys for Home and Belonging
Sangeeta K. Luthra

Until a few years ago, I took love for granted. I grew up oblivious to how lucky I was to have parents and grandparents who gave me unconditional and unshakeable love. They filled me with a lifetime supply, a reservoir that has sustained me. I am trying to pass that forward to my family and especially to my daughters. Writing about love is one way of doing this. It has shown me that love is precious precisely because we have to work at it every day—sometimes joyfully and, more often, painstakingly. Now that I am a parent myself, I truly appreciate how hard my parents worked to make their love seem effortless. *Sikhi* is at the heart of my parents' love, and like a double helix has expressed itself over time for family, for work, for community, and for life itself. My own love story unfolded on the move—in planes, trains, and automobiles as I spun around the globe. What began as wanderlust became a journey in search of home and self.

New Delhi, December 1974
A Grandfather's Love—Darji's Story

It was a cold, foggy, winter morning, around 3 a.m. in New Delhi, when my brother and I landed at Palam International Airport. I was eight years old and my brother eleven, and this was our first visit to India since our parents had made the same journey in reverse to the United States in 1971. We were traveling without our parents, chaperoned by a close family friend who was traveling back to India at the same time. My parents' decision to send us on that first journey back home was bittersweet. My father was going to miss the wedding of his youngest brother, Gogi, and my mother was going to miss an opportunity to meet her parents and siblings after three and a half years in the United States.

My memories of the journey are sketchy. I cannot remember what we ate, what we wore, or the toys and books we brought to keep busy during the long flight. I can remember the anxiety: looking through our bags again and again to check that our passports and tickets were accounted for. I was tense throughout the journey and can still remember the immense relief I felt when the plane finally landed and I knew that my grandfather, or "Darji," as he was known in our extended family, was waiting for us just a few hundred feet away. I was coming up for air after a long swim.

Crossing the threshold of the plane, we took our first breaths of the damp, musty air of a New Delhi winter morning and wound our way through customs lines and baggage checks until we finally got a glimpse of Darji waiting near the front of the airport. He was leaning against the rope barriers designed to keep the bleary-eyed but happy crowd of relatives, friends, and drivers from spilling into the arrivals and customs area of the airport. Some in the large crowd had garlands of fresh marigolds in their hands and others had handwritten signs with the names of those they were receiving. As we inched closer to the crowd, the sounds of the city—cars, taxis, and autorickshaws—grew louder. The air became heavier with vehicle exhaust, cigarette and beedi smoke, and more dewy dust as it wafted in, undoing the sterility of the airport. India was seeping in through doors that steadily swung open and closed as a stream of people moved in and out.

As we got closer, we could see Darji smiling broadly. His horn-rimmed glasses slid up and down the bridge of his nose as he called out to us through the hubbub of the crowd. He was a broad-shouldered man, six feet tall with a stiffly starched turban, salt-and-pepper beard and mustache, and a distinctive limp from a motorcycle injury of many years ago that had left his right knee stiff. He waved and smiled and laughed with tears in his eyes as he saw us pushing our luggage cart through the crowd. We were the children of his firstborn son who moved to the other side of the world, and for that I think he felt his grandfatherly love even more intensely.

We, Darji and my cousins and I, spent many hours in the Ambassador traveling from the airport to his home in Ghaziabad. Like nomads, we traveled to and from late-night dinners with relatives living in Delhi and for the late-night functions for Gogi Chacha's wedding. Once we had settled in for the long commutes, Darji made us recite *paath* (prayers) and *shabads* (hymns). In the morning or daytime, we would recite the *Mool Mantar* five or ten times and finish with the sweet, comforting words of the shabad, "*Tu mera pita, tu hai mera mata*," ("You are my father, you are my mother."). On evening drives we listened and try to follow him in the *Rehras Sahib* and *Kirtan Sohila* prayers. My cousins and I sat crammed together in the backseat, as if on an overstuffed sofa on wheels, moving through the cacophony that is Indian traffic. Along with other cars and trucks, Delhi streets were rivers of scooters, bicycles, pedestrians, cows, dogs, cats, and the occasional horse-driven tonga and donkey-pulled cart. Horns, bells, loudspeakers, and shouting commuters punctuated our recitations within the car. The aroma of peanuts roasting over coals, *aloo tikki* (spiced potato patties) frying on *tavas*, and sweet juice being squeezed from citrus and sugarcane was intoxicating, like incense for our prayers.

As we approached Ghaziabad, a sooty, bustling industrial town, another India began to come into focus. In those days, between Delhi and Ghaziabad were mostly small villages and farms that seemed to recede into the red-brown landscape. Only the smoke rising like a mirage from tiny homes seemed to give away their otherwise camouflaged existence. On a clear day we caught glimpses of children playing in dusty alleys and of cows, dogs, and cats foraging through piles of trash for something to eat. It was the quieter part of the journey before we reentered the purposeful chaos of Ghaziabad. Winding through the town, we entered our neighborhood by crossing railroad tracks hugged by a line of *jhuggis* (literally "shacks"). Darji often drew our attention to the *jhuggis an*d say, "You see the poverty; you won't see this in America. *Hai mera Baba, mehr karo . . .*"

Prayer and companionship within the car played out uncomfortably with the poverty and suffering outside. Blurry scenes of children living along the tracks silently seeped into me. I felt confused and shocked, but also alive and oddly at home. Many years later I began to understand why Darji made us look at this other world outside the car window. Over time and through Darji's eyes, the space between these two worlds became the foundation of my understanding of Sikhism. The Gurus' words hung in the dusty air of the Ambassador. I began to see the threads of the *gurbani* binding the ideals of Sikhism to an imperfect and cruel world. Sikhism was paath and *simrin* (meditation)—a new way of seeing and understanding. It was also *seva* (serving), not only serving others but also a new way of acting. Over the years, Darji and I traveled these roads again and again. In between, I finished school, left for college, traveled, and grappled with self and circumstances. Darji's words echoed back to me and kept me close to my Sikh heritage.

This experience of arrival and welcome was repeated many times over the years as I returned to India from the States—as a teenager, as a college student, as a graduate student, and later as a wife and mother with my own children. Almost every visit to India began in this way, until my last visit. In December 2005, Darji was not there to greet me at the airport. I had come to attend his last rites. Darji had passed away a few days earlier, and the cremation was already done. Only when I was waved through by the customs officials and had pushed my luggage cart through the crowd did I truly understand that I would never again see my Darji's face. The absence of my grandfather's rib-crushing hugs and breathless prayers of thanks left a hole in my heart.

My love story is about journeys and spaces in which I have found love in family and community—as a daughter, sister, friend, teacher, wife, mother, and Sikh. Darji was and still is a critical interlocutor, a constant companion in my journey, much of which I experienced riding in his Ambassador car.

Sangeeta K. Luthra

Pittburgh, Pennsylvania, October 1978
Going to the Gurudwara

Our Sunday-morning drive to the *gurudwara* (temple) was cheered by bright sun ricocheting off trees adorned with scarlet and amber-hued leaves made crisp by the cold but colorful autumns of Western Pennsylvania. The brightly colored leaves against graying tree limbs mirrored the ornate and brightly colored *ramala* (cloth) that covered the Guru Granth Sahib (the Sikh scripture) waiting in a gray-blue building. The luxuriously ornate ramala radiated warmth and drew me to the Guru as I bowed my head. Huddled together on the carpeted floor of the diwan hall, I sat close to my friends, cross-legged, knees touching. Side-glances, whispers, and smiles bonded us. The *sangat* (congregation) filled my heart with warmth and belonging. The *parshad* (sacred sweet porridge) filled my rumbling tummy.

The gurudwara was a refuge from feeling different, brown, or other. It became a place of culture, community, and belonging for the fifty or so Sikh and Hindu families that shared the rented space. Hindu *murtis* (idols) stood on the stage of the main hall. At the end of a *puja* (Hindu prayer) the curtains were drawn and the gods and goddesses were hidden from view. Like a scene change in a play, our parents placed the Guru Granth Sahib in front of the drawn curtain. After the service and *langar* (community meal), we children would sometimes sneak back behind the curtain and wonder about the elaborately decorated idols of Lord Ram, Sitaji, Hanumanji, Ganeshji, Lord Krishna, and others. As we recited Sikh prayers, incantations of a formless, infinite, timeless *Waheguru* (Divine), the idols seemed to bear witness. They were with us but not there. An older me would wonder about the undeniable but uneasy relationship of Sikhism to Hinduism. But at this point the relationship was more than politics; it was personal. It mirrored my own family's mixed experience of Sikhism.

In this community, my family away from family, I grew up. Like many adolescents, my mind began to turn toward the world beyond. Reading was another refuge. I remember being riveted by other people's histories. I read *Roots: The Saga of an American Family* and *Holocaust.* I don't remember why I was drawn to these books, but I

94

do remember the waves of indignation, guilt, and sadness I felt as I read. My own otherness, brown and exotic, chafed as I finished high school. At graduation I was dry-eyed and quietly ecstatic to be leaving the homogeneity and smallness of my hometown. College and life after allowed me to open up and play with many identities: woman "of color," student, activist, feminist, teacher, and eventually anthropologist. In each of these roles I found elements of Sikhism that were, for me, becoming about struggle: against sexism, bigotry, and exploitation, but mostly I was struggling for myself.

Dalhousie, India, June 1980
Love and Friendship in the Punjabi Homeland

My love affair with India took root in the warmth of Darji's Ambassador car, but its first blooms were in the mist-covered mountains of the Himalayas. At the time, I knew little of the spiritual significance of these mystical mountains for Indians of all faiths. I had yet to learn about Hemkunt Sahib and the tenth Guru's special relationship to this otherworldly valley. I didn't know about Lord Shiva perched as a yogi on a mountain peak, from whose hair emanated the waters of the Ganges. Nor did I know of the Kashmiri Muslims—descendants of the unions of Kashmiri Brahmins and Sufi Muslims from Afghanistan and Persia. When I first stepped foot in the Himalayas, it was with visions of Bollywood movies set in these ethereal mountains. These Indian fairytales, in which love is always fulfilled, made the town of Dalhousie feel enchanted to me.

When my brother and I once again boarded a plane destined for Dalhousie via New Delhi, we were older, more sure-footed, and we enjoyed the feeling of independence from our parents. Gone was the anxiety over a long plane ride, passports and tickets, and customs officials. We were filled with the excitement of going on an adventure in India with our Sikh American friends. We were participating in a Sikh Youth Camp in the Dalhousie Public School. The camp had been organized by our parents and their friends, and most of the seventeen youth ages thirteen to eighteen knew each other through family connections that originated in India but had become stronger in the United States. Given our ages, our youth camp relationships were a curious mixture of friendship, kinship, and crushes bordering on courtship. Whatever these relationships were, they were first and foremost shaped by the intense bond of being Sikh in America in the 1970s.

Within a few days of landing in New Delhi, my brother and I joined the rest of our group to drive to Dalhousie. Our time at the boarding school was structured around morning classes in spoken and written Punjabi, and learning religious hymns. The afternoons were for games and free time. Dalhousie was the perfect setting for an NRI (non-resident Indian) adventure in India. As a delegation of American youth, we were treated like minor celebrities. As if on cue with a Bollywood script, we obliged by providing our share of comedy and drama as we played pranks on each other; negotiated adolescent sensitivities and cliquish behavior; and suffered illnesses, cold beds, and even colder baths.

Often during our free afternoons we walked to the small town center to eat at local restaurants or to explore tiny shops jutting out of the mountainsides. The townspeople were a mix of local merchants and professionals, Indian army personnel, Tibetan refugees who set up stalls to sell paintings, jewelry, and other handicrafts, tourists traveling through the Himalayan region, and, of course, teachers and students from the boarding school. While the homes and shops were beginning to show signs of neglect, as much of the town had been constructed for colonials during the British period, the Himalayan scenery was otherworldly: green, forested hills with ghostly mist floating through them that suddenly banished by bursts of bright sun. After three weeks, I was ready to leave the school but sad to leave the hills, not knowing that I'd be coming back in a few years.

The second half of our camp was spent on dusty, treacherous roads in buses with no air-conditioning and lots of loud Hindi film songs. We left Dalhouse to tour northern India: Jammu-Kashmir, Punjab, Chandigarh, Agra, and New Delhi. Many of the stops in our journey were important places in Sikh history and culture, including pilgrimages to the holy sites of Harimandir Sahib and Anandpur Sahib. As we drove from the heights of Kashmir to the plains of Punjab, I began to see and hear a world that was familiar but not the same as the community I was growing up in. I thought a lot about my grandparents, great-grandparents, and Sikhs of so many generations past, and I was filled with a desire for belonging.

As we traveled through the land of our ancestors, the realization that my father's family wasn't a typical Sikh family became central to my sense of self. I had always known that my father's family was different because my father, grandfather, and my brother—as the eldest male descendants—were the only ones who were Sikhs with the distinctive beards, long hair, and turbans. According to custom in families like ours, the eldest son was a turbaned Sikh and the others were "mona" or "sahejdhari" (who cut their hair) Sikhs. My great-grandfather, Bansi Lal Luthra, who was a sahejdhari Sikh, had made his eldest son, Gopal Singh (Darji), a keshadari (with uncut hair) Sikh. For my great-grandfather, this was the greatest gift he could give the Guru and a sign of his great devotion to and love for the *bani* (words) of the Gurus.

Our extended family gatherings were colorful. Almost always we had at least sixty or more *chachas, chachis, bhuas* and *phuphards, mamas, mamis, maasis, massards* (uncles and aunts from the paternal and maternal lines) and of course the cousins, following Darji—often the only turbaned person in the room—in a recitation of Japji Sahib, Sukhmani Sahib, Rehras Sahib or Kirtan Sohila—whichever the time of day or occasion required. I imagine it would have been odd, even improbable, to those who came from Gursikh (orthodox) families to watch these people in saris and *ramale* (headscarves) reciting the Guru's bani. On my mother's side of the family all were Gursikh. They all kept their hair unshorn, were teetotalers, and followed only the ceremonies and traditions sanctioned by Sikh tradition. My maternal kin were soft-spoken, gentle, wonderful people but not necessarily more devoted to the words of Guru Nanak than my more raucous paternal kin.

As a teenager and young adult, I hated the ambiguity of my identity—Punjabi? Sikh? Hindu? American? I felt I was constantly dancing around my American habits and aesthetic, my accented Punjabi and Hindi, the "Namastes" (Hindu greeting) of my father's family and the "Sat Sri Akals" (Sikh greeting) of my mother's family.-

Bryn Mawr College,
Another Dark Day October 31, 1984

Almost eight weeks had passed since I moved into my college dormitory. I had just begun to feel comfortable in the new routine and living away from home. My roommate and I were getting along, and I was sleeping better in the small room with the sloped ceiling on the top floor of a coed dormitory. Initially both the coed living and the dusty warm air of the top floor made me uncomfortable. But I adjusted and was finally starting to relax and enjoy my classes. My favorite was a required English literature and composition class. The professor was a young English lecturer with a soft voice but provocative questions about gender and sexuality. We read Jane Austen and Edith Wharton. Over the course of the semester Jane and Edith began to feel like friends—young ambitious writers whose joys and struggles weren't all that different from mine.

It was a cool autumn evening. The walkway to the dorm was carpeted with red, gold, and burnt-orange leaves falling from the massive oak trees that stood statuesque throughout the campus. A few friends and I had just finished eating dinner. We were heading upstairs to our rooms on the third floor when I first saw the news. "*INDIAN PRIME MINISTER INDIRA GANDHI ASSASSINATED BY TWO SIKH BODY GUARDS*" flashed across a television screen in the common room below. I turned and walked back down the stairs to watch the news. My heart was pounding. My feet felt heavy, and I couldn't pull my eyes away from the screen. No one else around me seemed to react to the news. I felt alone and sick as a cold dread wrapped itself around me. The summer had already been full of bad news from India. In June, the Indian Army's Operation Bluestar had devastated the Harmandir Sahib (Golden Temple), the holiest of shrines, a kind of Vatican for Sikhs around the world; and we, half a world away, grieved for the Sikhs and other pilgrims who had lost their lives and for our beautiful Golden Temple.

Over the summer, as I followed the news and talked to my family in Delhi and Indore, I could feel the tension and fear in their voices. It was a sad time filled with dread of what more may come, but I could never have imagined *this*. Then it happened. Within a few hours, "the riots" started—first in Delhi and then spreading like wildfire around the nation. Years later, my family began to share their stories. My uncles described the mob that came for Darji but who turned away seeing that my uncles were not turbaned. Darji described how his driver, Harjit, had only survived by finding a place to cut his hair. My uncles in Indore described the mob that almost burned my sweet and frail maternal grandparents alive in their home! I could hear the hurt and deep sadness in my uncle's voice as he told me, "I feel like a stranger in my own home and in this place where I was born and have lived all my life."

I did not know then that I would soon see the scars of the horrific events of 1984 with my own eyes.

1986: From Punjab to Patna

In December 1986, while in India on a College Year Abroad program, I had an opportunity to visit a special Sikh historical site, Patna Sahib, in the eastern state of Bihar. Since September, I had been living in Varanasi, the ancient and holy Hindu pilgrimage center. I was working on a project studying the local Sikh community and the historical gurudwaras of the city. In the first week of December, I took a train to the town of Patna in order to meet Surinder Uncle, a close friend of my father. Surinder Uncle had offered to take me on a trip to Kathmandu, sponsored by his local Rotary club, if I could get to Patna. I decided that I would come a day early and visit the Patna Sahib Gurudwara, the birthplace of the tenth Sikh Guru, Guru Gobind Singh. I boarded the train with a letter from the president of the Guru Ka Bagh Gurudwara in Varanasi introducing me and explaining that I was an exchange student who needed a room in the gurudwara inn.

The train pulled into the Patna station at dusk, later than I had anticipated. By the time I found a shuttle that was willing to get me to the Patna Sahib Gurudwara, it was dark. I found a seat at the back, squeezed between a haggard-looking woman, her three children, and an old man. We drove for about twenty minutes when we were stopped at an intersection by a policeman. The driver put his head out the window and in an anxious voice asked the policeman, "Hey brother, what is the problem?" The policeman barked back, "The taxi is too full, I will have to fine you." The driver began to plead, "Please brother, it is cold and late. Let us go." After ten minutes of haggling, the driver slipped a wad of rupees into the policeman's hand, and we were able to continue. A few minutes later the driver stopped again. He turned to face us with his hand extended. Each of us had to hand over ten rupees in addition to the fare to cover the cost of the bribe. Some people grumbled as they passed the money up to the driver, but I quickly handed over the ten rupees and prayed that we would be left alone for the rest of the journey. The taxi was almost empty by the time I got out at the entrance of a long alley with small shops and stands on each side. Only a few tea stalls were open, and some shops were closed, but many others looked charred and boarded up. Walking down the ghostly alley toward the main entrance of the gurudwara, I began to regret my decision to come alone.

The next morning at around 5 a.m., I woke up to banging on the door of the small room I had been given the night before. Someone was yelling, "*Bhainji, uttho!*" ("Sister, wake up!") When I finally remembered where I was, I replied that I would be ready in ten minutes. To my surprise, the guide who was to show me around the gurudwara complex was a young *granthiji* who was a local Bihari Sikh. We quickly had *langar* in the main gurudwara and then got a rickshaw to visit smaller gurudwaras and sites associated with Guru Gobind Singh's birth and childhood. As we rode along, the young *sevadar* (volunteer) told me of the 1984 mobs, of the shops and homes set on fire, and of the many Sikhs dragged from their cars and homes to be beaten and killed. The alley of shops that I had walked through the night before had been one of the main Sikh markets and was also the first to be burned and looted. Some Sikhs, especially those who had family in Punjab, had already left. But many of the Sikhs in Patna, like my young guide and his family, were not Punjabis, and they had no desire to leave. Their ancestors had been devotees of Guru Tegh Bahadurji and Guru Gobind

Singh when they were living in Patna. My guide and his family did not speak Punjabi, but they did read the Guru Granth Sahib in Gurmukhi script, and they had served and would continue to serve these sacred and historical sites.

As I listened to the young Sikh's story, I wondered how Guru Gobind Singh would have reacted to the storm of violence this beautiful place had just weathered. I felt close to Guruji while standing in the place in which he was born and had played as a boy, and imagining the young man who had weathered so many storms himself. It dawned on me that he was a migrant like me. He had lived a life on the move: He was born in the eastern state of Bihar, came of age and "gave birth" to the Khalsa in Punjab, the Sikh homeland, and ultimately left this world in the western state of Maharashtra.

Los Altos, California December 2012
Home Alone with Jolly Jawanda, Sant-Sipahi (Saint-Soldier)

I reluctantly pull my eyes away from my book. The silence of an empty house is broken as I hear the front door opening. It can't be two hours already? The girls had taken the dog for a walk to a nearby Starbucks, and as soon the door closed behind them, I let myself fall back into the world of J. K. Rowling's new novel, *A Casual Vacancy*.

In the novel, Jolly aka Sukhpreet aka Sukhs Jawanda is the quiet ugly duckling of the Jawanda family. Her parents, Vikram and Parminder, are successful doctors and the only Sikhs in a small English parish that is the epicenter of the story. Jolly's older brother and sister are athletic, attractive, and popular in school. Jolly lives on the edges, in the shadows. At home and in school, she quietly, carefully cultivates her own disappearance. Her nonpresence seems impervious until she is reeled back into the world by her mother's prodding, who sighs, "Jolly, what are we going to do with you?" At school, the jeers of a bully, "Hairy, gorilla Sukh-Winder," drag her, like a fish on a hook, from the cool, wet darkness of anonymity and cast her about gasping in the dry air. I dive back into Jolly's world as if immersing myself in a pensieve, the magical time machine of Harry Potter's world. The fictional Jolly becomes my own daughter.

When she finds her niche in sports and wins a race with the girls' crew team, I feel the warm surge of satisfaction that comes with her recognition. When she starts making friends with the beautiful, enigmatic, and fearless Gaia, I feel the joy of her belonging. When, in the story's climax, she heroically dives into a cold English river to save her teammate's baby brother, I am frozen with fear and awe at her character, her courage, her personhood. When her darkest secret is revealed to her parents, I cry out in pain as if the blade of shame and self-doubt is slicing my own skin. I agonize that I don't know her, one who could be my own daughter. I didn't see this quiet *sant-sipahi* in front of me. Her enemy is indifference and cruelty in a world that too often ignores and discounts her. Her battlefield is too often her own body, home, and community. Her weapon is the Guru's double-edged dagger. Her victory is love for herself.

Los Altos, California, January 2013
Sikhi for the Next Generation

7:29 a.m. "Mommy, hurry up, we need to be in the car right now or I will be late! Didi! Hurry up! I am always late and today I will definitely get detention."

I shuffle through the house as I try to finish my morning tea, open the back door to let the dog back in, put some food in the cat's bowl, look for my keys. *Where is my phone? Where is that phone?* My younger daughter stands outside, her face in a frown, fuming as she waits next to the car for her older sister and I to come out of the house.

7:42 a.m. We are finally in the car. I buckle up, and as I back out of our driveway, I announce, "Let's do Japji Sahib (morning prayer) today. Get out the *gootka* (small prayer book); it is in the glove compartment." They groan and simultaneously reach for their headphones. "Put those away!" My voice is straining, getting higher pitched; my patience is dangling like a spider clinging to a strand of a web that has just been broken. "Once in a while we can start our day with paath." I start my usual lecture. "You don't go to Khalsa School anymore, I don't expect that much from you . . . But *this* is something you have to learn . . . gives you strength and . . .

perspective . . ." Their eyes glaze over. It is hard to stop even as I hear myself nagging. *This is not going to make them want to learn it.*

I take a deep breath, and soon they join in, mumbling, *Waheguruji… Ka Khalsa, Waheguruji . . . Ki Fateh.*

Ek Onkar
Satnam
Karta Purakh
Nirbhau
Nirvair
Akal Murat
Ajuni
Saibangh,
GurPrasad,
Jap.
My heart feels full.

A Different Kind of Love Story
Mandeep Kaur and Neesha Kaur

We sat side by side on the roof with our backs against the concrete wall. I could hear the drumming of the music from inside. It was pitch-black out, with a cold cloud cover cutting through the sky. I sat there devouring the sandwich she had made me, sneaking a look at her between bites. Mandeep wasn't a stranger, but she wasn't quite a friend. I had originally pinned her as being the shy type. The party was raging inside the apartment, yet we sat there in the cold shivering, me getting lost in the memory of how we met freshman year.

I stood in the elevator and saw my reflection in the brushed metal door. I quickly adjusted myself before I reached the second floor. It was my first time visiting my new friend's place. She was practically a stranger to me, but I was a freshman, and I hardly knew anybody. Hearing the *bhangra* music getting louder as I walked down the hall, I managed to find her apartment. I knocked on the door and it opened quickly, with the hostess standing there to greet me.

"Hey, *kuriye!* Come on in! Everyone is here!" Gurpreet said.

Walking in, I quickly realized that "everyone" was a bunch of strangers spread throughout the apartment staring at me as I removed my shoes. Most of the crowd was older and intimidating, so I scanned the room to see whom I could gravitate to. I spotted Mandeep and her roommate standing by the speakers that were blasting music through the room. Quickly, I made my way toward her, and the sound of the music I followed through the hall slowed to a halt. She quickly noticed me approaching.

"Neeshaaaa! Hiiii! Come here!" she exclaimed. She jumped side to side, tapping her Oxfords against the carpeted floor to the beat. Her long black hair danced along with her.

"Hey, Mandeep! The party's obviously over here!" I replied, excited to join in on the fun.

"Dance!" she yelled as she grabbed my hand and thrust it into the air, still bouncing her hips side to side. She took her other arm and pointed a finger up to the sky, doing her so-called "bhangra," really starting to get into the music. I couldn't resist dancing along with her. We were having an amazing time, and I quickly forgot about the others in the room. As we danced, I started to realize that Mandeep was using my hand to hold the weight of her body. She couldn't stand up straight. I noticed both her movements and words were twisting into a blurred mess.

"Neesha, uh I, uhhhh, Neesha . . ." she mumbled. She was beginning to slow down. I looked over to the kitchen counter next to her and spotted several empty cans of Red Bull. Mandeep had clearly been juggling several midterms and had too many tests to be drinking. She went from having a huge smile to barely being able to talk, her eyes heavy and glazed over. Rushing toward the bathroom, she ran into a trashcan and used what strength she had left to purge the energy drinks from her system. She was too sick to stay there. I knew I had to leave with her; I wanted to make sure she got home safely.

"Neesha, I think I ate something funny," she mumbled.

"Okay, Mandeep, I'm going to take you home now," I said, prying her arms from the trash can. She groaned, exhausted and dishevelled. I kicked the door open and coaxed her to make her way towards it. Mandeep nestled her head against my chest as I held her close. As I looked down at her, I was glad I came.

That night was my first real encounter with Mandeep. She ended up in one of my classes the following semester, but to my dismay, we didn't talk much. Maybe she was embarrassed by what had happened that night. If only she knew that seeing that side of her had made me want to get to know her more. I was quiet and waited patient. Sooner or later it was bound to happen.

Now, in the midst of another party, this mysteriously intriguing girl was talking to me. The same girl, with her long dark hair parted to the side, fair skin, light brown eyes, and adorable glasses. I, on the other hand, had changed quite a bit since freshman year. My hair was cropped short and dyed red, my nose was adorned with a green stone ring, and my arms were covered in random bangles. I really made no sense aesthetically, but by that point I had started to act and look how I wanted. I was "odd" as some would say, and many were taken aback by my appearance. But Mandeep wasn't. Talking to her was easy, and we had so much in common.

I heard people's voices permeating the music inside and asking, "Where did Neesha and Mandeep go?" We both pretended not to hear them and kept talking. I was surprised that I would rather be outside sitting next to her than inside partying the night away with everyone else, but in that moment, getting to know Mandeep was worth it. It seemed like we were finally becoming friends.

It was summer, and I was dying a slow death taking organic chemistry courses. I had just finished lab and was walking home when I saw a message on my phone from Mandeep: "Are you home? I have something for you!"

I thought for a moment. Curious, I turned the other direction and walked down her street to see her sprinting down the stairs of her building with a sunflower. She hopped in front of me, excited to give me the now droopy bloom she had collected on her way back from work.

We spent the rest of that night sitting on the couch just hanging out, our laughter echoing up to the angry neighbors above us. Before the night came to an end, she invited me to a concert for my birthday, a definite step up from the previous year's Eminem CD, which I never understood why she chose. This year I found myself falling asleep at her place, lying next to her, conscious of every movement she made. There was a brief moment of silence during which I felt something odd, and I sensed it in her, too. Before I could think anything else, she started tickling me. We laughed, soon grew tired, then lay there and rested—side by side, calm and relaxed, just like before—but I was nervous in my sleep and for some reason, afraid to open my eyes.

When the sun rose the next day and I woke, she wasn't there. I saw her in the kitchen waiting patiently for waffles to toast. She was making me breakfast! Flattered and starving, I jumped out of bed. In addition to waffles, there was a huge plate of eggs, toast, fruit, and yogurt waiting for me at the table. I think it was the first time someone had done something like that for me.

Mandeep left the huge bright sunflower from the previous day at the side of my plate. I grinned like a child holding a lollipop, the flower in one hand, devouring my food with the other. She made me feel special. It could have just been a sign of what a great friend she was, but I couldn't help thinking more of it. At the time I couldn't put my finger on the feeling, but walking out the door the next day with the sunflower she gave me in hand, I started to think of her as more than a friend.

Two years from the day we met, we had become good friends and roommates. We went from constantly hanging out among friends to spending entire days sitting together on the couch watching TV. It was our excuse to spend time with each other. I couldn't admit to her I just wanted to spend time with her, so I'd pretend that I sincerely enjoyed the things we would watch. Mandeep was opening a window inside of me that I hadn't acknowledged before, shedding light on a part of me waiting to be brought out. She was a woman, and so was I, but it didn't matter to me. I kept feeling pulled toward her, like a moth to a flame. I would often lose myself in these reveries when we lay silently on the couch, only Mandeep's voice bringing my trailing thoughts back to reality.

She had changed so much since we first met. Her hair was still dark and deep, but much shorter, grazing the bottom of her chin. She was no longer that young, shy freshman girl. She had grown into a beautiful, confident, and outgoing young woman. All those moments I spent with her in the past, all the second thoughts, pent-up tension, and attraction had built up to these moments. We were living in a fantasy world where we were able to indulge in our attraction without openly admitting it. My daily mission was finding ways to get close to her; I'd hold her hand for hours, only to stop when our roommates came through the front door. I was willingly giving in to her, savouring all her affection, and slowly going insane with every touch.

We ran through the streets at night, she held my hand, and I couldn't help but smile. I would be jumping off the walls, out of control, on a high; then Mandeep would grab me and I would stand still. She had no clue how much power she had over me; she played the tune, and I danced to my heart's content.

Afraid to completely let her in, that my feelings were growing too strong, I purposely made myself difficult to understand. The more mixed signals I sent, the more Mandeep pushed away from me. One night, things came to a head: I watched her walk away from me in the arms of someone else. My heart was ripped out of my chest.

I tried to come to terms with the idea that Mandeep and I could never be. My family and culture would never accept it. The harder I tried to compose myself, the more my heart hurt. I couldn't get myself to move on. Unable to deny it any longer, I blew up.

"I hate you!" I cried.

"Neesha, what happened—" She came toward me with a helpless look on her face.

I pushed her away.

"Don't!" I yelled at her as she tried to grab me. "You were never going to tell me!" I was distraught. I felt as if I was insignificant to her now.

"Neesha, I don't know what you're talking about!"

She was crying now, more than I was. She started to break down, and I sobered up as I realized she was having a panic attack. She started panting, breathing rapidly, and choking air. I held her, tried to console her. I talked her through it, calmed her down, and led her to my bed to sleep as she huddled against me. When I awoke to see her still asleep beside me, I was filled with both love and disappointment.

Two days later, Mandeep asked that we talk. I looked at her, both scared and excited. Was she going to say everything I was feeling, or something else? Was she going to tell me that we had to stop?

"You have to listen to me. Yes, I did talk to that guy, but I was trying to push away how I felt. Neesha, I like you. I'm sorry for complicating things because I know you can't do this, but I can't have you thinking that I meant to hurt you. I don't know how you feel, and I know this is going to make things hard, but I had to tell you."

I was shocked. It wasn't because I didn't know she felt that way, but that she had admitted it. That was the first time we spoke about being more than friends. I was so scared—she had only confirmed the way I had been feeling for a quite a while.

"Okay," I said. "Let's just be friends."

She gave me a half-smile. I needed time to decide what I wanted and whether I would go against what my family and culture expected. More importantly, I needed time to gather the courage to say that I, too, wanted to be with her despite everything. But even with nothing resolved, I knew she liked me. She really did like me. There was hope, and I lived with that hope for a very long time.

For a few weeks after that, we had kept up a façade, pretending to be normal, just friends. Eventually, she stopped talking to me, stopped looking at me. Our roommates learned what had happened, and Mandeep would stay out as long as possible and rarely come out of her room when she was home. When I ran into Mandeep at the library and asked if she was okay, she just shrugged. I grabbed her arm and squeezed it tight; I missed her.

Days later, I caught her as I was coming off the elevator to our apartment. She walked out the door with a backpack, a large shoulder bag, and a rolling suitcase. The hope of being together was fading. The more time we spent apart, the more I realized how hostile things had become. I was angry at myself for taking so long to admit what I already knew. I had grown accustomed to riding waves that other people made for me rather than making my own. This was the first time I had to decide something for myself. I needed to take action.

I texted her that I was going to do something about us. After not receiving a reply for hours, I started to doubt my decision. Maybe it had been too long—what if she didn't feel the same way? All my insecurities flooded back. I prayed for both of us to be happy regardless of what happened. I had never prayed with such passion and desperation.

I waited for what seemed like hours. She was late, and I didn't think she was going to show up. She had taken hours to respond to a text and had written a simple, "We need to talk." I sat in the back of the restaurant, and the heat of my body and of the soup in front of me wrapped tightly around my neck. I wanted to know whether she still wanted this. In that moment, I saw her shuffle in, tightly holding the straps of her backpack against her shoulders. She seemed nervous and uncomfortable.

She sat down in front of me without looking directly at me. I was afraid our eyes would meet, too, but I couldn't help but admire her face. I hadn't seen her this close in so long.

We had an awkward back and forth, then ordered food, and she started smiling. She always smiled when she got nervous, so I still didn't know what she was thinking. But she was so sweet, and everything I felt for her flooded through me.

I talked about how I felt. I apologized for taking so long. She was upset. Finally, I stopped and blurted, "Mandeep, I really like you, and I've taken a long time to think about it, but I really want to be with you."

She avoided the topic.

"Can we get the bill?" she asked the waiter.

We walked out of the restaurant, headed home, and talked as we did when we were friends. When we got to our building, she stopped for a second and looked at me.

"Let's go to the park. I don't feel like going home," she said. I followed and we sat on a bench. It was dark and chilly. We sat close to each other but didn't speak.

"Can I hold your hand?" she asked.

I looked at her. I couldn't tell if she was joking.

"Yes?"

She grabbed my hand. Hers was cold.

"Sorry, I was just really nervous. I've been waiting to ask since we left the restaurant."

I knew she was the one. She had always been the one.

I squeezed her hand to make sure she was really there.

I am a Sikh woman, and I fell in love with another Sikh woman. It didn't matter that she was a man or a woman because I fell in love with her soul. Love is meant to be the harmony of two souls, not two pieces that fit the puzzle of what our culture expects. Within the realm of society, our love story puts us at risk of discrimination and harm from our own families and community. We struggle with the thought of the future, but we hope for better. For me, *Sikhi* was always a personal experience of the *gurbani* that should not be judged. I never felt rejected by Sikhi, but rather the culture associated with the religion. Sikhi does not teach hate or discrimination, but people do. We do not write this to debate on the teachings of Sikhi, but rather ask for the equality and acceptance taught by Sikhi.

I am just a woman. No one could have told me that I would love a woman. I am just like any other woman. My ability to love cannot be seen in the way I dress or talk or walk. It can only be seen it in my heart, a heart that cannot be controlled, a heart given to me to love whomever I choose to love. This is why we share our story: to show that our love story is a Sikh love story, perhaps a different kind, perhaps with unusual actors, but a love story nonetheless.

My Sikhi *Simarna*

Harsohena Kaur

This summer, my son and daughter took their place at the *tabiya* in the *gurudwara*, Sikh house of worship, in the presence of the *sangat*, the congregation. They turned to the first page of the Guru Granth Sahib and began to recite the first verses of the *Japji Sahib*. This was their *Charni Lagna*, and they had worked hard for years in preparation for this day. I listened to them, with joy in my heart, hoping they would treasure this moment, for it was my gift to them. I hoped this moment would be like a shining bead in their *simarna* of Sikhi. I had begun stringing beads in my own simarna a long time ago. . . .

It was a summer evening in 1972 in a small town in northern India. The air was still and hot. The power was out. Tiny fireflies winked their light in the garden, mocking our darkness. We sat in the verandah as *Naniji* related the story of the martyr Guru Arjan Dev Ji's *shaheedi*. She spoke of the terrible torture inflicted upon the Guru by the Mughals on just such a hot June day. Afraid of His growing influence and wanting to intimidate His followers, the Emperor had ordered the Guru's execution, ostensibly for failing to pay fines. The Mughals tortured Guruji for five days, placing Him on a hot griddle and pouring hot sand all over Him, and then they put Him in a cauldron of boiling water. Naniji told us that He suffered without a grimace, just reciting *gurbani* and simply accepted this as the will of Waheguru. She admonished us for our petulance

113

with the heat and urged us to remember Guruji's suffering, to gain strength from it. She extolled the gentle beauty of Guru Arjan Dev Ji's composition, *Sukhmani*, and its power to soothe away pain.

But her words were a lilting background score in the background; I vainly tried to fan myself with a hand *pakhi* until I heard a stifled muffled sob, and then more. In the candlelight, we saw my older cousin crying, her heart breaking as she felt the burning suffering of Guruji. Suddenly it was a story no more, the words no longer just words in that hot stifling darkness. Like the clarity when vision comes into focus, those tears brought the story alive for me. I felt the reality of that history, the searing heat of Guruji's torture, and the link through the ages to this moment and our lives. Looking back, I think it was that evening, that moment, at age six, that I was born into my Sikhi. It is my earliest memory of identifying as a Sikh. This eventually transformed into a love that has found its way into every nook and cranny of my soul. My simarna of Sikhi is strung with the beads of numerous such instances, each moment that sparked for me and became a gleaming bead to hold onto.

A few years later, we spent the winter in Punjab and visited many historical gurudwaras. During those years, I had been reading stories from Sikh history, but they where just that: stories from a long time ago. Visiting the historical gurudwaras gave me an amazing, concrete connection to that history and elicited an intense emotional response in my young, imaginative self.

The sun was setting just as we reached the old *garhi* of Chamkaur, where Guru Gobind Singh Ji and a small band of followers had fought a large Mughal army. I wish I recalled the building, for it has since been destroyed and replaced with a large "modern" marble gurudwara. I was able to touch the thin bricks that showed in those old walls, pockmarked with bullet holes; I remember the thrill as I recalled that a few centuries earlier, Guru Gobind Singh had walked those same halls. In fact, His hand just might have brushed the very brick where my hand lay. I remember standing there, thinking of this Man, who gently tied the *dumalas* (turbans) on His two older sons and sent them out to fight a terrifyingly large foe. From the little crevice where I now looked out, He must have watched them fight to the death—two among the many who believed in Him implicitly and went to their deaths with a smile.

Days later we were in Sirhind, where the younger sons, the *Chhote Sahibzade* of Guru Gobind Singh, had been bricked alive for refusing to convert to Islam. At the time, the gurudwara was a small unassuming building holding in its heart the remains of the brick wall that had held the Chhote Sahibzade—held their breath, their faith, and their courage. I looked at that wall and wondered what the Chhote Sahibzade had thought as those bricks got higher and higher. Were they granted the vision to see beyond? To know they would be in safe sanctuary soon and therefore fearless? Did their courage falter? What about the bricklayers? Did they meet the eyes of the Sahibzade? Did their hands tremble? Did their hate quake? Did their eyes tear as the last brick went into place? How did they live out the rest of their lives?

Just a few steps away was the old tower where the two Sahibzade had spent their last night with their grandmother, Mata Gujriji. We stood in the old tower, with its crumbling bricks and open walls and a few pillars connecting the arches that held the roof. On that gray January afternoon, a bitter cold wind blew, much like it must have on the night the tower held its prisoners. I closed my eyes and could feel the presence of the two Sahibzade as they snuggled into Mataji's warmth and courage, listening to her reciting gurbani. I felt that I could hear the whisper of that Waheguru echoing from those pillars, like a blessing from Mataji.

Darbar Sahib or the Golden Temple in Amritsar is the most revered gurudwara of the Sikhs. my favorite memory of it happened one morning when I was ten years old. It was the time before the population explosion, crushing crowds, and television broadcasts. There was still a quiet serenity and a sense of mystery. We went there early in the morning, before the processional entry of the Guru Granth Sahibji. It was a gentle morning—the blue sky glowing luminous and the stars twinkling. The *Asa Di Var* floated softly across the water of the *sarovar* like a healing caress.

We climbed up and sat by a window on the first floor, overlooking the main hall. Suddenly, there was an electric current of anticipation as the Guru Granth Sahibji was brought into the main hall. The kirtan stopped mid-sentence, and the entire hall began to echo and resound with the collective chant of *Wahe-guru*, over and over again. My hair stood on end as I felt my heartbeat link with that rhythm and pulsate.

Once the Guru Granth Sahib lay on the *palki sahib*, the chanting stopped as the *prakaash* ceremony began. One by one, stalwart Sikhs stood up to recite a verse each of the *Bhattaan Di Bani*—a singsong cadence that has been part of the *maryada* for centuries. If I closed my eyes, would I see Guruji sitting right there, too?

There was magic there that morning. The sun was rising in a curtain of gossamer pink and those rose-gold rays came shining in through the outer windows. As I turned to look at the light, my gaze stopped. An American Sikh woman sat by the outer window, her white *dastaar* shining in the light like a halo, eyes closed, face glowing with peace and radiance. I stared at her for a long time, fascinated by her meditation. I was used to seeing people sing along with the hymns, or get emotional and tear up, or just come and go as they paid their respects at the gurudwara. Her stillness was mesmerizing as much as her foreignness. I was curious about what had made her choose to join my religion and what it was that she had found as she sat there, for the aura emanating from her was amazing.

These were pivotal moments for me. My heart resonated with emotions I did not fully comprehend, but that shone so brightly in my memory, they have served as emotional connectors to my faith. Unknowingly I was falling in love with Sikhi and laying the the foundation of my beliefs. Those physical connections with the Gurujis were the framework on which I would go on to build the walls and roof of my faith.

Gurpurab celebrations were always big festive occasions when we were growing up. A large colorful tent would be constructed and the Guru Granth Sahib would be placed on a palki on a high platform, both decorated with fresh flowers. The best *ragis* would sing shabad-kirtan all day long. Outside, it was like a carnival, with stalls of food and wares. There was always a sense of excitement and a wonderful feeling of coming together. One particular Gurpurab gathering stands out in my memory. I was sixteen and living in Lucknow at the time. As I listened to the kirtan, out of the blue I felt the music entering me and dissolving me. I could not stop crying. This was a wholly new experience, and I could not fathom why. My mother turned to ask me what was wrong, and when I told her what I felt, she gently said, "Sometimes our hearts are particularly receptive to the grace of the *Paramatma*. Repeat Waheguru at this time. When your heart has softened like warm wax, it is time to stamp it with Guruji's *chhap*—it will stay forever and be with you when you are in need. You won't even have to search for it." I believe I grew up in my Sikhi that day, for my faith moved from what I could touch and feel to within me. I believe I really began to carry the *Gurmantar* in my heart as my mother promised, for it has been there to sustain me time after time as I called upon that power.

As childhood gave way to adolescence and young adulthood, my Sikhi touch points moved inward as I strove to understand what Sikhi meant, and more importantly how it interwove with my world at the moment. Ah—those times of teenage angst, trying to understand my identity and purpose in life, and wrestling with the contradictions I saw while trying to fit them into a coherent whole. It was a kaleidoscopic time; each time I thought about things, they would shift ever so slightly, and a whole new perspective would shine out.

It seemed so ironic to me that we began with the gentle trailblazer *Guru Nanak Dev Ji*, who clearly asserted the equality and oneness of all humanity, only to have His followers, centuries later, organize into their own religion. The Gurus also spoke against mindless rituals and emphasized both spirituality and activism. I wondered if today we truly comprehended or trusted the purpose of Guruji's teachings, or had we resorted to blindly following ritualistic traditions? Should I mumble my daily *nitnem* or wait till I cultivated the mindfulness to appreciate every word? I have doubted and questioned and evaluated both my own faith and the tenets of my religion; I still do. As I have read, I have also learned that Guruji expected us to question and to think, as much as to believe. That, too, is a bead in my simarna.

I am proud of the equality Guru Nanak Dev Ji promised women

and the opportunity Guru Amar Das gave to his women *Manji* leaders, and for His categorical denunciation of denigrating practices like *sati* and *purdah*. But I remain troubled by the lack of women among the *Panj Pyare*. Where were the women at the moment in *Anandpur Sahib* when *Guru Gobind Singh* asked for a Sikh to give up his life? Why didn't He call for the women? Why didn't they answer the call? Were they even allowed to answer the call?

Mai Bhago's fearless determination and loyalty as she lead the forty soldiers who had broken with Guru Gobind Singh back into battle, was salve to my soul. But, I am still saddened by the silence among women that could not be broken even by our Gurus. Not one verse from a woman in the entire Guru Granth Sahib!

I marveled at the generous welcome of the Darbar Sahib, with its doors open to all four directions. Yet it is also appallingly true that even now, neither my sister Sikhnis nor I are allowed to do *seva* (community service) in the inner sanctum. The hurt, anger, and frustration at the broken promises and the unfairness against women are a pulsing bead in my simarna.

In the early'80s, Sikhs in the Punjab were in political turmoil. While the primary thrust was increased political autonomy for the state, there were factions demanding a separate homeland, and a few using violent means to make their point. The political machinery of Prime Minister Indira Gandhi effectively labeled all Sikhs as separatists and terrorists. Then came 1984, a year that burned holes in the fabric of our lives, leaving an acrid stench that still lingers just beyond the pale of everyday memory. In June of 1984, Mrs. Gandhi ordered the army to attack the Darbar Sahib, or Golden Temple, our holiest gurudwara. That horrific attack led to a stupendous loss of life of innocent pilgrims, the destruction of the *Akal Takht*, the devastating loss of the *Tosha Khana* and our historical relics, and all our broken, betrayed hearts. In October of that year, two Sikh men assassinated Mrs. Gandhi. In the days that followed, in a government-orchestrated pogrom, thousands of Sikhs were burned, chopped, raped, tortured, and killed maliciously by neighbors and acquaintances, all justified by Rajiv Gandhi because "When a great tree falls, the earth will shake."

Following the carnage, I went to the cantonment, or army area gurudwara. It was a "safe" place, and Sikh refugees from other parts of Delhi were living there, waiting for the fires to die down. I remember the woman who told us how her six-foot-tall husband and son had been killed by the mob. Her neighborhood was burning, and she had nowhere to go. She sat there, all night long, their dead bodies beside her, doing her nitnem. The mobs laughed at her, calling her mad, for still doing her paath while her men lay dead. She looked at me and said, "What else could I do? What else did I have left?"

Another woman who spoke of her two young sons. The mobs came by and mocked them. "Cut their hair, and we'll spare their lives," they called out, laughing and drunk from killing. She said she took her sons in, tied their *dastaars* and said, "They are not my sons. They are Guruji's sons."

"The mob just smashed kerosene bags on their heads and set them on fire," she said quietly.

Would I do the same? Is that courage or insanity? Was there even a choice, given the intent of that mob? Was she at peace that they had died in *saroop* rather than have their hair shorn? Or did she wonder if they would have been spared had she cut their hair? Was this vile hate really the will of Waheguru? Those questions grated on me like *rarak* in my eyes. That year shook me to my core; it's a bead on my simarna that still throbs with pain. Yet, despite the ash of those fires, I could not abandon my love for Sikhi. I had to continue to hold on, to have faith, to hope for courage. I also realized the importance and need of having a community, and the need to nurture that community and keep it safe. Now that I have children of my own, it hurts even more.

Life brings with it many challenges and choices. What we choose determines the course of our future. As an almost-adult, I fell in love with a non-Sikh and deeply agonized about my path and my choices. It was an oddly abstract situation as my entire "relationship" played out across a long distance via letters. I was never actually face-to-face with my "love." It did provide an amazing counterpoint as, day after day, I struggled between the reality and three-dimensionality of my flesh-and-blood love and the abstract reality and love for my religion. I wondered why it needed to be a choice. After all, love was the path to Waheguru Ji. Besides, Guruji had been the one to proclaim the brotherhood of all humanity and that we all were children of one God. The gurbani I read and the four open doors of the Darbar Sahib still asserted this message. Sikhi also said that good deeds were held more important than anything else: they were the key to a good life. And I saw Sikhs who did not live up to the ideals of Sikhi and non-Sikhs who did.

But time and time again, I would be drawn back to our history and to the sacrifices and blood that have irrigated the Sikhi's roots to ensure its survival. Through the centuries, Sikhs have had to fight, struggle, and suffer to freely practice their faith.

And it wasn't all old history! I had borne witness to 1984 and seen my faith's right to exist questioned and attacked. Did I have the right to give it all up for my personal desire? Or did I need to sacrifice those desires to fully realize my faith?

Along that path, in all my wrestling, I realized that it was not so much the values of Sikhi that were making me hesitate. It was pragmatism. Love would not be enough. I needed to share my life with one whose heart beat to the same Gurmantar, whose head bowed to the same Guru, who shared and understood and resonated with the same history and faith and belief. I realized that I needed that commonality to glue my life together. The deep certainty that I could not share my life with someone who did not share my love for my Guru and for my Sikhi became a bead in my simarna.

That bead became Guruji's blessing so that, a few years later, I found the life partner I was seeking. My favorite shabad at that time was *"Gur sant jano pyara main miliya meri trisna bujh gayi aase"* ("I have met my beloved Friend and my thirst is quenched." Guru Granth Sahib, page 776). Of course, the shabad refers to finding Waheguruji, but the parallel seemed prescient when I met my husband; we instantly felt a bond of love, friendship, and shared values.

I vividly recall our first dinner together. He was and still is an unbelievably smart and handsome *sardar* with a super-wattage smile and amazing energy. We started talking and the world just faded away. It was the easiest thing in the world to say, "Yes!"

Ironically, at the same time, I was facing some of the toughest challenges of my life. My sisters chose to marry outside our faith and left our family to do so. These were actions beyond the realm of even imagined possibility, and tore our family apart. For years, the sheer disbelief paralyzed us, and the hurt and pain bled like a non-healing wound. We struggled with the "right" and "wrong" of it. What would Guruji say about it? What should we do? Could we be together and safeguard our Sikhi? Could we walk such different paths and maintain the effortless sharing and sangat of Sikhi with each other? Given the place I had reached in my personal journey in Sikhi, my sisters' choices presented new challenges. Their decisions were valid as individual choices, but cut at the roots of what bound us together as a family and a community. Choices like these will occur with increasing frequency in our global, interconnected world. Beyond the black-and-white boundaries of any community, how do we deal with the widening gray zone? How do we keep our Sikhi strong and our community alive? How do we share our Sikhi across differences? Although we eventually reconciled and came together as a family, the turmoil and the heartbreak became another bead in my simarna. The questions remain, increasingly insistent as my children grow up in a world where they rarely, if ever, see a reflection of themselves or their heritage.

I thought I was aware of so many facets of Sikhi, but living with my Sikh husband has provided me with a whole new perspective. Growing up with two sisters and no brothers, my sense of Sikhi was primarily from the feminine perspective. Now as I walk beside my turban-wearing husband, I realize how much that charges him with being different. He stands out, stands apart, and stands alone. And my son follows that same path. From side-glances to surprise-widened pupils, to regular "random" checks at airports, to small transgressions of rudeness in a multitude of ways, to outright hate with both verbal and physical assaults—they face it all. It can be tough, troubling, and dangerous, and requires faith, confidence, and courage. I now carry that understanding with a prayer for their continued courage and safety as a large bead on my simarna. That bead does have a strong shine of gold in it from my husband, who carries his turban with pride and looks upon it as a way to leave his mark. He has built myriad connections through that recognition. As his friends say, he could walk into a black-tie affair with jeans because his turban would carry the day. I hope my son lives with that sense of pride as well.

Being a Sikh woman has its own difficulties. In our world today, girls and women face their own discrimination and derision. The ideal of physical beauty in today's world directly challenges keeping our *rehat*, our hair unshorn, and our body hair intact. Do we support our girls enough to be proud of their bodies and believe that they are perfect as they were made? Does it really matter? Are we getting stuck in the semantics of it? Is vanity to be condemned?

There are also other challenges from within our own community. I am grateful to my family for giving me the wings of freedom. However, despite the equality and respect that the Gurujis stood for, our community still has to live up to that promise. I rail against the inequities and injustices against women that continue to persist. Centuries ago, Sikh soldiers set an example by being scrupulous in their behavior toward women. Even after battle, they were known to treat their enemies' women with respect. But today our community struggles with domestic violence like any other, and the silence is deafening. How do we recapture that strong ethic? How do we give life to women's dreams? My hope for my daughter's dreams is a glittering bead in my simarna.

Today, I feel that my most important purpose in life is to give the gift of Sikhi to my son and my daughter. I see myself as a torchbearer who needs to pass this flame along. It's a step-by-step journey and a tough one at that. Every step has been a challenge—from teaching my children Punjabi without the context of using the language in their daily lives so they can read the Guru Granth Sahibji, to the discipline of memorizing their Japji Sahib every morning as we drove to school, to making the history of our community come alive in a meaningful way centuries and thousands of miles away from where it all began, to carving out traditions to celebrate Gurpurabs in the midst of Christmas glitter, to exemplifying the value of the collective sangat in a society that is built on individualism, to discussing the meaning of gurbani and its relevancy in our modern lives. I have come to appreciate that Sikhi is not a religion of once-a-week services. It is an active, disciplined, daily lifestyle that requires intentional choices every step of the way. I hope that my children will own that intention. Most of all, I hope they will find the deepest love for Sikhi.

Through all of the triumphs and troubles that come with life, Sikhi has been the bedrock of my existence, and my faith has sustained me. Time and time again I have felt the power of that love. As with most of us, I have had my share of pain and sadness and loneliness. At those moments, I turned to the Guru Granth Sahib, and amazingly, the shabad I opened to was, *"Jis ke sir upar tu swami so dukh kaisa pave."* ("Those who have Your protection will have no pain." Guru Granth Sahib, page 749) or *"Mere heare rattan naam har basiya gur hath dhariyo mere matha."* ("The jewel of Naam enters my heart as the Guru places His hand on my head." Guru Granth Sahib, page 696).

The surety of that love, even in the darkest moments, is the brightest bead in my simarna of Sikhi. That love has held me in despair, provided succor in pain and sustenance in good times, and filled my life with radiance. With that love I believe I can walk the path toward *sehaj* and *Chardi Kala*. With Waheguruji's grace, may that love beat in my children's hearts every moment, powering the actions of their lives so that they choose a Gurmukh life. That *Ardas* is the bead I am holding on to, right now, in my simarna.

Part 3: Sehaj

Graceful Acceptance

Circling The Sun
Jalmeen Kaur

The swirling pattern of the wood on the kitchen table gave me a point of focus as I tightly gripped it. I held myself still and endured the next contraction. At first I managed with various positions and encouraging words from my birthing team. But then the contractions became stronger and longer. I slipped into fear. How will I bear this pain?

My doula suggested I get into the tub. Somehow she knew that the water would soothe and support me like nothing else could . . . I eased myself into the warm water and as it circled around my belly and body, I felt like I was being held by my mother. I asked your father to go and get the *shabad*. Doing anything and everything he could for me, he unfolded the now worn and crumpled paper from my diary. I saw Mama's script scrawled across the page and I recited the shabad she sent to me. "This will keep you and baby spiritually and physically in a special bond and give peace to both of you," she wrote. "Satgur Sache Dia Bhej. Chir Jivan Upjia Sanjog. Udre Maha aye Kia Nivaas, Mata kai Man Bhut Bigas." (O' Mother, your face glows with Joy as you have been blessed! A child has been planted in your Womb and you are connected to the True Source of Life!)

The Zen bliss you must have felt—floating there—enveloped and cocooned in the warmth and stillness of the womb. Knowing that you were completely safe and protected. The warmth, the water, the nourishment, the peacefulness. It all seeped in through the umbilical cord, and you had the freedom to be. No demands. No expectations. Just love.

After hours of waiting and enduring for your arrival, a force started building and growing within. All of a sudden I lost complete control. My midwife told me it was not time yet—don't push! But it was so powerful that it completely took over, my muscles rapidly contracting and urging you to come. My body was in charge and I was relegated to watch, with no choice but to surrender as your life unfolded in front of me. I had never known a power like that. That force was so incredibly powerful, and after three hours of pushing, your ambivalence to leave that safety apparent to us all, you entered into this world. When I looked into your eyes, it was the first time I understood real love.

This is what Mama must have seen in my eyes when I was born. She demonstrated what real love was over and over and over in my life. Whether I was a small babe sick with fever or a lonely graduate student halfway across the country, whenever I was in need, she would say, "Do you want me to come?" But I always took it for granted.

A decade after your birth, I finally understood why you didn't want to leave the womb; it is like no other place on Earth. Caught up in my seemingly important details of daily life, I never appreciated how Mama's mere presence provided me with a sense of wholeness and safety each and every day. I didn't know until the precious vessel that created me was gone.

I received the call that morning, a horrific moment that replayed over and over in my mind. I denied it was true. It simply could not be. She had pneumonia but was being effectively treated. I had spoken to her on the phone just twelve hours earlier about how the antibiotics were sure to kick in. But in the background over the phone, my father's incoherent wails of sorrow flooded my mind. His cries replayed again and again as we boarded the plane and flew in desperation to get there and fix it. In my world I fix things. I was confused. Usually, no matter how difficult, nothing was insurmountable. It seemed so utterly impossible that Waheguru could make this sudden and cruel decision to take her from all of us. She passed peacefully in her sleep in her Suhag (husband's arms) and we didn't know how or why . . .

I moved through a heavy fog, everything seemed surreal as I sat in my white *salvar kameez* surrounded by all those who loved her in a state of disbelief and confusion. Mama was exquisitely dressed and peacefully sleeping in front of me. But there was no breath. And it was hard for me to breathe. How could it be that my Mama—my safety—was no longer on the Earth? I didn't feel safe anymore. And where did she go—this irreplaceable mother of mine—from whose womb I had come? I felt orphaned when she passed away. How could she birth me and then leave me here? Alone.

I reeled in the awareness that life and death were not in my control. That last night when I spoke to her it was the last time I would ever hear her voice.

Surrendering was always so difficult for me. Mama said I was always so stubborn, always wanting my way. And I was left wanting and longing for more time with her. At the time of the cremation, Bhai Sahib and our community elders led us into the stark white, cold room reciting Kirtan Sohila. I thought I was ready. I knew she was no longer housed in this body that lay in front of me. But when they started the process I screamed inside and wanted them to stop. It was unbearable that her face would be lost to me. I wanted one more look. One more moment. But I was frozen. I couldn't move. It was all too too fast. And then she was gone. The repetition and recitation of baani was sung as her body was taken, and it was the only thing that kept me slightly grounded in that moment. Kept me from going insane. Even though I knew she was no longer in that body, I felt devastated.

After the cremation, that void left me searching hard for her. How I missed her voice, her smell, her face. I became terrified that I would forget how she sounded, how she looked, how she spoke and giggled. I wondered if anyone ever recovered from this kind of loss. Now nothing would ever be the same. It could never feel "right" again.

The first few weeks were a blur. Amazing how your *sangat* just steps up and is there before you when you most need them. Family and dear friends took care of most things—arrangements, meals, details—while I functioned in that foggy haze. I went to work, but I didn't do my best work. I cared for you and your sister, but I'm sure you felt I was far away. I became very angry with time. Time did not stop for me. It did not stop for Mama. How could the world continue without her? Why couldn't everything stop for a moment? I wanted to breathe, and fix it. It wouldn't give.

It was a relief when your Nana Ji decided we needed to go to India to return your Nani's ashes to the Earth. Specifically, he said, we needed to take them to the Satluj River in Kiratpur, Punjab, so the ashes would mix into the running water of Mother Earth. I was eager to leave the overwhelming responsibilities of life it gave me a chance to be there for my father. When we boarded the plane, the look on your Nana Ji's face revealed how lost and bewildered he felt. He carried the beautiful engraved box with your Nani's ashes onto the plane on his head, giving them the utmost respect. He held onto them like he would never be able to let go. After the long and somber flight, we landed in India and drove the next morning to Kiratpur. And even though she was not in the physical form, Mama was alive for me during that long drive. Your Nana Ji and my *bhuas* (aunts) shared story after story about who she was here in this land that was so foreign to me. Nana Ji shared how she first served him tea when his family came to "see" this potential bride. She was quiet and sweet, respectful and not directly looking at him when the families first met during the traditional tea. Nana Ji was immediately taken with her unique beauty. He declared that she was "the one" and then sneaked visits to her during their engagement. As we drove through Panipat, I saw her and heard her laughter . . . a newlywed riding behind her husband on his motorcycle through the *kheths* (farms). This couple was so majestic, so handsome. I was in awe with the strength Mama must have had after giving birth to her son, my older brother, and then giving Nana Ji permission only two months later to fly to America to study. Moving in with her in-laws' and raising their son without him for two years, they communicated via mail, audiotape, and maybe a few phone calls. Her new home at her in-laws must have felt foreign to her—a new bride, daughter-in-law, and mother—just as this land felt foreign to me. I could picture her, determined and committed to make it work, and embracing her new family. My bhua told me of how my Dhadhi Ji asked, "Ramneek, sing that song once more." Mama was blessed with a beautiful voice, and she complied. She entertained those requests over and over. We sang her songs as we drove through Punjab. And as your Nana Ji shared more, it became clear that her beauty, her talent, and her courage served her in life. After trying for months, your Nana Ji got his first engineering job. He sponsored his wife and bought a ticket to bring her to America. Flying for the first time, alone with her little boy, she landed at JFK airport, and was lost in New York City after missing her flight to Chicago. She must have been terrified. There were no cell phones or Internet. Resourcefully and with some help, she found her way all the way to her apartment in the city of Chicago. Your Nana Ji was finally able to sleep after staying up for two nights in a helpless stupor not knowing how to find them.

She came to America and had the power to create a home here for us—sacrificing and leaving so much behind. During the drive, I was able to hear her voice and her song.

When we arrived at Kiratpur, I was comforted by the familiarity of the *gurudwara* (house of worship). *Kirtan* was playing, and the recitation of God's name told me we were bringing Mama to a good place. There was a long queue by the river, and we waited for our turn. The line of sadness stretched on as one by one others said good-bye to their loved ones. All of us bonded through our losses, holding each other up and moving each other along the line. We trudged along the narrow dirt path, and the sparse trees swayed and whistled a sad tune while we worked our way up to the small bridge. While your Nana Ji did the *Ardas* (prayer), I held your Nani's ashes, holding what was physically left of her and realizing that truly, none of us are our bodies. This is not Mama. Her essence, her love, her laugh is not this ash. And then he poured them into the slow river, and her remains mixed back into the womb of the Earth. As I stood there, a strong loving energy flooded my body. It filled me and held me up.

It was hard to leave her ashes, but others were waiting their turn. I wanted to stay. Just one more minute. But I had to turn and leave what physical piece was left, trying desperately to hang on to the intangible feeling inside me. His family held him as Nana Ji was taken from the river. We had completed the journey and returned Mama from where she had come.

As we flew halfway around the Earth to go home, I stared into the clouds and infinity of space above and wondered: Where did this loving, strong spirit go when she was freed from her body? The sun was so close I could touch it. Is she here in this sky?

As time passed, your Nana Ji wrote on his forty-fifth anniversary, one of his many writings to your Nani after her departure, and shared it with his children:

> *My dear beloved begum Ramneek,*
> *Tu Chhupi Hai Kaha—Where are you hiding?*
> *Main Trapata Yahan—I am wandering endlessly here.*
> *Tere Bin Suna Suna Hai Mera Jahaan—Without you my world is lifeless.*
> *I wish I had the wings to fly. I would find you and carry you on my back all my life. Together we would vanish in the outskirts of the sky.*
> *With love and peace. Wherever you are. Waiting forever . . .*

How blessed I was to be raised by a father and mother that shared this kind of love. And your Nana Ji will never stop while he is alive to keep your Nani alive for us.

In time, the family gathered to sort through the house and, as I entered into the home, your Nani's story was written throughout; her mark was left in every corner of every room. She was far from perfect, but the love she poured into her home and family was pure perfection. From the dishes on the shelf saved from our childhood, I heard her endless requests to eat more. From the stacks of phone lists and Post-it notes by the phone, I heard the constant ring of her endless, nagging phone calls. "Where are you? What's your plan?" I would give anything to receive just one more call.

She saved anything and everything that was meaningful to her, and I could see her in the "clutter." Your Nani drove me crazy all the time. And yet she was the person to whom I turned to when I was crazy. She was consistent, available, always there.

I didn't want to move anything. I didn't want to throw anything away. But it had to be done.

I needed something to hang on to. Where was Mama's *kesari kapra* that she slept with? I pictured that saffron cloth she wrapped around her head and went to bed with. I needed to find that kapra. I needed to have that to hold. It smelled like Mama, and I knew she had it in her last moments. I looked everywhere. I was inconsolable when it was nowhere to be found. My brothers joined me in my search, so desperate was I to have this cloth to hang on to. Despite all the things I could have from the house, I became fixated on finding that kapra, but it was never found. Without it to hold . . . it seemed too long . . . too long to be here until I could go . . . and see her again. You and your sister's need for constant attention and love kept me grounded. You needed your mother as I needed mine. I had no choice but to wait to "see" her. It felt like an eternity . . . so much life left for me to live . . . and I wondered if I'd be able to.

But then I saw Mama. She came to me in my dreams. She didn't speak. In one dream she was full of sorrow, and my brothers came running to get me and said, "Go to her." We were together, and I embraced her and comforted her. So much regret I had about not being there for her and being the daughter I wanted to be. Waheguru was giving me a chance to make up for missed chances. In another, my brothers and I were taking care of her. She struggled to keep her diabetes in check and had severe back pain, and we never paid enough attention. I hated myself for not paying enough attention. But Waheguru brought Mama to me in my dreams and let me be there for her. For these moments in my sleep, I am eternally grateful. Her presence was so "real." It was real. When I saw her face, I felt the lifetimes of love she gave me in the span of one life. It exuded from her and filled me up. I had been worrying. "How will she know how deep and wide my love is for her now that she is gone?" Even though it seemed I could never share or express it enough, I was given a chance to tell her. Even though she was not here with me, Mama came to me those nights and was telling me, "It's okay. I know. You're okay."

After some time passed, there were no more dreams. How I longed to see her again. Touch her. Hear her voice. I had found a way to connect with her, and I prayed and prayed for more. But no dream. People said, "Time heals." To me there was nothing further from the truth. Time afforded me more of a chance to numb out, detach, and feel sorrow that time was passing without my mother. My niece's birth, my cousin's wedding—happening without her. At moments my brain did not register that she was gone, and I wondered, "I haven't talked to Mama in so many days . . . I should call her." Maybe my brain was trying to fool me, to spare me the pain— part of me believing she was here, part of me knowing she was not, all in the same moment.

It had been a hard day with work, relationships, and life. Nothing was going right. I didn't feel right. I didn't feel like I was doing anything right for anyone. I fell asleep exhausted from crying. And then Mama was sitting at the kitchen table—*chaunkri marke*—cross-legged, elbow on the table and head resting in her hand. She always complained about those rolling kitchen table chairs. Her stacks of old pots and dishes sat behind her on the counter. She was smiling and said in Punjabi, "*Acha aaj pher ki karna?*" What do you want to do today? I went and sat in her lap as if I were a girl again and said, "Mama, let's pretend you've been here the whole time." And we laughed and carried on. I awoke to the quiet and stillness of the middle of the night. There was a strange tingling feeling inside. Like small bursts of sunlight breaking through the cold. Sunrays streamed down, washing over me, completely enveloping me and taking me in. I kept my eyes closed and felt a strange joy in the silence. I decided it was her. Who else was going to come for me when I was not even asking for help? Show up? Be there? I felt Mama and that distinct feeling of my mother's love.

"Jalmeen. You can do this. Just as I did. You have courage, and you have strength. And you are not alone."

And then I could breathe. She was breathing new life into my tired heart. In that warmth and stillness, there was no expectation. Time stood still. Time was waiting for me. And all that was in that moment was Love.

The immense power of what was given to me that day continues to cross the barriers of flesh and time and space. I can be here, circling the earth, and still be here with Mama. She is not lost to me. She never was.

When the family gathered at the Garden of Eden in California on Mama's birthday to plant crops to harvest for the homeless, it was clear to me that each of us felt we were overflowing with more than our share of love from Mama. This was a way to share the surplus with others. I asked you to rally your little sister and cousins to dig in the dirt and plant the tomatoes and herbs, but they just wanted to run around and play. You are growing fast, and it's time to decide how I want to spend the time that I have with all of you.

I remember your birth vividly. All your grandparents rushed to the hospital to hold you. And I can hear Mama's giddy laughter as she held you in her arms. And bathed you. Fed you. Held you while you slept, so I too could sleep.

I remember how I had to surrender—to trust—in Waheguru's plan then. My first lesson in surrendering control over to this force resulted in one of my greatest joys. My second lesson has left me with my greatest loss. But I will have to trust that only He knows. Birth and death are not in our control. I will have to choose to embrace this time and life I have with my children. Grateful that your gentle spirits have been entrusted to me. Appreciating that I have so much and thanking Him for the time that I had with your Nani. I now have the chance to live life in a drastically different way. Awake, aware, and fully present. The blueprint of real love was given to me by your Nani and is now etched into my being. I will pass that blueprint on to both of you.

When we are finished planting, your Nana Ji asks us to gather around the plot to say an Ardas to ask that Waheguru continue to bring peace to Mama's soul. I can see he is determined and committed to living the rest of his life in her honor. As he urges his grandchildren to fold their hands and try to stand still, I can see that he sees what I do. That we are all a part of your Nani's legacy of love. I see her face in my brothers when we remember and laugh and love her together. I see that your sister's nurturing, caretaking nature has clearly been passed through the generations to her. Your sister's name, Maaniya, means surrender, and she shows me daily that this is what I must do to be the mother to you both I wish to be. In you, my son, I see perseverance. Your name, Baaj, reminds me that the phoenix always rises. That we are strong. We are your Nani's legacy.

Now when I am overwhelmed, when I am sad, or when I just deeply miss her, I know I can reach Mama. When I search within, a rush of energy tells me she is here. Here within me. The love of a mother . . . a mother like mine . . . is eternal. I now know what that means. It seeps into your every pore. It is timeless like Him. It knows no limits. No boundaries. It stretches across dimensions. Across time and space. It is mine to keep and sustains me. It cannot be taken from me. And I will take it with me into every moment I live and take it with me when I leave. It is mine to keep. Forever woven into the fabric of me. When I need to be reminded, I close my eyes and envelope myself in Mama's warmth and love. And she is there, as she always was.

How My Mother-in-Law Became My Mother

Jessi Kaur

It was *sangeet* night at my wedding. Thirty years later the memories are as vivid as though it all happened yesterday.

After a trip to the United States, when I announced that I was marrying Gurjot, my friend of ten years, who was settled in California, my mother's joy was immense—not only because her daughter was not going to be an old maid after all, but also because she was extremely fond of Gurjot, just as my father had been.

Hosted at my aunt's house, my wedding sangeet was an intimate and modest affair. Surrounded by family and friends, I sat in the middle of a large family room while two henna artists painted intricate vines on my hands and feet. My aunt was singing Punjabi wedding songs that rejoiced a daughter's marriage while lamenting her leaving the family home. A warm glow enveloped me as I looked ahead to a new chapter in my life.

Out of the corner of my eye I saw my mother-in-law-to-be separate herself from the crowd at the far end of the room and walk determinedly toward me. I knew her well from my visits to Gurjot's house when he lived in India. She was always on the verge of a monologue. She shared her unsolicited opinion on all matters and could carry on uninterrupted longer than anyone I knew. To top it, her voice was rather loud and shrill. She was not one of my favorite people in the world.

When I met her soon after Gurjot and I had decided to get married, she said to me, "Please call me 'Mama'."

Gurjot told me that Mama had been miffed because he had "informed" her that he wanted to marry me instead of allowing her to find a bride for him, or at the very least seeking her opinion on whether he should marry me.

As she stood determinedly in front of me on my *sangeet* evening, the warm glow inside me turned into angst. The henna duo stopped their artistry and looked up questioningly at Mama, who stood tall at five-feet-nothing. Mama pulled out a bright red lipstick from her bulging clutch, leaned over me, and smeared it on my hairline. I cringed.

"*Baytay*, you forgot to put *sindhoor*," she said, oblivious to the fact that I was pulling away from her.

Sindhoor is a red powder-like substance that Hindu women typically put on their forehead close to the hairline to proclaim their married status. As a Sikh I had no affiliation with this custom, and certainly no desire to have her used lipstick smudged on my head.

I was embarrassed by the thought of how quickly I wanted to put the Pacific Ocean between my mother-in-law and me. There was no question this relationship was not going to be easy. Distance would be my best ally, I knew.

Perhaps I am sounding intolerant and brash. Perhaps I was.

In my defense, I have to say that I had been raised in a household that was peaceful and quiet. I was an only child and was not exposed to bratty siblings vying for attention or a mom yelling to be heard. My mother was a soft-spoken, gentle, and dignified lady who never did anything to draw attention. Mama liked thrusting herself in the center of whatever was happening. I certainly did not want to see her center-stage in my environment.

I did not let Mama's intrusion into my space ruin my *sangeet*. I was just happy at the thought that I would be saying good-bye to her within a week. But I had forgotten that Indian sons cannot be separated from their mom even decades after the umbilical cord has been severed.

Trouble started to brew when my parents-in-law visited us. The first day that Mama was with us, she commented upon the state of my husband's night suit.

"No one irons your clothes?" she asked.

Without missing a beat, I said, "He was waiting for Mom to come and iron his night suit." Ouch, the brazenness of youth. They did not call me "firebrand" for nothing. Being impatient, impetuous, and brutally direct were my virtues.

Mama smiled sweetly and said, "Sure." She was not one to shirk doing anything for her sons or their families, as I was to learn in the years ahead.

I was not appeased. How dare she spoil a grown man?

The next morning provided another moment that propelled the downward spiral of our relationship. Gurjot had made morning tea for me and was bringing it to the bedroom.

"Have you started drinking tea?" I heard Mama ask in a loud voice.

"No, the tea is for Jessi. Should I make a cup for you too?" Gurjot asked.

"No, thank you very much. I can make my own tea," announced Mama, her voice showing displeasure at her son's waiting on his spoiled wife.

I simmered while drinking the hot tea. The cold war was on.

My parents-in-law were keen to have my husband's younger brother settle in the United States. With my cousin's help, a suitable bride was found. Weddings are always a hotbed of tension. The larger and more elaborate they are, the greater the drama. Ours happened soon after his wedding at the hotel where we were staying. Mama had summoned a family gathering to open gifts the new bride had brought for our family.

"What are we giving them?" I asked, sensitive to principles of equality.

My mother-in-law was puzzled.

"It's the boy's family who gets the gifts," responded my father-in-law in a gentle, matter-of-fact voice that sought to educate me on protocols around Indian marriages.

My mother-in-law's furrowed brow indicated that there was no need to dignify my misplaced question with an answer.

"Well," I proclaimed, asserting my dislike of any sense of

entitlement by the boy's family, "I guess Gurjot and I are not accepting any gifts. It is against our principles." My husband stood firmly by my side and made me proud by nodding his agreement.

The look on Mama's face showed that her son's betrayal had struck a knife in her.

"Oh, and it is only you and your family who has principles," she threw a scorching indictment at me and walked away.

"Please keep my family out of it," I said to her retreating back, and stormed out of the room.

Oh Mama, if only I had understood that you were rising above Indian standards by not "demanding" dowry, I would have saved us all a lot of hurt.

The wall between us had come up—solid and inviolable. I did not have the maturity to see how self-righteous I was.

The next morning when we met for breakfast, I tried my best to avoid Mama. She greeted me with a hug and a smile as though nothing had happened. I was surprised by her congeniality but stuck resolutely to my hurt. I was still smarting from her comment regarding my family. I told myself that the hug was for the benefit of the new bride, who was also seated at the breakfast table. Or was it for the benefit of the waiter who was taking orders for sunny-side-up eggs? I couldn't have cared less.

Her sense of entitlement was a turnoff for me that no amount of superficial pleasantries could efface. It was evident in her demeanor toward my mother, who had come to live with us shortly after we got married. If my husband's standing by my side when I refused gifts that were part of a dowry had hurt Mama, having my mother live with us was the ultimate betrayal by her son. Without going into painful details, suffice it to say that Mama was far from pleasant to my mom. She indicated to her the inappropriateness of living with a daughter. Mama felt that her right had been usurped.

I heaved a sigh of relief when the in-laws returned to India. However, left to my own self-reflection, I realized how much I disliked the tension between us. Sometimes I wondered if Mama realized how little I liked her nitpicking everything I did, not to mention how much I disliked coming back from work to find her snipping coupons from newspapers strewn all around the family room. She would be waiting for me to take her to Kmart. I hoped that I would not run into anyone I knew as I walked the aisles stacked with bargains while she got her two-dollar rebate on a vinyl lace tablecloth. The next day when she told me she had found the same tablecloth advertised cheaper at another store, I was ready to scream. While I drove her from store to store, she talked incessantly, at times even reading billboards aloud when there was nothing else to say.

When Gurjot came home, he received a frame-by-frame account of Mama's annoying habits. Needless to say, my husband defended his mother, pointing out that her behavior was very typical of folks of that generation from India. I did not agree because that was not what I had seen. We would inevitably get into an unpleasant argument.

I did agree with Gurjot that Mama was not malicious, just annoying. He gave me examples of mothers-in-law who were much worse. Mama, he would tell me, was just looking for love and respect from her daughter-in-law.

Could I love and respect her? I wondered.

As someone who was trying to practice the nonjudgmental and nonviolent dictum of *Guru Nanak*, I found myself lacking.

Hum Nahin Changey Bura Nahin Koyay.
I am not good, no one is bad.
(Guru Granth Sahib, page 726)

Wouldn't it be nice to feel affection toward her even though I did not like all aspects of her personality? Could I suspend my judgment, stop comparing her to my mother because she was a different individual, and like her for who she was? Was it possible to accept her sense of entitlement as part of her upbringing?

I went on a forty-day meditation where I reiterated the phrase "I Love Mama" for forty minutes every day. I remember the first time I said it to myself, I choked over the words. But I remained persistent. I had read somewhere that such a meditation broke old patterns and created new ones. Something very interesting happened at the end of forty days. During the weekly call Gurjot made to Mama who was in India at the time, she asked for me. I reluctantly took the phone. I heard a cheery upbeat voice at the other end. "How are you, Baytay?" I mumbled some pleasantries. It was hard to pretend that everything was hunky-dory between us. She told me she had bought a pair of cloisonné earrings for me. My jaw dropped. I had admired cloisonné workmanship on one of her bracelets and looked for similar earrings when we were in Chinatown during her last visit.

Was I witnessing the power of thoughts? Was our relationship going to take a dramatic turn for the better?

It wasn't that easy. It would take a lot more than a forty-day meditation for the relationship to get better. A lot of chiseling of my mind, a lot of effort from both Mama and me had to be made before love transformed our relationship.

I knew creating walls or judging people was not the way to live. Respect for elders was a key virtue. But did the elders not have to earn, or at the very least deserve, that respect? Was it not up to them to be good role models? What if they were going against the principle of equality taught by the Gurus?

I may have been more inclined to put up with Mama's annoying and interfering nature if she had been more respectful to my mother. My mom, however, was a lot more forgiving than me. This annoyed me even further. I felt that my mom was ready to overlook Mama's behavior because in her mind the boy's mother was entitled to greater respect than the girl's mother. The lopsided equation riled me the most.

Gurjot felt that he had ignored his parents after he had moved to the United States. He was ready to overcompensate for his neglect. I was not concerned with my husband's past behavior with his parents. I was upset with his mom's current unpleasant behavior toward my mom. No amount of rationalization on my husband's part was good enough. The friction between my husband and me heightened, furthering my negative feelings toward his mother.

My mom tried to tell me that forgiveness was an essential part of life and that bearing grudges hardens the heart. I shared my discontent with my close friends at work. I told them that my parents-in-law had stayed with us for several months and the plan was for them to continue to do so each year. My situation was met with shock and dismay. "This is not India," I was told. "You don't have to put up with any of it."

The problem was not that my in-laws visited us. The problem was that after the first few extended visits, they started visiting with one-way tickets, and no one had any idea when they were going back. The first couple of months were fine. Mama made an effort to be pleasant, and so did I. But the sheer proximity of living together eventually caused friction.

Mama always wanted to be right smack in the middle of whatever I was doing. My father-in-law, who was diabetic, went for long walks and made friends with other Indians who lived or had businesses in the neighborhood. He also got a city transit pass made within the first month of coming to California and would go off to the senior center or the *gurudwara*. Mama always said the she was a "homebody" and did not like going off somewhere every day. I saw her more as a "busybody" inserting herself in my life. I could not have friends visit me without Mama firmly planting herself among us and answering every question that was put to me. I started taking my friends to the bedroom. To my dismay, Mama would follow us.

I found a clever way to not engage with her when it was just the two of us. I would cover my head, pretending I was reciting *gurbani*. She started to respect me for doing a lot of recitation from the scriptures. My deception made me feel guilty. I started to recite *gurbani* in earnest. As soon as I realized that Mama was about to ambush me with her verbal deluge, my *chunni* would come up and my recitation would begin.

And then Anhad was born, my bundle of joy. There was no way I was going to have Mama help me during my postpartum months. I requested my mother, who had started living with Bhapa (my adopted brother) in Southern California, to come and help me for a few months.

I am sure Mama felt marginalized. But she did not show it. Her joy at becoming a grandmother was too great to be marred. My mom may have been the official caregiver, but Mama was the one who knew every aspect of raising a child. And true to her nature, she voiced her opinion firmly and loudly. She had an opinion about everything. Anyone listening would have thought she was a pediatrician with decades of practice behind her rather than a housewife doling out old wives' tales. My answer to her suggestions was a clenched jaw, "My pediatrician thinks differently" or "Times have changed." Little did I realize that the old wives' tales were distilled Eastern wisdom that would over the years be vindicated by new research.

The kitchen was another battleground for us. She hovered around me as I cooked.

"You are burning the spatula."

"Lower the heat."

"Use ripe tomatoes first."

"Don't burn the onions."

"Add more turmeric."

The advice was as endless as it was unsolicited. I alternated between silently clenching my teeth or snapping at her. The latter resulted in arguments with my husband.

Our patterns continued. Many a time I thought of walking away from my marriage because I did not think I could take one more day of her proximity.

Bhapa, my brother, was my confidant and counselor. While he patiently listened to my rants regarding Mama's annoying behavior, he always reminded me that respect for elders was a core value of Sikhi, that I found faults because I looked for them, that my life's work was to develop patience and compassion even toward those I did not like, and that I would find grace and goodness in Mama when I was open to seeing it.

Ever since I found and embraced Sikhi as a teenager, I had developed a personal relationship with the Guru through *Ardas* (prayer) and *Hukam* (reading scriptures). The practice of pouring my heart out in prayer and reading a random passage from Guru Granth Sahib as the Guru's voice was, and continues to be, a daily routine for me. Every morning before I leave for work and every evening before I go to bed, I connect with my Guru. I take the guidance inherent in the Hukam very seriously. I believe that it is the voice of God steering me on life's bumpy road. The voice cheers me on at times, chides me on occasion, boosts my confidence when I need it, and reaffirms the closeness of the Guru's presence to me. Over the years, the direct response to my prayers during times of confusion and distress has continued to amaze me. During Mama's visits, I spent a lot of time in the prayer room.

When my heart was filled with judgment toward Mama's idiosyncrasies and what I considered bizarre behavior, the Guru would tell me:

Na Ko Murakh, Na Ko Syana
Varte Sab Kich Tera Bhaana

There are no fools or wise folks
All that manifests is the Will
(Guru Granth Sahib, page 98)

It has taken me many decades to grasp the depth of these lines. How is it the Will of God that some are fools and others wise? I had no clue. But somehow the verse calmed me down. Just taking my troubles to the Guru's door, praying, and being told to defer judgment abated the storm in my heart.

I prayed for peace. I prayed that Mama would stop bothering me. I prayed for harmony in my house.

Things were not all bad. Mama was a very helpful person. She was incredibly smart and well informed. In many ways she was ahead of her generation. She was organized and methodical as opposed to my fly-by-the-seat-of-my-pants lifestyle. I began to see aspects of her personality that I could admire.

Mama suffered from arthritis. One day when the pain in her knee flared up, I offered to give her Reiki (a spiritual healing practice where energy is passed through the practitioner's hands). Mama was a willing recipient. The very act of my giving something selflessly and her receiving it gratefully changed the dynamic of our relationship. I had often bought Indian outfits and other gifts for Mama. Even though she eventually enjoyed them, her initial reaction almost always was of finding something not right with the gift. This attitude had killed the joy of giving. Reiki was different. She was a grateful receiver and often asked for it.

Something akin to love began to flow between us. Mama tried not to nitpick when I gently told her that it bothered me. Her voice became softer when she figured out I was more willing to listen to her if she was not loud.

One day my father-in-law said to me, "We are getting old, *Baytay*, and traveling back and forth from India is getting harder."

He said they had two options. They would stay in India and not make frequent trips or stay in the US. He looked at me squarely in the eyes and said, "We would prefer to live in the US and make your home our permanent residence, if you are okay with it."

My heart skipped a beat. He had locked my eyes with his. I could not look away. He was waiting for an answer. The water running in the sink, where I was washing the dishes, was all I could hear. I was aware of the soapy suds on my hands. The silence between us was deafening.

"I will understand if it is not acceptable to you," Dad lowered his eyes and mumbled.

I gave Dad a hug, soapy hands and all. "Of course you may stay with us. This is your home," I heard myself say to my utter amazement. There were tears in his eyes when he looked up.

In those moments of suspended decision, loving gestures that Dad had made over the years flashed in front of my eyes. Upon hearing that Gurjot wanted to marry me, while Mama had pouted, Dad had picked up the phone and called me.

"Jessi, *Baytay*, I want to thank you for accepting my son's proposal. I am honored to welcome you as a daughter in my family," he had told me.

His affection had run like a steady stream even though the tumultuous relationship with Mama caused occasional ripples. The bond between Dad and me made me yield to my parents-in-law's wishes to live with us.

We were a family of five. I had voluntarily accepted that fact. The tears in my father-in-law's eyes bore a witness to my decision.

Something magical happened when I surrendered and accepted. Life began to flow. Little nuisances that had often become big battles lost their oomph. We settled into a comfortable routine.

We added a new room to our house that gave all of us more space. Mama pretty much took over the kitchen and made wholesome Indian food every day. She found a purpose in life—serving her children and their guests. When I felt like exercising my culinary abilities, Mama and Dad never failed to appreciate the pasta, the fajitas, or the Chinese fare I put together. In fact, Mama often told me that she preferred my less oily and more nutritious dishes to what was served in restaurants. I suspected that this was her way of discouraging us from spending money on eating out frequently.

When we entertained, Mama was my willing helper. She designated herself the "sous chef." One evening I was doing the dishes after the guests had left. Mama called out to me, "Jessi, come and sit with me. There is an interesting show on TV. We are both tired. Let Gurjot clean up." She had come a long ways from censuring her son for making tea for me!

Mama started appreciating the clothes I bought for her during my annual visits to India. In fact, she became completely reliant upon me and took pride in telling everyone that her "daughter" took care of her wardrobe.

Mama's demeanor towards my mom had gradually changed over the years. She became respectful and appreciative of her, often commenting on her graceful and loving ways. When my mom passed away, I was grateful for the fact that Mama had made peace with her during her lifetime.

Mama was not someone who paid lavish compliments. Praise was best given behind a person's back, not to her face, she believed. One day she surprised me.

"*Baytay*, all my life I longed for a daughter. God gave me two sons." Then she held my hand and said, "God gave me a daughter, too. A little late in life." I hugged her. The very next second she was worrying about the milk boiling over. She was in the middle of making *paneer*. Mama was uncomfortable with sentimentality and reluctant to show her softer side. That was just the way she was.

A few years after they moved in with us, Dad passed on. I was in Barcelona, and it took me a couple of days to get back home. Mama's instructions to my husband were that all decisions regarding Dad's last rites would be made in consultation with me. She had gotten into the habit of taking me into her room and consulting me whenever something of import was occurring in the family.

After Dad's passing on, Mama felt that Indian custom demanded that she retreat into isolation, clearly something she was not born to do. She started wearing white *chunnis* and reciting more *gurbani*. She would stay in her room most of the time. I told her that I did not want to see her in somber colors. Dad and she had had a good life together. A few years before he passed on, they had had a fiftieth anniversary celebration. She needed to live fully; in gratitude for the life she had been given.

Mama heeded my advice. She began to dress well again and immersed herself in a social life she created for herself. Her "kitty" group, her frequent *Sukhmani Sahib* recitations with friends, birthdays, anniversaries and weddings in her circle of friends kept her vibrantly busy. Mama lived her life fully until a severe backache started to plague her. To our dismay, it turned out to be lymphoma of the spine.

Mama's last four months are filled with poignant memories that will last the rest of my life. She was a fighter and kept her spirits high. Every day when I visited her in the nursing home, she received me with open arms. While my husband took care of her medical needs talking to doctors and arranging the next round of chemo, etc., she turned to me to take care of her personal needs. After resisting it at first, she looked forward to the oil massage on her parched legs and feet. She let me comb her hair even as clumps of it were falling off. She enjoyed the nice fragrance of the moisturizers on her hands and face. I would hold up a hand mirror and say, "See how nice you look in a side bun, Mama." She would humor me with a smile, knowing full well that her silky gray hair was rapidly thinning.

Throughout her illness, Mama remained alert. One day she noticed that the flask in which I brought tea for her was missing. She knew right away that I had left it in the nurses' kitchen where I was rinsing the dishes. She told me that I needed to be more mindful. She orchestrated a *Sukhmani Sahib* recitation while she was laid up. She provided a guest list and gave clear instructions on letting her friends help me with the *langar*. I could tell that she did not want me to get overwhelmed with making phone calls or cooking.

After the recitation, when I went to the nursing home with *parsad*, she was waiting for me. "Perfect timing," she smiled. "I have just finished my *paath*." And then, after she had tasted the *parsad*, her brows furrowed "Who made the *parsad*? It is a bit overcooked." I smiled. Some things never changed. Mama remained a perfectionist to the end.

When Mama passed on, I felt I had lost my mother all over again.

Soniye

Subrina Singh

Born into a culturally traditional family to not-so-religious Hindu parents, I spent a great portion of my life learning about my religion and asking questions about God and spirituality. I entered Stony Brook University in search of answers as I filled my freshman schedule with classes on the *Ramayana* and other great Indian epics. While I read and tried to understand the messages of the *Puranas* and *Bhagavad Gita*, it was not until a class on Northern *Bhaktas* that I was formally introduced to Guru Nanak Dev Ji. Guruji's works of bhakti literature, which eventually became part of the Guru Granth Sahib, captivated my mind, spirit, and soul. The *shabads* and *gurbani*, especially that of Mool Mantar, were mesmerizing to me, and I felt as if the spiritual void of my mind and body was nourished.

After attending *gurudwara* on a more disciplined basis and attempting to follow the path of *Gurmat*, I decided that I needed the discipline and spirituality of Sikhi to help control my life, my bipolar disorder, and, moreover, my mind. It was at this point I decided to make a commitment to *Waheguruji* and myself; I had already considered myself a Sikh, but for me, for my lifestyle, and for my relationship with Waheguru, I chose to commit to not only better myself, but also love myself, even with all my "defects." I now constantly say, while I am not happy with the pain and suffering I have endured as a result of being bipolar, I love the person it has made me—a strong, empowered woman full of love and hope for the future with complete faith in God.

It was the first week of September 2009, my second year at Stony Brook, that I met my soul mate, Amanpreet. Eager to learn Hindi, I strategically sat near a couple of familiar faces. I knew few people in class, which was rather small, so I was a bit excited to meet the unfamiliar faces. My professor pointed out the extremely good-looking *sardar* who sat behind me. I am not sure if it is unprofessional to mention how handsome a student is, but she blatantly said, "Amanpreet, you are so good looking." In addition, he was from Delhi, his Hindi was amazing; I'd strike up conversation, searching for answers before my professor randomly called on me. She might have noticed the sparks between us. We had some chemistry; I am no science student, but we clicked so well I would dread the end of class.

Like most girls, I tried to look my best when we had class together, hoping that Amanpreet—Aman—noticed me and see me in the same light as I saw him. Every Tuesday and Thursday, I woke up a littler earlier to straighten my long, black, naturally wild and curly hair. I searched the closet for the perfect outfit and tried on multiple ensembles for one to catch his eye. Finally, there was makeup and perfume—so many products to choose from. I even took extra time to pick a bag—this was my favorite part but probably the last thing he noticed.

We had many Facebook conversations before we exchanged numbers and began texting. While preparing a dance for a charity show, I would end practice late at night and call him, saying, "My dorm is on the other end of campus. Stay on the phone with me until I get back, okay?" Sweetly, he always replied, "Of course." He probably thought I was the world's slowest walker, as I would arrive back in my room but still keep him on the phone. I began realizing how much we had in common. We talked about our everything, and I told him about my three sisters and dysfunctional family that I loved dearly. He told me about his brother and the huge family that he lived with and their constant guests. He chuckled when I explained I was a legitimate Barbie collector. I described my best years in high school, and he told me about his very different experience going to a high school in Queens. I mentioned that I sang opera; he was a bit surprised at that one, but responded with, "I definitely have to hear that one day." I explained my decision to live a life inspired by Gurmat and my decision to take *amrit* to display my discipline to Waheguruji. Amanpreet questioned my decision and reasons for spirituality, and I knew I'd soon have to share the details about my illness.

As time passed, I wondered if we were just friends, or if he liked me. I asked my suitemate for advice. She replied, "Be forward; just ask him. Guys like that." I was a tad bit shy, but finally a couple days before Halloween, he said, "Wanna hang out?" I was excited, but casually replied, "Sure," hoping not to appear too eager. We saw a movie that day, *Law Abiding Citizen*. Not my first choice, but I was too happy to care.

I was convinced it was our first date, but after that movie—not exactly a romantic date flick—I wasn't so sure. I complained to my suitemates with anxiety in my voice: how long would it take for him to call or text me? Four long days passed, and finally he called. We spoke for hours and decided to study for a Hindi quiz the next day. Multiple hangouts later, I was seriously falling for him more and more.

November 5, 2009—just a few days after he first told me that I was beautiful—is a date I will never forget. Around 5 p.m. (yes, I even remember the time), I finally took the advice of my suitemate and asked him, "Do you like me?" With hesitation and sarcasm in his deep voice, he responded, "Of course, or I wouldn't even be here." Looking back, I cannot believe I then asked, "Are we in the friend zone?" He looked at me and smiled, "No, I actually like you . . ." I could not wipe the grin off my face, finally knowing the true feelings he'd so casually held back. It was coincidentally the same day of this charity show I had been preparing for, that he asked me to be his girlfriend. I did not even have to reply with a "yes." The smile and blushing cheeks on my face said it all. Of all the girls he could be with, he had chosen me.

About four weeks into blissful dating, with dates and late-night talks that lasted until morning, I felt it was time to be honest. At this point in my life I was in a sort of rehab program for people with mental illnesses, which required me to leave school early on Tuesday and come back Wednesday morning. When Aman asked, "Why do you go home every Tuesday?" I was stunned; I did not want to lie but was not ready to tell him yet, so casually and with much hesitation in my voice, I responded, "I like to be with my family." Wow, what a complete lie. *I would rather be hanging out with you on Tuesdays*, I wanted to say.

One Wednesday morning when he picked me up to go to Stony, I finally blurted out (after a few awkward silences had filled the car), "I have something I need to tell you; it is serious." He was bit shocked and inquisitive. I had rehearsed how I was going to tell him a million times, but nothing I planned happened.

"When I was in my junior year of high school, I had some problems and finally went to see a doctor, and I was diagnosed with bipolar disorder."

Silently and patiently I awaited his response. How would he react? Would he still want to be with me? Would he still like me?

"Okay, so you are bipolar . . ."

I answered back with a simple and very quiet "yes." It was the type of yes that was full of shame and embarrassment. Silence again.

"That is not that bad, I would have never known," Aman spoke gently. Then he laughed and said, "I thought you were about to tell me that you had a baby or something." Still laughing, he continued. "That's not bad at all."

A couple of days after my big revelation, he asked if my illness was correlated to my decision to live a life of Gurmat. I explained the reason I end my day with *Mool Mantar* and *Ardas*: "When you wake up in a hospital bed, not knowing how you ended up there, and cannot explain why a pill bottle of a controlled substance was empty on your bed, and then a doctor comes into your room as you lie there hopelessly and does not know how to help you or what is wrong with you, there is only one thing you have to hold on to—that is God and faith." During my worst panic attacks, the mere chanting of *Waheguru* eases the tense pain within my heart. I knew Aman understood; he was different.

This was a major turning point in our relationship, the point when we both realized how much we cared about each other. Never in my life had I ever told someone about my disorder and received such a calm and accepting response. He did not make me feel defective, inferior, or ashamed in any way. Never in my life had anyone been so supportive.

As if being bipolar was not enough, unfortunate events filled my life during this time. In April 2010, my family broke apart. My parents separated after we discovered that my father was unfaithful to my mother. I began to lose trust in people, and although Aman was with me every step of the way, it was hard to know how genuine he was and whether I could completely trust anyone, let alone him. We had something special still, and communicated our emotions constantly. "I know after all you have been through it is hard to trust people in general," he told me one day, "but I want you to know that I will never hurt you in that way. I will never betray you." This stuck with me, and even three years later, I still remind myself of the kind, loving words he spoke to me that day.

The next few months were close to the best months of my life. I was so happy. I was happy with him. I was happy being me, in my own skin. We grew closer, and eventually our first anniversary came. I grew accustomed to waking up to his good morning calls and falling asleep to his voice when he wished me good night.

I was not lying when I said bad things continued to find a way into my life. It was around our first anniversary that I was diagnosed with yet another condition, hypothyroid disease. Within mere weeks I went from a fit, petite beauty to a four-foot-ten-inch, 150-pound girl. I felt disgusting, ugly; "unattractive" was an understatement. It took weeks before medication worked and I lost some weight, but I was never going to look the way I did before; I was never going to look like that girl Aman initially fell for. I was scared of the hatred I felt toward myself, and I was scared that Aman would think I was ugly. To this day, he has never said one word about my weight gain and continues to praise me as the most beautiful girl in the world. If only I saw myself through his eyes.

Aman began to write me love letters and leave me little notes to try to boost my self-esteem and take me out of my depression. Through these little Post-its, he became my rock. After only one year together, I knew that regardless of what happened to me or my life, no matter what crisis came my way, he would always be there. More than a best friend, he was my confidant. I could tell him everything and anything and he would keep it safe. I felt so secure and protected in his presence. We told each other things that had never left our mouths until we shared them, and that brought us closer.

My trust in him finally let me breathe, as if I were no longer carrying the entire weight of the world on only my shoulders. From anniversaries to holidays to birthdays, he always found a way to make me feel like I was number one. Not only did I care deeply for Aman, I was madly in love with him. Without his ever saying, "I love you," I knew he felt the same way. Our unspoken love kept us close, but our friendship kept us together, and as each day passed, it only strengthened. Our bond was a force to be reckoned with.

Again God threw me a curveball, except not only toward me; it was toward my family and it changed our lives forever. On Sunday, March 18, 2012, my sister was violently murdered on the front porch of her home in Queens, New York. As my family and Aman gently broke the terrible news to me, I ran to my room, the tears unstoppable. He hugged me, held me in his arms, and for the first time said, "*Soniye*, we will get through this together. I am here for you. I love you."

At last, he said the words I had been longing to hear, but not out of sympathy or pity. When I later asked him why chose that moment to tell me, he said, "It was on that day that I realized how precious and short life could be, and that even though you already knew, you needed to hear it just in case we never got another chance."

It was that day, the worst day of my life, that Aman so gracefully supported not only me but also every member of my family. I always wondered how one knows when their partner is "the one." That day that I knew I had found the one for me. Like they say, "When you know, you just know."

The week following my sister's death was unbearable, but I had to be strong for my dear Vava. It was Aman who held my hand as I saw her deceased body for the first time, as I gave her eulogy, as I watched her body go up in flames during her cremation. As I laid my sister to rest, it was Aman who stood by my side, and I knew he would be there forever.

I have this theory that when God made every man he made a woman to go with him, to complement him, to create an unbreakable relationship. Part of life is going through experiences and places to find that person God has made for you. I am lucky enough to say that I have found mine. I have found my partner for life and can confidently say that I cannot wait to spend every day of my life with Aman.

Our relationship has been tested constantly, and he has had many opportunities to leave me, but he has not, and I know he won't. We are unbreakable. I thank God every day for bringing Aman into my life. It has truly been a blessing, and he is one I will never take for granted. Each moment I spend with him is a dream come true for me. To be honest, he is everything I never knew I always wanted and because of that, our love will only strengthen and continue to persevere. Aman and I complete each other for one simple reason: respect. We respect each other in a way some people find impossible. Even through our trials and troubles, we have always persevered. With Aman by my side, I see a bright light that shows me to the end and because of this, I am certain the best is yet to come.

The Boy is Pink!

Jasminder Kaur

Birth

The first grandchild was to be a boy, but something went marvelously wrong. My father stormed out of the hospital. My mother was comforted by the woman who delivered me. Shortly after came the second child, another girl. This time there was no need for my father to trouble himself with a hospital visit. Years later there was to be a third child, a boy who would not survive to meet his birth. Soon after, my parents stopped hoping for the offspring my father so desired.

It wasn't easy for him. Born into an orthodox Sikh family with immigrant parents who'd made their way from a village in Punjab to a developing Singapore in the 1950s, he grew up in a 600-square-foot flat with a violent father and seven siblings, one of whom committed suicide at twenty-one. Living in a Chinese-dominated society meant there was no value for his beard and turban, so one day he returned home without them. He had erased visible traces of his otherness. My grandfather disowned him.

It wasn't easy for my mother either. She too was raised in a conservative Sikh family by immigrant parents, with a brother twenty years her senior who rose to become one of Singapore's leading obstetricians. Barred from furthering her education, she fulfilled her familial duty by looking after her brother's children.

When she came of age she was promptly betrothed to my father. No longer her parents' responsibility, she was now answerable to her new owner.

Brought up by a devoted Sikh wife and mother, my sister and I were raised to not give our father further reason to resent our mother. We were pristine, obedient, and in bed by the time he returned home in the evenings. Neither he nor she had completed the equivalent of a high school education. For us, textbooks were paramount. School was the temple, and our father became God. There was a slight problem, though. God was often up in the clouds, and he was always getting into trouble. An accomplished pilot, a functional alcoholic, and a perpetual philanderer, eventually God no longer resided with us. He retreated to his haven, a small flat he rented on the far side of the city. Voluntary confinement, he called it. He left us with sporadic financial support and layers of bruises. He, however, never forgot his family. He visited regularly with harassing phone calls and drunken drop-ins. Our mother sought refuge in raising us, while always pining for him. One day he would return, she would say. After all, God never abandoned his followers. It was merely a test of her faith. She prayed daily. Or whenever she needed to. I did at first and then couldn't. There were too many contradictions, too many injustices tolerated in the name of *Waheguru*.

It wasn't always doom and gloom for my sister and me. We were told how very special we were by the "not-so-random men" in our family who felt us up every so often. These less-than-ideal conditions meant my love story had deferred beginnings. It meant glorious episodes of truancy, defiance of authority, and psychic rages. It meant questioning of tyranny in all of its magnificent forms. Birthed amid chaos and contradiction, often scared, sometimes fearless, I persevered. Imagination cloaked me. I sought refuge in the words of African American writers James Baldwin, Richard Wright, and Ralph Ellison, and through their stories of being "other," I became me—the one whose journey began when I left Singapore for university abroad—with one oversized pink suitcase in tow.

Transition

Arriving in England at age twenty-one to pursue a higher education ushered in my journey toward falling in love—with myself. Self-love arrived late. Or perhaps she was always a dormant presence. I lived, ate, studied, laughed, cried, and conversed daily with people nothing like me. Intellectual and personal dialogues with my British peers challenged me. I tugged daily at layers of deep-seated insecurities and self-doubt. My sharp distrust of others made relating almost unbearable at first. Time and distance, however, had healing powers. The halls of residence I shared became a sacred space of emotional growth and renewal. Slowly layers began to shed away. I learned to listen to myself by speaking to others. Through a communal living experience and the intimacy it fosters, my journey toward self-love unraveled amid strangers, far away from home.

Meanwhile, another very different kind of love story was unfolding. Before leaving for England I met a like-minded cultural other, a Canadian Hindu expatriate working in Singapore. From a chance encounter on the street, a different kind of love grew between Singapore, where he was residing, and England, where I was studying. We decided to get married after I graduated and returned to Singapore. Hindu tradition stipulates the wedding happen where the bride-to-be is from, but a Canadian of South Indian Hindu descent and a North Indian Sikh are never to cross. Our marriage also caused waves in the local Sikh community, disrupting cultural and religious convention. No Sikh temple would sanctify our transgressions. Our immediate families came around, but others would not accept our union. Our wedding was joyous nonetheless and marked my next big transition. Several weeks after our Hindu wedding nuptials, I left for San Francisco to join my "other."

The elsewhere I had imagined had arrived. Befriending a German "sister" and a Jewish American elder, as a newly wed immigrant in the Bay Area amid my chosen kin, I continued to find myself. Barred from paid employment while awaiting permanent residency was an invaluable gift. Several years of voluntary service to the financially impoverished and racially oppressed of America revealed my life path. Once again disrupting cultural norms and familial expectations, I applied to the PhD program in African Diaspora Studies. My Singaporean family could not understand why injustices to a people so different from us could be so meaningful to me. But their stories saved me as a young girl, and at age thirty I found my intellectual home in the African American Studies Department at University of California, Berkeley.

Renewal

Today, in connection with others nothing like me, my love of mind blossoms as I pursue an academic path. My journey toward healing continues. I harbor deep wounds from the past and live daily with the pain and possibility of renewal. Courage and defiance are markers that have followed me into my adulthood. Constantly going against God's tyranny made me infamous in my family at an early age. I became the boy, the one who could do things girls wouldn't, the one who challenged my father and also stood by him, glad when he made peace with his own father. My volatile, tyrannical, philandering, physically abusive, substance-using grandfather had found God one day, literally, under the hood of his car, or so the tale goes. He had heard the voice of Waheguru at the age of forty. Overnight he took on the vows of Sikhism, giving up liquor, women, meat, and dairy. What he couldn't give up was his reign. After his enlightened conversion, he continued to enforce his will upon us, this time through Waheguru. He met his fate the same place he found God—hit one day while cycling to temple and thrown over the hood of a car. He was eighty-five. I was sitting with my father when his father was driven to the crematorium, once again disrupting the patriarchal renditions of Sikhism by stepping into a role traditionally performed only by men.

After his father's death, my father descended into his own private hell. The one who stood over six feet tall, commanding our fear with his mere presence, became a prisoner of his addictions. Three years ago, on the eve of my sister's wedding, he showed up on the doorstep of my mother's flat—delirious; emaciated; smelling of whiskey, sweat, and excrement; wanting to be early for his younger daughter's wedding *phere*, or so he said. Maybe it was a cry for help. I will never know. What I do know is that he missed her wedding, just as he had missed her birth.

From that day he ceased being God. All I felt was shame as I walked out of the hospital ward where he had been taken in the throes of death. What became clear as my sister and I walked away from the hospital that day is that I might never see my God again. He had chosen his demons over his family. My sister's hands still stand out vividly in my mind's eye. Perhaps it was the intricate *mehndi* that adorned them, or maybe it was the lab report she held, a piece of paper that spelled out the depth of his torment.

Today, almost at the tail end of my doctorate, and as an adjunct lecturer, I continue to question what "being" Sikh means. As a Sikh woman, I inhabit multiple spaces. I am an alien resident and a woman who considers America my home. I challenge conventional notions of being and becoming a Sikh. The practice of Sikhism for me is the art of battle—the battle for inner peace, for self-love through relatedness and crossings. I transgress tradition by partnering with those from different castes, creeds, religions, and nationalities. I challenge norms by embodying knowledge and experiences of those nothing like me. As son and as daughter, as teacher and as student, as healer and as wounded, I manifest the battle. And what does my ongoing journey toward falling in love with myself look like? It means doing. Love. As it happens. Amid upheaval, and in connection.

Spark of Life

Gurpreet Kaur

When our twins were seven years old, we finally decided to further our family planning. I had always wanted a large family and lots of pitter-patter of tiny feet around the house, so we were joyous when the new pregnancy test came back positive. I was not sure if it was real, I waited for some pregnancy nausea to set in. Instead, at four weeks, I was greeted by intense cravings for hot-and-sour soup and pickles. "Pickles?" I thought. "So cliché!" We giggled and laughed as we enjoyed our daily dose of pickles, as I wasn't the only one craving them! This was fun!

A couple of weeks went by, and one day I woke up soaked in bright red blood. It was my first reality check. On the one hand I was terrified at the prospect of losing my pregnancy. On the other hand, I placed my faith in the hands of a higher power, *Hukam* (God's will and order). The physician in me thought of all the possible reasons for painless uterine bleeding . . . genetics, chromosomal aberrations, and uterine or placental abnormalities, to name a few. I thought to myself that no matter what was destined to be, I was going to accept the outcome with grace and gratitude.

Our first ultrasound confirmed the heartbeat. It was music to my ears to hear the sound I had heard nearly hundreds of times while performing the Doppler on other patients I had seen during my family medicine residency. Tuning in to the ultrasound image, there it was, an ant-sized beating heart nestled inside the warmth of a peanut. There was not one, but two! I tried to laugh with joy but couldn't. Only tears escaped, as I was too afraid to enjoy the pleasure. I cried on my way home in the car. My heart pounding. Then, in an instant, thoughts of miscarriage hushed, and I was overcome by double the pleasure again.

We let the news settle in slowly. After the scare, we were reluctant to celebrate. It was to soon. I prayed to *Waheguru* (God) to let the pregnancy continue only if the children were going to be healthy and not suffer. In that same breath, I vowed that I will love them and protect them and be thankful for them no matter what shape or form they came in. I never imagined that a life so small could promise pleasures greater than any worldly pleasure or what money could buy.

Several more weeks went by, and we dove right into the pregnancy. As my belly started to grow, I placed my hand on the lower half to support and feel the very active twins. My seven-year-old twin children joined right in. They wanted to enjoy every moment in anticipation of receiving their younger siblings. Aekash, my son, and Arzoe, my daughter, loved their unborn siblings so much they wanted to follow their daily growth pattern. We looked at all the ultrasound pictures and the recordings of the little hands and feet waving in my belly. We opened up all the anatomy books and followed my pregnancy one day at a time and discussed every anatomical change that occurs each week, and each month. At week ten, babies are building cartilage. By week twelve, they have doubled in size. Week thirteen, they are the size of a peach. Week fourteen, they have eyebrows and hair on their heads. This sparked very interesting conversations around hair and its significance—how in our family, babies are born with plentiful hair on their heads—and the significance of hair in *Sikhi*. Week fifteen, babies are kicking and active. A follow-up ultrasound revealed two very naughty boys, twisting, tumbling, and turning, waving and swimming endlessly in placental fluid. Oh, what a joy to have them look right at the Doppler and sense its presence. It was truly a miracle to see the sweet lips, noses, arms and legs, and teeniest tiny fingers and toes we had ever seen.

Around sixteen to eighteen weeks, I was having pain with minimal walking and activity. My obstetrician reassured me and said, "I won't keep you home from work just yet."

Love, Joy, and Connection

Our dreams began to unfold as our seven-year-old twins planned out our entire future. They each decided which baby to share a room with and that they would take turns babysitting. We moved the furniture around the house to accommodate the new baby furniture, which was on its way. The bassinets would be in the master bedroom. The cribs would go in the shared rooms with the babies' older brother and sister. My unborn children responded to my voice and touch. When they were restless, I soothed them with singing *kirtan* (Sikh hymns). The sensation of little bubbles in my tummy soothed to a whisper. They were behaving and learning to listen, already! I was now 23.3 weeks pregnant, and the four of us spent several dinners making a list of names. We could not commit to names, so we put the list away in a drawer for later reference. After dinner one night, I was full of love and asked my husband to take a family picture of us. I didn't want to forget this moment, as if I instinctively knew that things were going to change. I brushed away the uneasy sensation. I captured the moment of my miracle of life. While I was making active efforts to stay detached, I unsuspectingly became attached.

I slept well after having been showered with so much love and attention. At five in the morning, I woke up as usual to get ready for work and found myself soaked again in a pool of bright red blood. This time there was a cramping pain, and the fleeting possible diagnosis once again swam through my mind. The kids had to go to school, and I needed to remain calm. I asked my husband, Dickey, to drop off the kids as usual, and I drove myself to the Labor and Delivery (L&D) room. It was very difficult being an actual patient walking up to L&D when I wasn't used to asking for help. I couldn't hold myself upright any longer, and as I leaned against the entry door, I whispered, "I need help" to the security guard by the main entrance. The kind staff quickly ushered me into an empty room and hooked me up to the monitors. Unsynchronized and painful, untimely cramps turned out to be contractions and were becoming stronger and more frequent. The mucous plug was out, and with cervical dilatation, I was in premature preterm labor. With optimism by my side, I continued to breathe in and breathe out, working through the cramps.

The on-call obstetrician asked what I wanted to do if the babies were born.

"What do you mean?" I asked.

"Do you want to save them or let them go?"

A million swear words crossed my mind as I remained composed to collect my faculties. I wanted to shout out loud, "Why do you think I'm here? Why do you think I want to let my children die? What kind of question is that? Why the hell would I come for help if I didn't want any help? Is this a joke? Keep the babies or let them die? Is it really a matter-of-fact decision? How dare you ask me, just like that, without hesitation or remorse?"

I was angry. My professional peers made assumptions about my decisions not only because I am a family physician, but also because I am a hospice physician. I see death every day. I see my patients wither away little by little and fade away. Nearly every day I hold their hands at their deathbeds, if they allow me this honor. This was neither the time nor the place to question the sanctity of life. At any stage in a human being's time on earth, life is a blessed precious gift.

"Save them, of course!" I said. What other option was there?

I was transferred to a higher level of care at another hospital with a neonatal intensive care unit (NICU). The bumpy ambulance ride accelerated the contractions. With each squeeze my little babies were pushed down the birth canal. I wanted to pray, but overcome with fear, I could not bring myself to do it. I have always received everything I have prayed for, and I was afraid to ask this time. No amount of medication slowed down the contractions. They became stronger and more forceful as the hours went by, as if a force of nature was unleashed on its charted course, and there was no stopping it. The resident who came to check on me said, "I have no hope." Her words were sharp and unfeeling and without any sorrow or grief. It is never the right thing to say to a patient, and certainly not to a palliative care physician who is holding on to any glimpse of hope that her children will be born alive and will thrive in the face of adversity. After much deliberation and a few conversations with the specialists, we agreed that resuscitation would be attempted only if the children were born active and kicking. If they were still, they would not be resuscitated. They jumped inside of me, there was no doubt that even when their heartbeats were not being monitored, they would be kicking on their way out.

Several hours into a painful labor, I was offered no pain medication. I finally had to ask. The bedside nurse who was sitting with her back toward me sparingly gave me small doses of opioid, which seemed to wear off within minutes.

"You have had so much medication that if I were to give you more, it would be lethal," she said. Each contraction tore and ripped through the inside of me, and she thought I was at risk for respiratory depression due to too much pain medication?

I howled, "Do I look like I am having respiratory depression?" I was screaming at the top of my lungs while my husband, stunned, stood by helplessly. I was pleading for more pain medication and had to keep asking the nurse to get additional orders from the attending physician. I insisted upon seeing an anesthesiologist. It wasn't long before I had an epidural and there was finally calm in the midst of the storm. Numb from the waist down, I received a few hours of rest. I was fully dilated twenty-eight hours into labor and was rushed to the operating room as the children tumbled in the womb so much they were now breach. We prepared for a crash C-section in the event that manual repositioning was not successful. I was quickly taken to the operating room, where the additional staff called in for the night was waiting, and within seconds my water bag broke and the obstetrician along with her resident attempted manual manipulation to turn the babies around. I imagined how they were beaten up by this process, and I cried the whole time. A few minutes later, Baby A was born kicking and moving. Twelve minutes later came Baby B. They both had to be swiftly intubated, as they did not breathe on their own for too long. Their lungs had not yet matured.

The doctors quickly whisked the babies away to the neonatal intensive care unit before I saw them. I tried to sneak a peek through the stream of unending tears but could not. I was taken to recovery. I longed to see my children, and the endorphin surge in addition to the effects of the epidural did not let me feel the pain from the process I had endured. A few hours later, we finally met our newborn children in the NICU bundled up inside their warm incubators. They looked almost alien-like with the multitude of tubes attached to them. The loud respirator, the beeping essential units, the numbers flashing on the screen, and the intensivist trying to talk to me over all the background noise were all blocking my view. We were afraid to lose them, so we were reluctant to name them, but we had to choose names for the birth certificates. We quickly opened up the *gutka* (prayer book), and it brought us to *Jaap Sahib* (one of the daily prayers), my favorite *paath* (prayer), and landed on the letters A and R.

Abhey Ajay Singh and Rafiq Amitoj Singh

The names suited them. Abhey, the fearless, and Rafiq, the friendly one. Abhey was a bit pale and had light skin, and Rafiq was the older one who took most of the beating during the delivery and was dark with all the bruising. Rafiq instantly became my favorite as he managed to get all my sympathy. Some people refer to their newborns as monkeys, and mine really did look like monkeys. The cutest monkeys I had ever seen. They weighed one pound ten ounces and were born with functional body parts. We examined every inch of their bodies, which were visible through the tubes and the tapes. Hairy scalps, long eyelashes, flat ears—just like their Daddy. Lips red and long fingers with overgrown fingernails—just like mine. Abhey's diaper had just been changed. We saw them in the world's smallest diapers and we were ecstatic! They both looked like little wax dolls. When I touched them, they would calm down for the moment. I could see the blood vessels under their skin, which was so thin it stuck to my hand. I was afraid to sheer the skin, so I held myself back and just consoled their silhouettes.

The intensivist continued to tell us how fragile the kids were and that the likelihood was that they were going to have some brain damage.

"They are born so young that their eyes are fused. They may have an internal brain bleed," and so on and so on. My brain was on overdrive. We tuned her out. How much more did we need to hear? The ultrasound of the brain was normal. There was no brain bleed. This entire time I was crying so much that my vision had become blurry and my eyes almost shut from being swollen. My tears wouldn't stop, as if they were flowing from an unending source. We spent any available moments caressing and cooing to our children. We talked to them, and they responded to our voices. Abhey turned in the direction of his father, who was speaking to him, and grasped his finger. He then opened his eyes and looked right at us with his big black eyes.

"Their eyes aren't fused!" we said to each other. "They are open and beautiful!" His forehead furrowed, and he started to pout. With his thin red lips, he suckled on the breathing tube in his throat and grasped onto it like a bottle. "He thinks he is drinking milk!" we exclaimed. We rubbed his forehead, and he calmed down.

Then Rafiq, who was several feet away in another incubator, opened his eyes. He was more startled, and he loved being touched and caressed, which we could not do much of because his skin would get stuck to our fingertips. Our tender moments continued to be interrupted by the frequent blood transfusions and medication adjustments. Abhey turned paler, and we didn't know where all the blood was going. The breathing machine wasn't helping anymore, and his oxygen levels kept dropping.

"We have him on an experimental machine now. Other than manual CPR, there is nothing else we can do." He was turning pale, and his lips were blue. Glued to his monitor, I knew better. He continued to suckle on the ventilator tubing and look at me every time I spoke to him. He looked at me with his big blackish-brown eyes, closed them for the last time, and turned his head toward me. His doll hands, curled around my index finger, opened and released their grip. A swarm of intensive care team members rushed to tend to him. I asked for him to be taken out of the incubator, so he could die in the comfort of my warmth. It seemed like an eternity until when I received Abhey and wrapped him in my arms. My little monkey died very quickly as I rocked him back and forth. We hoped for a miracle: that Rafiq would live.

The next day, Rafiq, who was a fighter, met the same fate, although he hung in there longer. I didn't want him to hang around for me, and he was writhing and wincing as our destitute hearts watched him die. We asked him to go to Waheguru; we begged for him to leave us and be at peace. Even in the last moments, the boys' personalities were apparent. Abhey was the quieter and younger of the two. He did not protest his death. Rafiq left declaring and crying as if he knew that if he died, then I would too. The rise and the fall of his chest, consistent with breathing, slowed to a halt. A shadow seemed to have escaped and brushed past my cheek. The pink moist inside of his mouth turned dark as if a light switch had been turned off. A big chunk of my heart went missing in the instant when I witnessed the last exhalation with which his warm body became cold and still. This is death. I have seen it many times before but not held it in my embrace. I wanted to follow my children and was frustrated that I could not. I have never felt smaller and more insignificant in my life than at that moment when life slithered and escaped through the spaces in my despairing grasp. I was reaching for air as if I could hold on to their souls just a little bit longer. I fell to the floor of the intensive care unit, and my husband escorted me to the room where we were allowed time together as a family. We lay with them on the bed and tried to wake them up as if they were just kidding and were going to spontaneously wake up and smile. I listened to their hearts with my ear on their chests, in case they were still beating. They were not. We examined every inch of their bodies in wonder that these were real miracles of life. We kissed their ears and their hands and their tiny little feet. The skin was no longer sticky. We were finally able to hold them close, yet there was no joy in that. This is *moh*, this is love and this is attachment, yet we had no control over it.

With the death of my two children, a part of me died too—not a proverbial death but a real one. A soul cannot be contained or arrested; it must move on. I had to accept this and yet know that this was for the better for me and for them. How? I do not know.

The Abyss

Surviving the traumatic death of a loved one is a long, arduous, and convoluted journey that each one of us must travel alone. Crying hardly seems like a part of the healing process. There are so many questions and no answers. No evidence was found of an infection, a ruptured uterus, or any other known cause. Just "sheer bad luck" said the perinatologist. I wanted to ask, "What is luck? Show me the numbers and show me the evidence!" I don't believe in luck. I know that this happened for a reason. I needed to talk to a *Bhai Sahib* (Sikh clergy). I needed some cultural and spiritual context shed on this situation. None was available at the time, in the hospital or after.

The funeral coordinators took their bodies, and stored them until we released them for the next step. I do not remember much between life and death conversations around the dining table where we spent most of the next few days. My scientific mind kept me sane, stronger than I thought. Between denial, anger, and confusion I opted to stay home while my husband made all the arrangements. I went to the funeral home with him, but I did not dare step out of my car, as my body did not want to move. I wanted this nightmare to end. My Bhai Sahib from Chicago called. He said that what belonged to Waheguru had returned to Waheguru, that I should do *simran* (recitation, meditation upon the name of God), and it would give me *bal*, strength, to deal with this. I wanted to hear that if I did simran, then my children would be returned to me. I heard no such thing.

The funeral home asked if we wanted to hold services. We did not. We needed for the pain to end as soon as possible. We needed closure. I did not have the courage to ask for help. We had not told many friends that we were pregnant, much less announced that now we needed support to get through this. Our family flew in from Maryland and Chicago; cousins who lived nearby and one of my childhood friends were our sole support.

"You shouldn't go," said my husband. "Let me just take care of it." I disagreed and frantically got my guts together and put on the maternity tunic that I had bought just weeks before. We drove to the crematorium, which seemed a very long way, in Oakland. Hidden among other industrial-appearing buildings, it was a very unsightly place, which gave me shivers down my spine. This is where my children were, awaiting a prayer in their name and a farewell to their earthly bodies. After working against all the resistance in the room, I finally penetrated through the line guarding the entry to the viewing room. "I need closure. It's my right to say good-bye." What if the funeral home mixed up the bodies and tagged them wrong? I needed to confirm with my eyes, one last time, to really believe that they were gone!

"They have blood in their eyes," said the administrator of the crematorium.

"Oh no, are their eyes closed?"

"Yes," she said, "but their skin is fragile and may break, so don't pick them up."

I agreed to this ridiculous request. I wish I hadn't. My dad was the first to step forward; he kissed their foreheads, one by one, and gave them his love. In that moment I realized that their *Naanke* (maternal grandparents) were grieving the loss too and their *Mamaji* (maternal uncle) had just lost his nephews.

"They are so little, and look at the hands and the toes," said a voice from the back.

The viewing was a bit blurred; my eyes had been swollen from incessant crying for days. I tried to remember their tiny faces; I longed to finally see peace for them. We begged for forgiveness and for any trespasses against them.

"I'm sorry," I cried. "I'm sorry . . . I couldn't save you. Forgive me for your suffering . . . I'm sorry . . . so, so sorry."

Ardas

My brother led the *Ardas* (prayer). Standing there in the viewing room, Veerji's voice trembled under the weight of his tears. He paused as if he did not expect the emotional outpouring and we all wept quietly.

I did not want to do simran. I did not want to have a conversation with God at that time. "I am angry with you," I said in my mind. "You are causing so much pain without any explanation." It took another twenty-four months before I willingly bowed to my Guru again. My faith remained unwavering, while my relationship with my Waheguru, whom I had thought of as my best friend and my keeper, had now been altered. I was not going to ask why this happened. All I knew was that this did happen.

Against the grain of my upbringing, I mustered the courage to seek help. I summoned resolution and valor and walked into a therapist's office. "Would you like an antidepressant?" asked the therapist. "No, I just want my babies back, and then everything will be all right." She was quiet. We ended our session. I did not need antidepressants two weeks into my loss. I was grieving.

What I needed was a ray of hope, something or someone to tell me that I would survive this. I questioned my own existence and the possibility of seeing another day. I felt detached, weightless. I felt as if God could do no further harm. "You've done your worst!" I challenged God. "What's next? Losing the roof over my head? My job? It matters none, as the breaking point has been reached, and the pain threshold has been raised." Life, as I was concerned, had ended. My Waheguru, who was my friend, my father, my mother, and my caretaker, had breached my trust. My creator had hurt me in a way I never thought was possible. "Fix it!" I very arrogantly demanded, as if I were entitled to happiness beyond what had been granted to me.

I watched my sons' bodies incinerate. They were now gone, and along with them any hope of a future we had imagined with them in our lives. As soon as we entered the front door of our home, my daughter Arzoe ran into my arms with tears rolling down her cheeks in an unending stream and asked, "But Mom, why would God do this to us? Why did God kill the babies?" I had nothing to say; she knew too much already. We just held each other and cried. My son Aekash consoled me, patting his tiny little hands on my head. "It's okay, Mommy. It's okay." In that moment, I felt unconditionally and absolutely loved. Like the flicker at the end of the candlestick, I felt alive for a moment.

No one could have prepared us for what was to follow. My breasts continued to be engorged, with no baby to feed. It made me angry. I iced for days and avoided bathing or showering, as it might stimulate more milk production. I stepped out to get some fresh air, and at the grocery store there was a baby crying at a distance. Without warning, the profuse lactation became apparent, and I stomped out of the store to turn it off. How long is this going to go on? I asked myself. Isn't there a book on this? Isn't there a *How To Live After Your Newborns Have Died for Dummies?* Infection soon ensued, and my body continued on its predetermined course, thinking it had a child to nurse.

Some friends and coworkers sent flowers. I didn't want any dead things in the house, so I tossed them out. People around us tried to comfort us, yet nothing seemed to help. There was nothing that could be said or done to help, but people felt like they needed to do something, and we appreciated the gestures, knowing how difficult it was in situations like those to say the right thing. Even Dickey and I didn't know what to say to comfort each other.

We paid for a biodegradable urn, which we would drop right into the ocean. After two days of deliberation, we decided to go with the place we all love the most, Half Moon Bay, California. I was relying more on *Gurbani* (Sikh teachings from the Sikh holy scripture, the Guru Granth Sahib) than I knew, and more than I wanted to believe. I knew I couldn't shut out God for too much longer, as the teachings permeated through to guide our family along every difficult decision we were confronted with.

The Dove

The captain of a twenty-foot yacht agreed to take us to Half Moon Bay. We rode the turbulent waters, which turned blue to black as we drove five miles into the ocean. I smelled the remnants of my boys in my hands. No matter how gently I cupped the salt and pepper ashen remains, there was no choice but to release them to the ocean's fury. I wept and kissed the urn as if the kisses could be felt by my children, whose spirits I knew were with us. "Let's do this quickly," said my husband. Without much hesitation, we lowered our twins' ashes from a plastic bag into the water. The crashing waves quickly engulfed every last bit of dust. Within seconds, there was no evidence left. My womb was finally empty. I felt a sigh of relief. I could breathe again. I wished them well.

I leaned forward on the railing and continued to reach with both arms into the ocean as I heard the abyss calling me. I obliged. Dickey pulled me back, "For our living kids," he whispered and ushered me to safety. I agreed to stay. He put his arms around me as we embraced Aekash and Arzoe.

As the yacht started for land, a white dove came out of nowhere and hovered over the sea. The dove circled the boat and we started to head back, and it followed the boat all the way to the shore for its five-mile-long journey. We fondly took a video of the dove following us, and it was enough to keep us distracted on the way back to shore. It seemed that of my countless open wounds, one of them was capped with a flap and secured with a Band-Aid by that dove. After that, I allowed a little bit more light to come into my heart.

Perspective and Healing

As enlightenment slowly filled my heart, connecting my past gave me the strength to bear the present. I thought of all the mothers who had lost their children in the 1984 genocide in Amritsar and later in Delhi, and the pain they endure even in this present moment. It opened my eyes to help me realize that I am but a small drop of water in this ocean of a world. It pains me disproportionately to admit that I am a better person for having carried, given birth to, and lost my twin boys. If it means that it makes me a better mother for my living children, then the loss was not in vain. I know that we are not the ones in control; there is a greater power at work. We have to be willing to lose our most precious assets at a moment's notice since they don't belong to us anyway and will not accompany us on the next part of our spiritual journey.

As Guru Angad Dev Ji (the second Sikh Guru) says, we are guests here on Earth. The homes, the wealth, the children, the spouses, the siblings that we believe to be ours do not belong to us.

I am no longer caught in the illusion of life and death. I know the

Guru Granth Sahib is the ultimate embodiment of love, and I do my best to merge with that everyday.

Every year on their birthday, I retreat from the world for a few days to allow myself time for reflection. It allows space to heal and remember. When I open the memory box, I am hesitant but not fearful to see the pictures, videos of them alive, the footprints, the birth and death certificates, the body tags, the little booties and caps, the little *karas* (iron bangles worn by Sikhs, one of five articles of faith) that their grandfather carved with his hands. Something tells me that we will be reunited again. The priceless time I spend with my living children, my family, my friends, and my volunteer work in medicine and outreach to the underserved members of the community have filled in the wounds with purpose and hope. I look forward to meaningful interactions in the limited and borrowed time that we have with each other.

Part 4: Sanjog

Written in the Stars

God's Flow

SatJot Kaur

I've always been a spiritual person. I remember being about four years old, not long after my father died, wondering what I was doing in this human body. I distinctly remember looking at my hands and arms thinking it was so crazy and weird that this thing was attached to my soul. When I learned the Lord's Prayer at my grandma's Baptist church, I remember thinking "Our Father who art in heaven" was referring to my father who'd died, and I wondered how everyone knew. When I found out God the father was different, I still imagined my dad sitting up on a cloud beside God, who was sitting in a king's chair. My mother sent me to Lutheran school, not because she was religious but because she didn't think the public schools in Los Angeles were good enough. I, however, appreciated the spiritual aspect of the school and enjoyed praying multiple times a day with my classmates and teacher. I thought the stories in the Bible were pretty cool too. A few years later I attended a Catholic school. When all of my friends started taking Communion class in sixth grade I wanted to take it too. In reality, I was longing for a spiritual family— a group of people whom I could trust like my relatives and talk with about God. I didn't have that at home. At the time both my mother and older brother (by ten years) were atheist as far as I knew.

Then one day my mom decided she wanted a religion. We hung out with the Hindus for a bit and noticed some people in the crowd wearing all white and turbans. They were American Sikhs, introduced to the religion by Yogi Bhajan, a spiritual teacher from India. One of them ended up being a chiropractor, and my mom needed help with her back, so we started going to his office regularly, which was located in a Jewish neighborhood just south of Beverly Hills. That's when my fascination with Sikhi began. At the time I was a curious ten-year-old, pretty confident and happy with myself. I remember being so captivated by the chiropractor's physical appearance. Never before had I seen anyone wear a turban, beard, and long, flowing *kurta*. What topped it all off was the dazzling all-white attire that he wore every day. He looked like a very holy man, and my soul nudged me to learn more.

Every time I saw him, I asked him questions about his religion. Finally one day he told me to go to *gurudwara*, the Sikh temple literally meaning Guru's Door, to understand the true essence of Sikhism. I protested, wanting him to be my personal live Sikhi encyclopedia, until he told me about *prashad*. The sweet nectar of God's name, prashad is what lured me to my first gurudwara. We went to the nearby Guru Ram Das Ashram Gurudwara, which was founded by Yogi Bhajan and attended mostly by American Sikhs. Once there, I felt so much love from the Guru and the beautiful *sangat* (community) that I knew my soul had found its home. I led the *kirtan*, the devotional music, and was instantly good at it since I took piano when I was younger. I also loved that everyone could reach their own enlightenment through God and Guru by themselves. This was different from what I had learned in Christian schools, where priests and pastors were the middlemen to God. I remember the first time I actually meditated in the morning hours of the *Amrit Vela*. I had been trying with much frustration for a few months and one day it happened! I became inspired and took *amrit*, Sikh baptism, that same week. My mother was supportive of me but hadn't yet taken amrit herself. As I learned the history of my religion, my dream of going to India began—and eventually came true sixteen years later.

Between these years of finding the Guru and going to India, I went through periods of ups and downs with my devotion to my religion. I found it hard to wear a turban, keep my hair, do my daily *nitnem* prayers, and keep up with my promise to the Guru of living an honest Sikhi life. I descended into the deepest of Maya's pits, coming up for air occasionally, then diving back down again. I experimented with alcohol, drugs, and sexual partners. My longing to belong and be accepted was so intense and so skewed. I thought what I was doing was the only way to be a part of a group of people who I thought were my friends. I was caught in a cycle of disrespecting myself for the sake of pleasing others, and it was so difficult to leave. I wanted to escape, but it was hard to do alone. I moved to New York to get away from it all and start fresh. Maya followed me there as well, but this time I was committed to changing myself for the better. A Sikhi sister of mine suggested I join Alcoholics Anonymous since it had helped her get sober while deepening her connection with God and Guru and separating her from her obstacles. Between the meetings and my sponsor, I was finding my true self, the God within me, while being of service to my community. I never realized how much ego I had in everything I did—even praying! I was shown that God is ultimately in control and that all is according to His will. That realization was so powerful to me. I had always pretended I believed it, but for the first time I actually lived it. It was so exhilarating! The universe opened up and I finally was able to breathe, catch a break, and let God guide me. It was the first time since I was a child that I was truly and sincerely happy. I found myself riding my bike around Prospect Park with a big silly grin on my face, in love with the trees and the birds, taking time to actually ask my roommate how she was and listen with true interest, pushing shopping carts back to their rightful place to help out, looking every single person I met in the eye and smiling . . . the list goes on. I was a new person. My change was so noticeable and so positive it even got my roommate going to twelve-step meetings! I loved myself and honored the God within me. I was content being a single young adult rather than looking for a partner to save me, like I had in the past. Life was good.

I was feeling so good and so in tune with my soul that I decided I had to go to my soul's home—The Golden Temple. I had seen so many pictures of my religion's spiritual center, but I had never been there. Spring Break was coming up (I was a teacher at the time), so I took the opportunity and booked my plane ticket to Amritsar, India. I was told that ten days was not long enough to fully appreciate what India had to offer, but I went anyway. I had wanted to go for a long time, and when this opportunity presented itself, I knew I had to take it. When I told a friend of mine that I was visiting India for my vacation, she mentioned she would be there with her in-laws during that same time and that I could stay with them. I wasn't surprised—this was how life operated in God's flow!

My friend came with her husband to pick me up from the airport and took me to the Golden Temple first. When I stepped onto the marble *parkarma* that surrounds the gurudwara, I was in such awe that bliss overtook me. I felt the light of the ten Gurus, who paved the way of life for all Sikhs, beam throughout the space. Just looking at the *sarovar*, the body of water surrounding the Golden Temple, I felt at peace. I knew I was home. I can still feel that feeling now. My heart melted. I was so in love. I wanted to spend the rest of eternity there, but my friends insisted we go home, promising me we'd return.

A ten-minute drive later in the same city of Amritsar, Punjab, I met my friend's parents and experienced living the Panjabi way. Most important, I watched what it was like to be in a marriage, both old and new, and was quite surprised by the reality of it. Like many of my American counterparts, I had a seriously unrealistic and selfish view of love, marriage, and how to have a happy life. Both my friend and her husband, as well as his mother and father, taught me, through their actions, that marriage is all about serving the other. My friend and her mother-in-law spent countless hours in the kitchen cooking, cleaning, and serving their creations to their husbands. I was so used to doing everything for myself that seeing their actions was mind-boggling! The husbands didn't fall short on their end of serving, either. My friend's husband gave her a back rub daily without her even asking for it, while her father-in-law made and served chai for everyone after lunch. It was beautiful to watch them. I realized that if I wanted to be as happily married as they were, I'd have to give up my selfish, individualistic ways and be of service. I was starting to recognize a theme here: it all came down to *seva*, the Sikhi way of selfless service. Serving God and His creation would then in turn serve me. Upon realizing this and seeing the beauty and love of their successful marriages, I wanted to get married. But it wasn't the same as times in the past when I wanted to get married because I thought it would make me happy. Rather I already was happy, and I wanted to get married so that my husband and I could grow together while serving each other and God.

During the next few days I visited the Golden Temple, went shopping, and ate many rich, creamy, spicy, delicious foods, truly savoring the local cuisine. I had a long list of things to do and buy in India, and I was sure I wouldn't be able to do it all. Of course my hosts found an English-speaking bicycle rickshaw driver, since I was still operating in God's flow, so I managed to get everything I wanted done in one day. I also managed to miscalculate the exchange rate and gave my rickshaw driver a seriously generous tip. Though my host family was appalled, I was happy for him.

The next morning I received a call from my Sikhi auntie/kirtan music teacher from New York. (Shortly after I moved out there, she took me under her wing as her niece and student and has been a great source of Sikhi inspiration to me ever since.) The reason for her call was to check in on me. During the conversation she suggested I take classes from her kirtan teacher in Amritsar. I told her I wasn't interested, that I wanted to spend the second half of my trip meditating at the Golden Temple, since that was my main reason for going. I was finally at my soul's home; it felt so good to be in the Guru's presence and in the space of many great Sikhs before me that I didn't even want to consider going anywhere else. I wanted to soak up the sweet blissful amrit nectar that permeates when in the presence of the True Guru. I had waited my whole life to come here, and I didn't want to get distracted from my goal of making peace with my soul. Auntie Ji listened to what I had to say and then continued insisting I at least give her teacher a call, so I agreed just to get her off my back. As a woman of my word, I called her teacher and ended up making an appointment with him for the next day. Then I called my friend Patti, who happened to be staying in the house next door to him (God's flow!), and she said I could share a room with her for the remainder of my trip. So I packed up my bags, thanked my hosts, stepped outside to find my rickshaw driver waiting for me, and set off for a new adventure.

Upon arriving, I met my friend for long enough to set my things down and check out the beautiful two-story home (with a toilet!). I was in the outskirts of Amritsar in Chheharta, about eight kilometers out from the Golden Temple. Things were quiet here, with nice big houses and fields around them. I gave my friend a quick kiss and then ran next door to get to my kirtan class on time. My new teacher, Ustad Ji, was a very sweet being with so much love for the Guru; I immediately felt grateful that I was there. After an hour-long class, though, I was exhausted. Between the challenging lesson and the heat, I was ready for a nap. Ustad Ji insisted I stay for a group lesson. I tried to say no, but a student arrived just as I did, and she then also insisted I stay. So I did one more hour-long class—more challenges, same heat. I was really tired! Just as I thought the class was ending, two more students arrived. One of them was Ravinder Singh.

I remember thinking they were really late, and then wondering if that meant I had to stay longer. I was so tired! Ustad Ji began explaining the essence of kirtan and switched to speaking in Panjabi. Ravinder spoke up to translate for Ustad Ji, and I remember being surprised at the Australian accent coming out of his mouth. He was obviously of Panjabi descent, but apparently he was visiting India as well. He translated for the rest of us, and it was quite beautiful listening to the words of a devoted *ragi*. It went something like this:

Ravinder translating for Ustad Ji: "Life is like an ocean, and we are meant to cross it by Guru's Grace. Singing *gurbani kirtan* will elevate your soul and cleanse your mind."

By this time we were all entranced with his words, leaning forward with our eyes locked on him so as not to miss a thing.

Ravinder translating for Ustad Ji: "Then your parents will die and all happiness will come to you . . ."

At this point, our faces fell. Everyone started looking around at each other with confused, sad looks. Ustad Ji saw our reactions and realized Ravinder must have mistranslated.

He clarified himself in English: "Once Maya is gone, only then can you be truly happy." Phew. We all eased back and let our faces relax a bit. A few smirks were stolen.

I remember thinking this Ravinder guy must be a joker, between arriving to class extra late and translating things wrong. After class all the students went next door to the house I was staying at and hung out. By then I was high on the Guru's love, so I was doing okay! I found myself joking with Ravinder a lot, and it seemed almost as if we had known each other before. Later that night my friend Patti teased that I had a thing for him, but I dismissed it. I still thought he was too much of a joker for me.

The next morning, by the grace of the Guru, I was able to do *ishnaan seva*, marble washing, at the Golden Temple with the kids from the nearby school founded by Yogi Bhajan, Miri Piri Academy. There was so much love in the air and in my heart as I stood in the sarovar and scooped buckets of water to give to my fellow brothers and sisters to help clean the sacred grounds. God's love was everywhere, and I couldn't have been happier. When we were done I was in such bliss, I looked forward to doing it again the next day. Patti and I went home and napped for a few more hours of the morning. We woke up and began chatting. She again turned her attention toward Ravinder and me, taunting me in her charming Mexican accent.

Patti: "Soooo you and Ravinder, hey?!" She was giggling and winking away.

Me: "No, Patti, stop it." I gave her the "You gotta be kidding me" look.

Patti: "I think so! There is something there! Ooooouuuuooooo!"

Me: "Patti, he is way too much of a goofball for me. I am in no way at all interested in him like that."

Patti: "You should text him! See why he didn't come with all of us this morning for ishnaan seva." I still thought she was being silly, but I decided to text him anyway.

Me: "He says he wasn't feeling well."

Patti: "You should tell him to make it up to you by taking you out on a date."

I was in a cheeky mood, so I did, figuring I was leaving in a few days anyway, so it wouldn't matter if I acted a bit sillier than usual. To my surprise, he said yes, and that's when my mind started to catch on that there might be something worthwhile about this guy. Of course Patti teasing me the whole rest of the time about my "lover" probably had a bit of an impact. Our first date ended up being a group lunch, which was just as well. We all joked the whole time and had lots of good laughs. They were all genuine people, and I was happy to have met such sweet souls. Ravinder made it to ishnaan seva the next morning, and I surprised myself with how excited I was. He stood next to me in the sarovar, passing buckets and joking around. My experience was definitely different from that of the previous morning, but I went along with it. After we finished the seva, we went our separate ways.

The following morning a group of ragis from our American Sikh community, Chardi Kala Jetha, was scheduled to sing kirtan in the first slot after the doors to the Golden Temple opened. I hadn't entered into the gurudwara yet; the line had been too long every time I went. A group of us went together from the house and stood in line, waiting on the bridge for the doors to open. I was so excited to finally be going inside. Ravinder said he'd hold a place for me inside in case I got left behind. Naturally I did, as I bowed for a long time and looked around for a bit, took it all in, understanding it was the only time to do so. I made my way upstairs and found Ravinder by the window. It was so serene to be sitting inside the Harmandir Sahib, listening to my friends play kirtan, and looking out over the sarovar with my soul mate. It was so much to take in I felt overwhelmed. I was truly blessed and grateful to God for His kindness toward me.

We walked outside once our friends finished playing and meditated underneath a tree. I decided to do 108 *Mool Mantras*—the root prayer of the Sikh faith. Ravinder lent me his *mala* and sat with me. An intense energy emanated from him, and I wasn't sure what it was. We had a great connection, but I wasn't sure if I was imagining it. I'd mistaken this feeling before, so I was unsure about it. At the same time, I was at my soul's home, meditating since the morning hours of the Amrit Vela, so I knew something had to be right about it. After I'd completed my 108 Mool Mantras, I wanted to keep going, so I told Ravinder I changed it to 1,008; he was cool with it and stayed with me the whole time. We walked all around the Golden Temple, explored lots of nooks and crannies, had tea and *langar*, dipped in the nectar tank, and eventually talked about ourselves in a serious way. We shared our pasts, presents, and what we wanted for our futures. I found myself interviewing him to see if he was husband material. Our hopes for our futures were in sync, so when we finally decided to leave the Golden Temple, I was prepared to say something to seal the feeling before it was gone, but I was scared. We were meant to meet up with a friend for lunch, so I stalled until I saw him in the distance. That way if I embarrassed myself, I could use our friend to distract any discomforts.

Me: "So I wonder where our friend is going to take us to eat."

Ravinder: "Ya, I dunno. I'm sure there are lots of good places around here."

Me: "Ya, probably. Sooo . . . when are we getting married?" I had a big goofy grin on my face, ready to play it off as a joke at a moment's notice. I was so nervous about his response, but something told me it was going to be okay. Our friend was barely within earshot at this point. It was perfect timing.

Ravinder, obviously caught off guard, stammered: "Uh . . . well . . . um . . . uh . . . I . . . I guess my parents should meet you then."

Woohoo! Success! Victory! On the inside I did a "cha-ching" motion with my arm and said "Yessss!" The biggest sigh of relief, followed by the most exhilarating feeling of my life. However, on the outside I said very coolly, "Ya, sounds good, and I'll introduce you to my family." By then our friend was in front of us, and we welcomed him as if nothing had happened. Throughout the rest of the day we stole many cutesy glances and smiles at each other but didn't talk about it. We just knew. And just like that, in the span of one short week in Amritsar, God led me to my husband.

Handing my life over to God was the hardest and most reward-ing thing I've ever done for myself. It's still a daily commitment, and when I can do it, I feel the happiest and in turn I can do more for my community. Of course, living in God's flow doesn't mean I bludge around and wait for things to happen. Rather, I'm proactive with my life but unattached to the consequences. If I see something isn't working, I let it go and move on. But I always go for it! I went to my soul's home, the Golden Temple, selfless and full of love for all of God's creation. He prepared me for marriage and then presented me with my husband. I was told trips to India were life-changing; I had no idea this trip would fully change my entire existence. By God's grace Ravinder Singh and I have been married for over three years and we have a beautiful, loving daughter, Bhakti Kaur, who was born last year on Valentine's Day. My life is blessed in so many ways I cannot even begin to count them. Every day I bow before the Guru and say, "Thank you, Lord, now and always. Thy will not mine be done. *Wahe Guru Ji Ka Khalsa! Wahe Guru Ji Ki Fateh!*—"The pure ones belong to Waheguru! Victory belongs to Waheguru!"

Diving In

Manbeena Kaur

I can say a lot about my partner. I could describe his unnatural fixation with all things Apple, his unexplainable aversion to leftovers, his preference to only use half of a walk-in closet, or even his impeccable sense of style: 80 percent preppy and 20 percent California cool. But that's really just skimming the surface. Because underneath, after I allowed myself to really dive in, eyes wide open, heart in my hand, I saw him for what he really is: a love that was made just for me.

Swimming at Midnight
(Ironic, since I can't swim.)

He taught me. One night, we both had a craving for ice cream, and for me, if that doesn't involve some element of Heath Bar, it's not good enough to be called dessert. We found the only Dairy Queen open that late and ordered our mini Blizzards at the drive-thru. We thought it might be fun to relish our treat overlooking the pool in his apartment complex. As we finished the last spoonfuls of this guilty pleasure, we dipped our feet in the pool.

I looked over at him as I edged myself off the side and asked, "How deep do you think the water is on our side?" He must have seen something in my eyes—the slight hint of spontaneity, maybe?

"It's not that deep—" he began, but before he finished his sentence,

I had made the plunge. My grin broke the surface of the water as I came back up. I expected him to be shocked, but he just gave me a small smile. What's more romantic than taking a midnight swim on a weekday?

I thought I'd float around for a few minutes, and then we'd walk back to his apartment. I was fully clothed—in jeans no less—and didn't know how I was going to drive back home in my wet garments. As I was thinking that maybe this wasn't such a great idea, he jumped into the water next to me.

We spent the next two hours playing, laughing, racing, and perhaps, most importantly, relishing the moment. Our über-type-A personalities became childlike, splashing water on each other and playing pool games. At the time, I was caught between the drama of my personal life and the stress of work. I didn't let myself truly rest. So in that moment, I unleashed my mind from my responsibilities and endless color-coded to-do lists. I let my body stretch out and unwind. That night, he taught me how to swim. How to float. How to take a deep breath before you dive in.

What's ironic is that in this relationship, I dove in from the very start. After only a few months of getting to know him, neither of us ever missing an opportunity to take a dig at each other or incorporate a funny accent to elicit a bonus laugh, I completely trusted him. That's one lesson that I hadn't learned from my past failed relationships. I still hadn't learned to keep my cards close to my chest. Others wear their hearts on their sleeves. I wear mine on my face.

That night we swam together wasn't a spontaneous act of two working professionals. It was the night that I saw, crystal clear, that this man had all the right components. I learned that he was a patient teacher; that he could be playful but also stern when he needed to be (like when I kept splashing water on him, and he insisted he didn't want to get his *dastaar* wet). That he took care of me, never letting my nose go underwater when teaching me how to float. That he was strong, placing his palms under my lower back as I tried to stay above the water. That he was competitive, always beating me in our races to the end of the pool. I also learned that he encouraged me to take risks and try at my own pace. When I thought I could hold my breath and travel the length of the pool only five minutes into his lesson, he let me try. When I came up for air after only making it halfway across, he greeted me with a smile and told me I would be able to cover more distance the next time I tried. He was right.

When I had practiced swimming a bit more, I let my competitive side get the best of me and challenged him to a race using the two techniques he had taught me—the frog and the freestyle. Every time I lost, I immediately challenged him to another race, suggesting a new part of the pool, hoping the new environment would give me some kind of advantage. My theory proved false every time. I laughed and said, "Again!" not wanting to admit defeat. As I prepared myself for the fifth race, I took a deep breath, bent my head underwater, and flashed back to a time in my life when I thought I'd never feel this kind of joy again.

Several years ago, I had gone through a gut-wrenching, cliché, New York City breakup. Of course, now that I've had some distance (and I'd like to say maturity), I recognize that there was a reason (or several) that we didn't last. But it took me many years, many introspective moments, many episodes of *Sex and the City*, and dare I say it, my *new* relationship, to help me grasp that it wasn't really a good partnership in the first place.

As I came up for air in the middle of the race, I saw him at least four strides ahead of me. I swam harder, pushing my feet away from me and stretching my arms out, trying to catch up to him. Many of my friends have teased me for calling him "my partner" instead of using the word "boyfriend." But I really feel like his role in my life, and my role in his, is most accurately defined by this word. I wanted a partner who had just as much at stake as I did if our union were to fail, and who'd be just as happy if it were to succeed. I wanted someone whose priority was to see the relationship grow and thrive. I was confident knowing that, like me, this beautiful man had a vested interest in seeing our mutual venture succeed, taking risks when necessary, making cutbacks where appropriate, but always knowing that we had each other's backs. That after everything life might rain down on us, we would take it all in, holding hands, chins raised in the direction of our goals.

I blinked once more and saw the wall of the pool within my reach. *Just a few more strides.* As I swam toward my goal, I remembered that it took me a little more than six months after my breakup to begin thinking about being with someone again, of opening myself up to someone else's observations, critiques, and appreciation. After a few more months, I met *him*. Looking back, *Waheguru* must have known that I didn't have the energy to last through more waves of disappointment and heartache. I was only strong enough to swim through a gentle tide of first dates and e-mail exchanges.

I smiled when I finally came up for air at the finish line and launched myself into my love's arms. He had been waiting there at least a few minutes, but he whispered, "Good job!" in my ear as if I had won. It was just a few months after my first date with him that I realized: I had dived in. I had completely immersed myself in him and was surrounded by his positivity and light. He lifted me out of the ditch of past relationship baggage and heartache and plunged me into a pool of warmth and tenderness that always accompanies a new love.

As I looked up at him, finding his hands beneath the water with my own, I closed my eyes and savored the moment. I heard the quiet lap of the water as it hit our bodies in the dark. I smelled the chlorine and the way that grass smells after a light rain. His hands curled around my waist. He dipped his head lower to kiss my neck, and I giggled and pushed him away, because his *dhaari* always tickles when he kisses me there. I finally let myself release, relaxed my shoulders, and exhaled.

The man standing in front of me had brought me back to life. He had re-sparked the energy, the passion, and the love that I was suppressing and hiding from the world. I had tried not to wear my heart on my face anymore, but when I met him, he managed to take that invisible mask off. Since he saw me so clearly, he allowed me to see the rest of the world clearly too.

He breathed air into my lungs, closed the wounds in my heart so it began to beat, and kissed my lips until they were pink again. I've never told what a significant role he played in bringing me back. And I don't need to. He must have seen the potential in me—in *us*—to take the plunge. I'd like to think that this journey to find my partner was completely self-guided. But that's not entirely true. The way I found him, the way I flowed into him, mind, body, and soul—it could only have been the work of something Divine. I thank Waheguru for giving me the strength to dive into him and never look back.

Girl Reads Boy, Boy Reads Girl

Prabhjot K. Ahluwalia

Our story began in fall 1991, when my parents saw an ad in the then very popular and highly circulated publication known as *India Abroad*. This paper consisted of many articles about Indians living outside of their motherland and all of their accomplishments. But, most important, it contained a matrimonial section. My parents saw a small ad seeking a match for a Gursikh boy, age twenty-six, EE (electrical engineer), six feet tall. Literally, that was how much information was given. Having grown up in the United States, I was having a hard time grasping the concept of arranged marriage, much less that of finding my life partner in a newspaper! I couldn't believe that my parents were even considering this ad.

I immigrated with my parents to the United States in 1975, when I was six years old. I grew up in Silver Spring, Maryland, in a middle-class neighborhood. I had a lot of family around, but the majority of my friends were Americans. My friends were from all different backgrounds—Jewish, Christian, Quaker, Mormon, white, and black. They all came from families where going steady with a boy or going to a dance with a boy was part of growing up. For me that was definitely not the case. My parents were always there for us: They worked hard and provided for us. We always had a nice home, nice things, and a used car to get around in when we turned sixteen. However, if I had a crush on some boy or another in middle and high school, I never went to a dance or went out with one. In my home, it was never explicitly stated that I couldn't—it was simply understood.

But when I was twenty-two, my parents responded to an anonymous PO box from a marriage ad. Shortly thereafter, they got a call from the father of the Gursikh boy. As he and my dad talked, it became clear that we knew common families. After both sides had spoken with mutual friends, we decided that our families should exchange pictures. I felt a bit relieved by this first step; I wanted to have an idea of what I had to look forward to (or not). When the picture finally arrived, it was a picture of three boys, brothers. I was a bit confused until I looked on the back and saw the names: Gurpreet, Gurinder, and Jasjit. Realizing I was supposed to be considering Gurinder, I was happy to see that he was tall, wore a nice *dastaar*, and had a nice smile and a full beard that he did not trim. By that I mean he didn't have spots on his face where the beard hadn't grown yet. That was not going to work for me!

Both the families and Gurinder and I decided to meet. Gurinder lived in Milwaukee, Wisconsin at the time and was planning a trip to Washington, DC for a family get-together at his brother's home in early February. So on Saturday, February 8, 1992, Gurinder and his parents came to our home.

The meeting was conducted in typical and traditional Indian style. I made tea and brought it out to the dining room. Gurinder and his parents and my parents and brother were all seated at the table in the dining room. Everyone spoke with each other, including Gurinder, making jokes and laughing; I sat and watched and listened, and really didn't participate in the conversation unless asked a specific question. During this interaction, I did notice that Gurinder was very funny and had everyone relaxed and laughing. Laughter had been a big part of my life growing up, so Gurinder definitely had that going for him.

And he was kind of cute.

After tea and chatting were over, Gurinder and his family left. A few minutes later, Gurinder's dad came back to the front door and asked my father if it was okay for Gurinder to meet me the next day for lunch. In the meantime, my parents had asked me what I thought of Gurinder, and I'd responded that I'd like to talk to him again. So when my dad was asked about another meeting, he agreed, knowing that I was also interested. That night, I remember thinking about the refrain all of my cousins sang to me growing up all the time: "You love to laugh so much, you have to marry someone who will make you laugh." I wasn't nervous about meeting Gurinder the next day. He piqued my interest, which no one else had done so far.

The next day, I drove in my recently purchased Mitsubishi Diamante to the home of Gurinder's older brother, Gurpreet, in Crystal City, Virginia. I met both of his brothers, his sister-in-law, his younger sister, and, of course, his parents again. I was a bit nervous about meeting the whole family, but it turned out that I had actually met Gurpreet before at a party through some friends, and his wife and I had gone to a Sikh camp together, so I felt a bit more relaxed and comfortable being there.

Gurinder suggested that we go to Georgetown for the day. I drove us there, and we walked around the waterfront area. We ended up at Tony and Joe's Restaurant for lunch. We talked nonstop about everything; from how many kids we wanted (he wanted four, and I was undecided) and how we wanted to raise them in Sikhi to where we wanted to live, what our beliefs in education were, and where we saw ourselves in ten years. This was the most intense conversation that I had ever had. It was going so well that we lost track of time. What was supposed to be a simple meeting turned into a five-hour lunch, and Gurinder missed his flight back home to Milwaukee.

A week passed, and Gurinder's father called my father to ask if Gurinder had permission to call me. I had already told my parents about our lunch in Georgetown and that I would like to see Gurinder again. So when my father got the call, he agreed to let us talk. A few days later, on Friday, February 14, Gurinder called and we talked for five hours, from 10 p.m. to 3 a.m. I hadn't realized that I had that much to say, but apparently I did (and so did he). We talked in more detail about our interests, friends, and families. I had always been a social kid, so I didn't have a problem talking, but

I was somewhat overwhelmed with this kind of conversation. It was serious and could have a big impact on my future.

Our phone conversations continued for another couple of weeks, and then Gurinder flew back to see me for a weekend. Now we were both nervous about seeing each other. Was the person I'd built a phone relationship with going to be the same in person? Even though we had met a few times before, we would now be meeting after having shared many intimate details about our private lives.

I wasn't sure how this weekend was going to turn out. Gurinder came to my house and picked me up, and we spent all day Saturday in Washington, DC, walking at the Mall and talking some more. Then we spent all day Sunday at Baltimore's scenic Inner Harbor. Both days were filled with lots of walking and talking. I had come to know Gurinder better in the previous few weeks than I had known some people all of my life. We "clicked" and shared many of the same values and aspirations for the future. However, Gurinder was not able to make a commitment for marriage based on a couple of meetings. I was the first person he had met in this arranged manner, and in his mind the process of finding a wife/life partner couldn't be this easy. How could everything be great with the first person you met?

When Gurinder dropped me off on Sunday night, he stopped short of my house and parked the car. He said that maybe we should take a break for a while . . . take some time to think things through. Although I had become fond of Gurinder in the short time I'd known him, I was not in love with him. I agreed, and we said good night, leaving things between us undecided.

Gurinder flew back to Milwaukee on Monday morning, but our decision to "take a break" did not last long. The very next day Gurinder called me and wanted to talk again. Finally, on Tuesday, March 2, 1992, Gurinder called once again and this time asked, "What would you say if I asked you to marry me?" And my response was, "I wouldn't say no." That was it . . . that was the marriage proposal. We decided to get married and let our parents know our final decisions. The rest happened rather quickly. We had an engagement in April, and were married in June of the same year.

Because of this very fast meeting, engagement, and marriage, Gurinder and I didn't really know each other all that well . . . despite the many long phone conversations. Marriage, as I was figuring out, was all about adjusting to a new home, a new person, and a new lifestyle. The early years of our marriage were a bit tough as we lived apart because of Gurinder's job. However, that job allowed us to travel all over the world and carry on a "dating" type of relationship for the first four and a half years of our marriage. Ever since this initial separation, we have been inseparable.

About ten years into my marriage, I remember thinking that something had changed in our relationship. I don't know exactly when it happened or how it happened, but we had fallen in love. It started with how appreciative Gurinder was of all that I did for him and our daughters. He thanked me and told me that he loved me all of the time. He never left the house without giving me a kiss, and he always gave me a kiss immediately upon his return. He was amazing with our two daughters: overprotective yet very fun and loving. I started to see him as a loving husband and father. Even though his work took up most of his time during the week, he always tried to protect our weekends. Weekends were family time and we tried to never compromise that. Over the years, the little things aggregated into a larger feeling that we have preserved ever since.

Looking back now, I can reflect on what has made our relationship work. It is mutual respect, it is commitment, and it is a lot of compromise and hard work. We made a decision to never go to sleep angry at each other—and even though we've broken that rule a handful of times in our twenty-plus years together, the majority of the time we've stuck to resolving issues immediately. I think these qualities—the respect, the commitment, the compromises—all contributed to turning our "liking each other" into our loving each other.

My Love

Manpreet Kaur Singh

My parents were married in India during a time when romantic love was considered an antonym to the more widely accepted "arranged marriage." My father recalls that on their wedding day there were a few people who had become suspicious that my parents had a "love marriage" rather than an "arranged marriage." In truth, my parents' introduction and nuptials had been completely arranged by my mother's sister, but community members were perplexed by why my mother and her family, coming from an urban background, would choose to marry a man from a rural background. But neither my father nor my mother saw socioeconomic status or caste as a critical criterion for their life partner. Up until the time they met, they had both been completely immersed in the teachings of Guru Nanak, which resonate in the celebrated lyrical hymn in *Suhi raga*: "One who has a basket of fragrant virtues should enjoy its fragrance. If my friends have virtues I will share in them. One should walk life's path by sharing virtues and discarding vices" (Guru Granth Sahib, page 766).

Their "love letters" to one another were often an exchange of verses from Sikh scripture, and that was enough for them to know they were talking to each other as soul mates. My parents were also raised on the egalitarian Sikh principle that caste has no place in the value system of a Sikh. So, to those who were most curious whether my parents had a "love marriage" or a traditional arranged marriage, my father would answer a question with a question: "What marriage, arranged or otherwise, is without love?" This anecdote was my introduction to the nuances of love.

I grew up the daughter of a Sikh scholar, always in the watchful eye of the North American Sikh community. I knew more Sikhs than most, yet I struggled through the course of my formative years and education to find companionship within our community. My father's career caused my family to move around a lot, but wherever we were, I would always find ways to attend Sikh youth camps, retreats, and singing and speech competitions locally, regionally, and nationally. My father inspired me, and like many daughters who admired their fathers, I always hoped I would marry someone who was as passionate about Sikhism as he. When I graduated from college, I got into medical school and toiled with the thought of deferring admission for a year so I could go to India and engage in a yearlong community service project—kind of like a Sikh Peace Corps. Ironically, my parents were not supportive of this idea, thinking I'd be better suited to help people in India once I was equipped with medical training. So off I went to medical school and then residency, inspired principally by my sister, who had Down Syndrome, and who had taught me that it was my calling to care for chronically ill children.

Medical school and residency were both in regions where there weren't large Sikh communities, so to prevent myself from isolation, I continued to attend Sikh youth camps and retreats, finding comfort in the company of Sikh friends in other states and in Canada. Nevertheless, it was challenging to meet both the demands of medical training and those of my parents to find a spouse and settle down. More Sikh men and women were marrying people from different religions and cultures, so the pool of eligible Sikh men in my age range was shrinking. In other instances, the timing wasn't right, or our family values were not compatible. My search for a suitable spouse became a game of discerning the year one had immigrated to North America. In other words, were you an ABCD ("American-Born Confused Desi") or an FOB ("fresh off the boat")?

These identity assignments were common in the new millennium and seemed as silly as the love marriage/arranged marriage debates my parents had experienced twenty-plus years earlier.

A few years went by, and the topic of love arose in a conversation with my grandfather. I was growing exasperated by the challenges of finding love and the chronic pressure from my family to marry before my biological alarms went off. My grandfather comforted me, claiming that the love of my life was already born, living, and breathing somewhere, and that it was just a matter of time before I found him. In fear and doubt, I was struck both by what he said and my self-focused perception that my love would only come into existence the moment we met. I fantasized he was someone who could inspire me to lead a balanced life much in the way I was inspired by the teachings of the Sikh Gurus as described in *gurbani* ("Utterances of the Guru").

I guess you could call me a late bloomer, because I didn't really date much until after medical school. I had a steady boyfriend for the first time during my first year of residency, starting a series of disappointing interactions with men who sang the same insecure song as soon as they saw my ambition. I began to really wonder if a successful woman in medicine could find companionship. By the time I turned thirty, my parents were happy if I had any prospects on the horizon—even if he wasn't a Sikh.

Lots of well-meaning family and friends offered me advice: "Find a nice Gursikh boy from India . . . someone local . . . a doctor . . . anyone but a doctor . . . older . . . your own age . . ." etc. I wasn't intending to waste time or be particularly selective, but I was also wary of rushing into a bad situation. A few years of this went by before a friend finally pointed out that even though I might want to settle down, my doubt in destiny and pessimism about finding my soul mate was not helping the situation. This moment of self-realization finally dispelled my fear and encouraged me to open myself to the world around me—to signal that I was ready to meet my love. I took this experience and translated it into a meditative effort on the divine Name (*nam simaran*) while singing the following hymn in supplication: "Bring that blessed union into reality, O my Beloved" (Guru Granth Sahib, page 743). Perhaps cliché, but I recall singing this hymn at a New Year's *kirtan* and feeling more hope than any well-meaning friend had offered up until that point.

After two months of this concentrated effort, I received two signals in return—about the same man, though through independent channels, curiously. One came through a traditional matrimonial site. Another came from a middleman (*vichola*), a man who was mutually known to us. Not surprisingly, my first encounter with Mandeep was a carefully articulated but honest introduction by e-mail succinctly summarizing our life stories—and sufficiently piquing further interest. In this busy day and age for thirty-something professionals, there was no time for games, and technology was our friend. After the customary presentation of "biodata," our exchange went something like this:

Me: "I love children and am an avid fan of music and traveling. I'm looking for a partner who embraces my career choices and strives with me to balance work with a rich personal life."

Him: "I love all things related to food, including cooking many types of cuisine. I have recently rekindled an old passion for photography. Ideally, I would like to meet someone with similar family and religious values, who I find attractive and interesting, but who can also relate to my own experiences . . . bridging two cultures, balancing the demands of family and career, and working in an intellectually demanding environment. I hope I haven't completely overdone it. As a scientist, I'm assuming you will value data more than chemistry at this early stage of the game, but perhaps we can work on the latter."

A few days later, he followed up with a phone call that lasted seven hours; a week later, he flew out to meet me. His determination to win my affections demonstrated chivalry, and for once, I felt hope that good things indeed come to those who wait. In the short week leading to our first meeting, our words seemed enough to convince us that we had fallen in love. I learned that Mandeep was an

American-born, Oklahoma-raised Sikh man who had been raised by his mother after his father had died when he was just ten months old. Somehow, with no paternal role model or Sikh community to guide him, he was more steadfast in his identity than most Sikh men I had met. In spite of our divergent circumstances growing up, we had remarkably similar values. Never were our words sweeter than in our initial courtship, and by the time we met, that part was a mere formality. It reminded me of another verse by our fifth master, Guru Arjan Dev Ji, that expresses the sustaining power of a meaningful conversation: "Sweet-spoken is my noble-hearted Beloved. I have grown weary of testing him, but still, he never utters a harsh word." (Guru Granth Sahib, page 784). Our beloved Guru Arjan in his wisdom is referring to a higher power with characteristic compassion and forgiveness, but in the midst of losing ourselves in the words of romance, this verse reminded me of the deeper ideals to strive for in love.

My father called this the "poetic phase" of our relationship, one that he hoped would continue to inspire us to live in ever-rising tides (*Chardi Kala*). He shared the poetry found in gurbani that encapsulated the feelings I had developed for Mandeep: "I am a sacrifice to my Beloved who is without any blemish. I have exchanged with him my mind, body and soul. How can I forget him even for a moment? Seeing him brings joy to my heart; I keep him clasped to my soul." (Guru Granth Sahib, page 765).

This verse connected my experience of being in love to something spiritually transcendent.

We had our first trial in this spirited existence when Mandeep and I attended my friend's wedding in Chicago. Mandeep was the perfect date: handsome and a complete gentleman, impressing friends and family alike with his charm. However, when he returned home, he developed a persistently high fever that very quickly became life-threatening and required hospitalization—a physician who on a daily basis treats and teaches about the dangers of septic shock was now a patient himself. In a matter of days, I felt like I had awoken from a dream and would need to brace myself for the possible tragic loss of my Prince Charming. Helplessly worrying for him from a distance, I tried to comfort him on the phone through his moments of feverish delirium. Weeks passed, and devotion and antibiotics were perfect complements for recovery. Before we knew it, Mandeep was back to his usual self. Our devotion was also a mix of abiding faith in our love and faith in our Gurus through reciting scriptural hymns and humbly asking for restored health. Our visits to one another resumed, and we began plans to spend the rest of our lives together.

Three months after our first meeting, my love, Mandeep, proposed to me on the banks of the California Pacific Coast. After all that we had already endured, it was back in nature where everything came together. We had ventured to the Pacific Coast to join the vastness of the ocean, which we felt was akin to our future. Mandeep and I came across a patch of lush green grass along the coastline that compelled us to pull over. We wandered toward the ocean when another couple approached us and let us know that we were traversing Jade Point, a region where jade stone and fertile ground abound. I bent down, picked up a stone shimmering in the sun, and gave it to him.

"Here," I said, "a souvenir from Jade Point."

He scrambled to find one in return and said, "Here's a stone that's a little shinier," and placed a beautiful diamond ring on my finger. I was speechless with surprise and felt like my knees were going to buckle. We gazed upon the ocean, like our future, quietly and confidently.

A week later, we formalized our engagement with our families. The order of the day (*vak*) by Guru Arjan was hopeful, suggesting that true love, above all, needs to be based on spiritual compatibility and self-realization: "In this age only such a one is designated as true hero who is dyed in the love of the Divine. Instructed by the Perfect True Guru one conquers the self and thereby subdues everyone else." (Guru Granth Sahib, page 680).

In three months, we were married. My father presided over our wedding and gave an inspiring explanation of the *Anand Karaj*, the Sikh wedding ceremony that is thematically focused on the life of a householder:

During the wedding ceremony, the bride and groom circumambulate the sacred scripture four times, once for each of their four vows. Let me explain the dynamics of this most beautiful wedding ceremony. In English, we use the word "Universe" to describe the whole cosmos: literally Uni means "one" and verse means "to revolve." Creation is revolving in set orbits around the One Reality, the central focus of life. For example, the sun, moon, Earth, and other planets all revolve in their own particular orbits, a movement that sustains life. The moment a star breaks away from its orbit, it withers away. We have seen broken stars, meteoroids, falling on the ground. Because they moved away from their orbits, they lost their balance and harmony, and perished. In the same way, a Sikh couple circumambulates the Guru Granth Sahib four times to take four vows to stay within its orbit. In this analogy, the Guru Granth Sahib is the center of their lives. They will always seek guidance and blessings from it throughout their lives. The circular movement around the scripture symbolizes the primordial cycle of life in which there is no beginning and no end, while the four marital vows reflect the ideals that the Sikh tradition considers to be essential for a blissful life:

1. ***Lead an action-oriented life (parvirti karam) based on righteousness (dharam) and never shun obligations of family and society.*** *Performing good deeds requires one to make adjustments in life. In fact, an ideal life is the result of a series of adjustments.*

2. ***Maintain bonds of reverence and dignity (nirmal bhau) between one another.*** *Here I would like to share with you*

the blessings that Guru Amar Das gave to his daughter, Bibi Bhani, at the time of her wedding. Bibi Bhani is an important woman in Sikh history: she was the daughter of the third Guru Amar Das, she was the wife of the fourth Guru Ram Das, and she was the mother of the fifth Guru Arjan. At her wedding, her father gave her the following blessings: "My daughter, Bhani, mind three things in your interaction with your husband. First, take care of your eyes. Always look directly into each other's eyes with love. Second, mind your noses, as this reflects in Punjabi culture one's social standing and reputation in the community. Keep the honor of your family intact. Third, mind your ears. Speak gently to each other without being hotheaded."

3. **Keep the enthusiasm (chau) for life alive in the face of adverse circumstances and remain detached (bairagia) from worldly attachments.** *For Sikh couples, joys and sorrows are integral to life. In this context, Guru Tegh Bahadur proclaims: "The one who grieves not in grief and is never affected by the pains and pleasures of life, such a one alone is a true devotee. For this person, gold is as good as dust. Such a one is never affected by praise and blame showered by others." This is an ideal for families to rise above life's inevitable circumstances.*

4. **Cultivate a balanced (sahaj) approach in life, avoiding all extremes.** *The final vow reflects the ideal state of marriage that avoids all extremes in life. This vow suggests one to follow a middle path. Most individuals have to work hard to attain this state of equipoise when the power of lust is sublimated and limited to normal family life, when anger becomes courage of conviction, when attachment becomes "love" for humanity, when greed is replaced by hard work, and when pride is sublimated into self-respect and dignity. This is the blissful state of marriage. That is why we call the Anand Karaj "The Ceremony of Bliss."*

My father concluded by saying that an ideal bride prefers the company of the Beloved to worldly things, just as Guru Nanak explained in the definition of a "cultured bride" (*Suchajji*) in Suhi raga: "When I have you, I have everything. O my Beloved, you are my wealth and capital. In your company, I abide in peace; in your company, I am congratulated by everyone. Both by the pleasure of your will, you can bestow thrones and greatness or make us beggars and wanderers." (Guru Granth Sahib, page 762).

My love and I celebrated our union with friends and family and then went off on our honeymoon. Upon returning from our tropical island paradise, we faced another challenge: living apart for the first year of our marriage. We had both devoted so much of our lives to developing our careers that the logistics of being together were going to take more time to sort out. The job opportunities were bleak where I was, and Mandeep was not happy with his work environment. We traveled across state lines to see each other once or twice monthly, appreciating the precious time we had together as if it were going to be our last, reminding ourselves that we wouldn't be doing this forever.

Then a blessing came along that set us into motion: our baby! I carried our daughter while living on my own and was fortunate to have the support around me. Mandeep moved to be with us just in time for her birth. He chose to extend his training and expertise in the care of critically ill children so that we could be together. Despite a nationwide recession, we took it on faith that an opportunity would open up. Having been on faculty at his institution for five years, my love set aside his pride and braced the discomforts of being a training fellow for one more year. He applied for several positions nearby, so I could continue to pursue my aspirations of becoming an established clinician and scientist at Stanford. Amid the stress of uncertainty, all the knots unraveled and life flowed smoothly.

You could say that our children brought us luck, because around the time that our daughter turned one and our son was in his eighth month of life in utero, my love got an incredible opportunity to work at a children's hospital in the area. But this was not just any children's hospital, it was *the* hospital—the one where my husband would find career fulfillment; his esprit de corps. He landed the job that many in his line of work would say was ideal for him.

Our experiences before and after love prepared us for the marathons of life rather than the sprints, and we start each day afresh with the feeling that our journey together has just begun. One final inspiring thought from the Guru Granth Sahib eloquently expresses what I hope will be the way we live our future in gratitude: "We seek all gifts from You alone, O Lord! You alone are all my adorning jewelry! Whatever comfort You give us, we gladly accept in gratitude. Wherever You keep us, O *Vahiguru*, that place will be our heaven on earth. You are the Cherisher of one and all!" (Guru Granth Sahib, page 106).

The Way Home

Meeta Kaur

It never occurred to me that I'd marry a Sikh, let alone a *sardar*. I grew up with sharp, well-dressed Sikh men. My father's and uncles' turbans were always neatly tied, and their beards were neatly set for both professional and social events. They often matched their turbans to crisp ironed shirts, neatly tailored slacks, and perhaps their outlook for the day. That, coupled with their charm, intelligence, and an undeniable work ethic, planted a seed of expectation within me, but I was also determined to make my own way in the world.

When friends and family asked me if I planned to marry, I'd respond, "I don't know how to answer that question." Call it a life sabbatical; I wanted time to ponder the larger questions. This, of course, exasperated and exhausted my parents. They wanted me to "stick with a professional career" and "have a steady life," not question "every little thing."

My parents found love easily. In Chandighar, India, 1965, my father heard my mother's shoes clicking down the sidewalk outside the dormitories of their medical school. He looked up and saw a petite, bright-eyed, outspoken medical student carrying her future in the click of her heels, and he knew she was the one. That moment led to a colleague-ship, an engagement, and then a marriage. They eventually risked crossing three oceans and two continents together to land in Cleveland, Ohio, where they raised me and my brother.

The power of that one singular moment when my father was moved by the sound of my mother's shoe steps is how I came to be.

Unlike my parents, my self-discovery was different and a slow-to-brew sort of process. I continued to question, "Who am I?"—something my parents never understood. "You are a proud Sikh," they'd tell me. "You are a lion. You are our future." In their minds, what more did I need? "Sure," I'd say. But I wasn't so sure. As the years passed and I found more and more of myself, I began a spiritual journey I never imagined, and it led me right back to my parents' dream come true. Funny how that works.

In late summer 2002, I stood on the steps of a Manhattan apartment building waiting for a man I had yet to meet in person. I had officially met him over IM—an AOL chat set up a month earlier by a mutual friend. Our mutual friend held a firm optimism I'd like this man, even though I had sworn off marriage and was contemplating buying a backpack, taking rock-climbing lessons, and traveling the world. I was determined to be the community Auntie on a consistent global adventure—not a wife and a mom. In spite of myself, however, I was intrigued.

My coast-to-coast blind date began with a charming message in 11-point Geneva font that popped up on my computer screen to say hello every so often. I scoured the Internet for a picture of my IM suitor and found two. In one, he looked sweet and youthful, smiling ear to ear with a peer camp counselor he used to work with at youth camps. The other picture showed an attractive man in a neatly tied turban and beard. Banjot looked like he had knowledge of the world, like my father and uncles.

We talked a few times on the phone. He lived centered in composure, a placid pool of calm. All of it was expressed through his voice, and the pace at which he carried conversations. He naturally slowed me down from my so-called "schedule" and the ways I kept myself busy to not feel so alone in the world. I had good friends and family, but I realized I was looking for a life partner. We decided to meet.

I flew from California to New Jersey for a South Asian Women's conference. He was in Manhattan. I was on a budget, but I managed to get a cab from Jersey to the bus station and then took a Greyhound to Manhattan. Had my family known, they would have had the police, the FBI, and a SWAT team looking for me. But I knew I could handle myself, so I decided to let fate lead me.

He breezed down the steps, tall, latte-skinned, and handsome. He wore a black turban, jeans, and, layered over a white T-shirt, a light-blue sweater. A hint of a black strap inched its way out from under his T-shirt. It was his *gathra*, a strap that holds his *kirpan*, a sacred dagger, in place. It captivated me. I had met people who wore kirpans but never entertained dating a person who wore one. For me, seeing that gathra secured me in the present moment, and the ground beneath me became a little firmer.

I waited patiently for him to say something about it. Break out into a lecture on Sikh awareness or how important it is to be an *Amritdhari*, a Sikh who volunteers to be initiated into the *Khalsa Panth*. I waited for him to ask me if I was one, or say that he expected me to be, but he never delivered the lecture. From that very first meeting, he let me be me.

We walked through Central Park, attempting a conversation in broken Punjabi with our American-educated, English-stained tongues. He sang Sting's "Fields of Gold" to me. There was that voice again. It was deep and calm, like a solitary walk through Muir Woods. His voice could carry warring nations to peace it was so comforting, so reassuring.

We had sushi in his neighborhood. It was one of those meals where the conversation had no end, and I didn't want it to; occasionally I would glance at my plate, the rolls of rice and fish seeming like pink and green blossoms as rain poured down outside. He mentioned his mother was a vice president at Citibank. It caught my attention, because I too had been raised by a mother who loved her work and was ambitious in her own right. I instantly knew he'd understand my need to pursue my ambitions and be self-sufficient.

And all the while, his spiritual status never came up—nor did mine. That private world where he prayed was his and his alone. It simply was none of my business. And yet I realized the commitment the gathra represented was something I wanted, too. His spiritual world wasn't mine to step into; I needed to create my own world centered in faith.

Our future togetherness was something I sensed. None of it was spoken; it wasn't revealed in a clever chat over coffee; it was in the squeeze of his hand, and the lifetimes I saw in his eyes, which also expressed how much he valued himself, his roots, and his love for the world.

As I saw him more, and spent time with him, I realized we were having a much deeper dialogue. My questioning of the world met with his unspoken faith in it. His reserve equalized my chatter. My heart opened and invited his in. His resolve anchored me in my own spiritual journey. I started to think I could spend my life with this quiet strength, this unwavering faith of a man.

Our relationship unfolded in ways that I could not have imagined. It went past the limitations of the label "love." Yes, love served as the toolbox, the vehicle by which we "loved" each other, but he also pushed me to understand and discover myself. He understood that the greatest gift he gave me was the space to realize my purpose in the world.

Connecting to Banjot reconnected me to my parents. He became the translator for their silence—all that they felt was expressed through his simple presence. If they had the words for it, I believe they were trying to say, "He is so satisfied within himself as a Sikh. This is what we want for you, so you can live a life of *sukh*." And he translated what my mother could not say: how critical it was for me to discover who I was as a Sikh woman in the world, a Kaur, a daughter of Singhs and Kaurs, a carrier of the Gurus' lineage for future generations.

Throughout my marriage with Banjot, I have discovered the vast universe within myself, an entire solar system revolving around my faith. It has given me an unwavering peace, a steadiness—solid ground to walk on. The private conversations I have with *Waheguru* are my favorite time of the day. The more I stay in touch and talk my heart out with Him/Her, the more I celebrate every blessing, every gift, every dream come true, every chance to dream some more, and the easier it is to hand over every hurt, every doubt, every worry, every concern—to lay them all at His/Her feet and simply step away knowing all will be taken care of is a relief. Handing over the burdens and staying in gratitude for my boon on Earth anchors me in a joy that language is incapable of expressing.

My faith has also helped me shed the confines and labels the world places on me as a minority woman or a strong woman of color or a Sikh woman who is brave and courageous or an emotional woman—a *this* woman, a *that* woman, *a woman*—and instead become a beam of light that can merge with the greater world and universe. In turn, I can see the light in everyone I meet.

These days, when Banjot and I visit my parents with two kids in tow, my retired father might be counting rasgula packages in the freezer, to which my mother will declare, "Your father is getting on my nerves." My father often laughs at my mother's editorials. And as always, they tease each other, make fun of each other, scold each other, bicker with each other and then—when it counts—love each other tenderly, quietly, with their full hearts. When they address the children as, "our leader, Benanti" and "Sidak Singh the Great," I know my children will also go out into the world and find the greatest of loves. Knowing my parents' story, and now my own with Banjot, my history and storylines fill me with endless hope and possibility for us as human beings who live for, endure, and sacrifice all for love. And when we leave my parents' home to return to ours, the look of relief and peace on my parents' faces is all I need.

In the deep recesses of our fleshy, beating hearts, those defining moments when lives intertwine, grow, and expand—these are our greatest blessings. All of it is written in the stars. Such a moment comes in the smallest of details; all it takes is the click of a heel or the slip of a sweater to know—yes, we are onto something here. And this moment is ripe for everyone at the right time and in the right place. I truly believe it is pre-written and we have to do the work to get to that singular instance that can change the course of our lives. It takes effort to fulfill the plan laid out for us, but it is such a glorious plan, the effort involved is worth it.

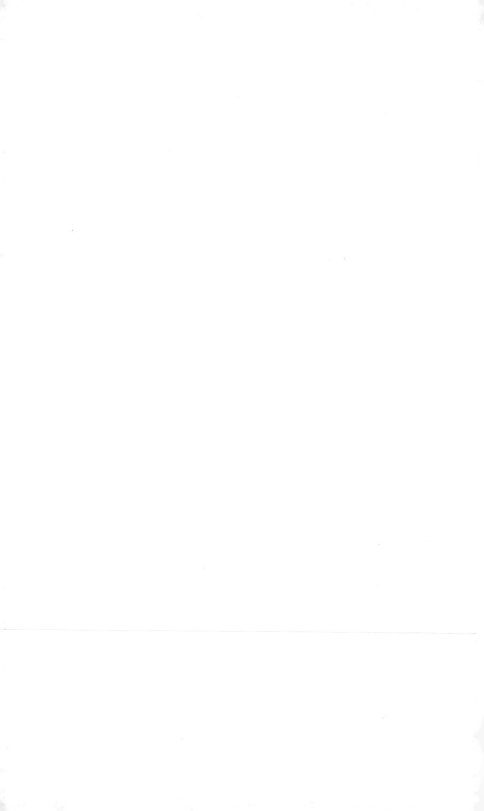

Part 5: Dharam

Our Sacred Work in the World

Love: The Most Lasting Form of Activism

Simran Kaur

The year 1984 was a starting point for me. I remember little else of that time. A voice is etched in my memory: a newscaster was reporting on violence in Amritsar, where a sacred space had been attacked and hundreds of men, women, and children had been killed. The phone was ringing constantly and my father was gone for days and days, attending meetings in the *gurudwara* and at the homes of friends. The pages of *Des Pardes* were filled with images of bodies, destroyed buildings, and lots of bloodshed. These are some of the earliest memories of my childhood, and they have helped shape my life's path.

My father has always been an activist, and it was not unusual for political leaders from Panjab to visit our home. Sikhi taught him never to stay idle or apathetic during times of injustice. It was not surprising that he was so politically engaged during the events of 1984; what also impacted me deeply was the role my mother played during this time. My mother, whose pride and joy was her family, embodied her role as a daughter of the *Khalsa*. She was not silent during those challenging months for our community. When my father organized and attended rallies and protests against the Indian government, my mother was right by his side. She, along with other women from the community, packed *prantay* and *cha*; pushed their children in strollers; and marched alongside their brothers and husbands. My mother never spoke to me about her actions because for her it wasn't activism—it was her identity, inspired by her faith. It was only when I went on a school trip to a museum many years later and came across a picture of my mother—her fist in the air, surrounded by her children and other Sikh women—that I really felt the importance of her role in formulating what activism looked like for me.

Without a doubt, my faith played a major role in my growth as an activist. It would be impossible to separate my activism from my faith; I am an activist because I'm Sikh and the essence of Sikhi is in its activism. My parents were unique in their teaching of Sikhi. While we were taught the *rehat*, they also showed us, through their actions, how Sikhi should be practiced on a daily basis. We were raised to be well read and engaged in global issues, to help people in need, and to always stand against injustice in all its forms. Stories also helped, and there were many in our home—about our Sikh history, about Guru Nanak, Bibi Nanaki, and *Janamsakhis*. We talked about issues happening in Panjab, about Jarnail Singh Bindrawale and Sant Longowal. We discussed the Anandpur Sahib Resolution and the Green Revolution. And there were the stories about my parents' childhood—how my father's *Chacha* had saved his life when he was a young boy or how my mother would visit the home of her blind neighbor with *rotis* for them.

It wasn't lost on me how much my parents had sacrificed for their children. Soon after their marriage in Amritsar, my parents immigrated to England, where my father found a job driving buses in town, not an easy task for a turbaned Sikh at that time. Their faith in Sikhi continued to be resolute as they settled into their new lives as immigrants in a country that had a new language, a new culture, and new expectations. The stories about our own history were not labeled as revolutionary, as activism or social change, but that's exactly what they were. Knowing the revolutionary tradition I came from helped me understand who I was meant to be. It gave me the motivation and drive I needed to be involved in social activism, to stand up for the truth. It provided me with a voice and a platform. Over the years, my faith and identity grew, and throughout this journey I always came back to one value: the divine love of *Waheguru* exists within all of us. Finding that divinity was a transformative experience, and the more I nurtured this love, the more I became committed to social change.

They say that love is our most powerful, lasting form of activism. One doesn't need to attend protests to be an activist, because our relationships can often be the very sites of radical transformation. Relationships have the capacity to change the world within and around us, to drive empathy and passion and a desire to leave the world much better than we found it. Whom we love and how we love is as much a statement of our social consciousness as the petitions we sign. Love itself is radical, and while finding my one true love, I, too, was transformed.

Early in life, I often gave too much of myself in a relationship— unlike my work as an activist, which was much more freeing and forgiving. Being an activist is unconditional—the way true love should be. The act of giving to others is empowering and liberating; we don't expect anything in return. I would often meet the men I dated through the activism work I did. It made sense; it's where I spent most of my time. I have always known that this is part of who I am, and being with a partner who feels the same passion has always been attractive to me. Perhaps the problem with activists, however, is that we focus so much on interacting with our communities that we don't realize that relationships and our intimate interactions could also benefit from that same kind of passion. Activists often get so caught up in being there for others that we forget how to be there for ourselves and for those closest to us. In fact, I was so busy sharing my love with other people that I forgot the importance of also sharing that love with myself.

I didn't realize how intimidating it could be for a man to date a strong and driven woman. While I felt I lived my life according to what my faith had inspired within me, I was stuck in a maze of dating that was uninspiring, painful, and left me feeling empty inside. It was everything that my activism was not. I quickly realized in my development as an activist that true love has a strong, sustaining effect. Although I had a strong support network of family and friends, I recognized early on that what I needed to do this work was the unconditional love of a partner, a partner who could support and sustain me through my growth as an activist. Time after time, I reached out to the wrong men for this sustenance. I didn't know what I was looking for, exactly, but I did know I would feel it in my heart when it was right. And even when it wasn't right, I made lots of excuses because I wanted so much to move on to this part of my journey as a woman. That's what is amiss with the strain that I, and many of my girlfriends, experienced in our twenties: we were constantly given messages from our families and from society that unless and until we were married, we were not quite whole. It wasn't enough that I loved what I did for a living or that I felt fulfilled by my life choices. There was also the spoken and unspoken pressure to be constantly searching for a partner. It wasn't until my late twenties that I finally felt ready to transition to the next step.

In some ways, he was there all along. We met several years ago, initially brought together by our mutual interest in Sikh civil rights issues. At the time, we were both in the midst of relationships and transitioned easily into being friends; it wasn't until much later that our paths became inevitably intertwined. Maybe because I was not looking for love, I finally found it. Perhaps because I didn't rush into it and was thoughtful about my decision (for once not feeling the pressure from anyone), I was finally able to see his love for what it was—sincere, unconditional. Although it didn't come in the package I was expecting, and it challenged my entire growth as a Sikh, it was exactly what I needed. I had always grown up with the vision of being with a turbaned Sikh; I subconsciously thought someone who practiced his Sikhi externally meant that he also practiced it internally. But Sikhi teaches us to find the light of Waheguru within everyone and now, for the first time, I finally understood what that meant. You don't know true love until you find it, and when you come across it, it feels different.

It was months before I realized what I was experiencing, and I almost overlooked it, but I gently reminded myself that this time it would be different and I would take my time. Today, we adore each other and are inspired by the love each of us has for the world around us. Our love is growing each and every day, and it inspires me. I've found someone I want to build a future with, someone I want by my side as I continue this journey as an activist. Our relationship helps me feel what Professor Puran Singh wrote about when he described "Ajar Vastu." My Sikhi has helped me find this love, overflowing the boundaries of my heart.

I don't know what the future holds for me, but after years of looking and shedding too many tears, my heart is full. I know that my partner and I are equals and will continue to uplift each other to put into practice what our Sikhi teaches us. We continue to be inspired by our faith and history, grateful to our parents for how much they sacrificed for us, and motivated by our desire to better the world we live in. We hope to teach our children to live out Sikhi the way the Gurus intended. In many ways, ours is a simple love; we have nothing except devotion for one another. It is the best kind of love.

Amritsar

Gunisha Kaur

The smell of freshly cooked *dal* and perfectly round *rotis* fills my lungs. I take a deep breath. As I exhale, the sound of *kirtan* fills my ears. The bustle of people speaking Punjabi behind me is over-shadowed by the noise of children splashing water. I lift my bowed head off the ground, allowing my fingers to linger on the warm marble for a fraction of a second. My eyes flutter open, and in front of me I see the beautiful golden reflection in the rippling water. The whole world around me is at peace. Slowly, purposefully, and freely, I begin to walk. Each step covers the story of a hundred years. The clockwise journey takes me past a portrait that captures my atten-tion. I pause, my feet rocking back and forth on the hot stone, and I resume my walk again. I reach the entry point for which I have been longing; the covered path of the *Darshani Deori* invites me in. It is a place that hundreds of thousands of souls have visited in the past, yet none experiences it as the others. Each story is unique. The golden image before me is flawless.

My love story begins in 1984. I was born in Amritsar, Punjab, in a charged social and political milieu. My dad was a victim of the 1984 violence in Delhi after the assassination of Indira Gandhi, when thousands of innocent Sikhs were targeted on the basis of their faith. Mobs charging the trains identified him as a Sikh, beat him, and left him for dead. For over a week, my mom, with her infant son and newborn daughter, sitting in her in-laws' home, had no idea if my dad was dead or alive. As the preparations were being made for my dad's funeral, a couriered letter came that changed my mother's world.

We moved to the United States almost immediately after my dad was found, miraculously alive. The pull towards the United States let us leave India behind. We were still Punjabis, but we were no longer Indians. We moved to Iowa, where we lived as first-generation immigrants. We grew up as Americans in the Midwest, disconnected from the past that we had narrowly escaped. Perhaps it was a tactic of self-preservation; perhaps it was an opportunity for rebirth.

It took a decade and a half for my parents to explain our family history to me. What I learned about our life in Punjab and our politically charged asylum moved me. A place within me felt a unique connection to Punjab that shifted to the forefront of my conscience. It troubled me that, for nearly two decades, I had not known the history of my own family and community. I wanted to know more, and I wanted to share this knowledge with others. I was thirsty for answers, for understanding.

After having learned about the violence that shook the state and my family, I returned to Punjab and began to understand what had happened in my city of birth. The city, state, and country were palpably different from any time I had been there previously. When I saw *darjis*, *cha-valas*, or *rickshaw-valas*, I wondered whether they had lost children to the violence. I wondered if the easily identifiable drug addicts roaming the streets had suffered torture at the hands of the government that was in place to protect them. I wondered how many of the *dhobis* that I passed in the streets had lost their loved ones to the violence that shook the state to its very core. I felt a granular connection to each and every Punjabi with whom I spoke, as if our homeland's history entangled our personal histories. And with this bond, our narratives were inextricably intertwined.

What moved me the most was the connection I felt with women who had lost their husbands, sons, and brothers to the violence in Punjab. I identified deeply with these women. In a way, my life story should have been their life story. Yet somehow my father had survived. Somehow I had made it to a better life. Rather than evoking guilt within me, this recognition engendered a sense of responsibility.

I embraced the responsibility I felt to provide a voice to those in the faraway depths of Punjabi villages, whose words cannot be heard by the rest of the world. The concept of defending the oppressed is rooted deep in *Gurmat* and reverberated in my conscience. But my connection to these women created bottomless crevices in my soul that echoed louder than just the moral obligation that I had based on my understanding of Gurmat. As the one that made it out, I had a responsibility to tell their story, our story to the world. It became an all-consuming driving force behind my work and my spirit. This responsibility did not frighten me; it empowered me.

My path as a physician and human rights activist has provided me the good fortune to base much of my work in Punjab. From documentation of human rights violations to advocacy for survivors, my history has become one large circle, interconnecting me with individuals whose stories are so similar to mine. When I initially began my work, the overlapping problems of socioeconomic issues, violence against women, drug and alcohol abuse, environmental destruction, and debt and farmer suicide were overwhelming. Not only did I have no sense of where to begin my work, I also felt the problems to be insurmountable. It was overpowering and nearly debilitating to see what had happened to some of the people who had not been as fortunate as my family and me, who escaped the trauma and started our lives over.

Yet as I work on real-time solution-building on the ground, my response becomes ever more hopeful. There is so much potential for positive change and revolution. And whenever my tasks seem burdensome or my emotions consuming, I seek solace in my connection to Punjab, Amritsar, and the Darbar Sahib. As I enter the beautifully engraved archways and lower myself onto the marble ground, the vibrations of the music, water, and souls uplift me. I come here with a heavy heart, and my mind is freed. It is an everlasting source of inspiration and connection to my history and an eternal refuge that asks only for love of all humanity in return.

My love story begins in 1984. I was born in Amritsar, Punjab, in a charged social and political milieu. And though my life is rooted outside, we will forever be connected to Punjab. This is the birthplace of Gurmukhi, the language of the Gurus. This is the home of the Singh Sabha Movement and the Jallianwallah Bagh Massacre. This is the earth that is nurtured by the Ravi, Satluj, Beas, Jhelum, and Chenab Rivers. No matter how we flourish in our communities in the diaspora, Punjab will always hold our roots. It will always be our home.

A Revolution Called Love
Harbani Ahuja

aavahu bhainae gal mileh ank sehaelarreeaah ||
mil kai kareh kehaaneeaa samrathh kanth keeaah ||

Come, my dear sisters and spiritual companions;
hug me close in your embrace.
Let's join together and tell stories of our All-powerful Husband Lord.
(Guru Granth Sahib, page 17)

As a little girl, I crawled into my mumma's lap at night; she sang *shabads* and whispered *saakhis* of Mai Bhago. I listened, in awe of the strength and unwavering loyalty of Mai Bhago as she rallied the soldiers to reignite their commitment to the Guru. A courageous warrior, she fought valiantly, unafraid of death to defend Sikhism during the sixteenth century in India. I'd drift into sleep dreaming of a fearless Kaur riding a horse onto a battlefield, a warm light radiating from her silhouette.

At that young, impressionable age, Sikhi was not much more than my birthright, a safe place to retreat to where there would be warm *langar*, a meal served at the Staten Island *gurudwara*, and Gurmukhi books filled with *Oora, Aara, Eeree*, the Punjabi alphabet. Sikhi was my long braid that Mumma weaved in the morning, and the soothing *kirtan*, spiritual hymns, that echoed through the rooms in our home. It was the *Japji Sahib* prayer I read from a small red *gutka* every morning before school, my head bobbing with sleep every so often. Sikhi was attending our local gurudwara every Sunday and learning how to recite shabads on the harmonium. It was the answer I gave my friends when asked about my religion. But as I got older, Sikhi became so much more to me than my birthright. As I began to fall deeply in love with Sikhi, I found my life's calling.

I realized early in life that being a Sikh woman and being an Indian woman is a contradiction. The countless martyrs in our rich history and the revolutionary words of Guru Nanak inspired my passion to fight for justice and equality. To me, equality was an ocean of *amrit* (holy water). Refreshing, awakening, transformative—it washed away all barriers and biases. Mata Jeeto, Guru Gobind Singh Ji's wife, added sweet *pataase* (wafers), to the amrit that Guru Gobind Singh prepared for the *Khalsa*, a community of purity in consciousness and actions. By adding sweetness and love, qualities personified by women, she made the Khalsa genderless. The Khalsa was to me the very essence of equality, but I found myself infuriated by the discrimination in our Sikh communites across the globe.

When I was fourteen years old, I attended the wedding of my eighteen-year-old girlfriend from our gurudwara. She was fresh out of high school, and her parents had arranged her marriage. She was the first of a series of girlfriends at our gurudwara who were married off at early ages. They were never asked if they wanted to attend college or have a career. Each time it happened, it was if their futures had been snatched away from them. It was as if their opinions about their own futures were not necessary.

At home, I found myself listening to cousins say that they'd marry a housewife over a woman with a good career, and elders who wouldn't be happy with the birth of a girl in the family. I realized that I was surrounded by Sikhs who chose to view Sikh women through the Indian cultural lens, with its patriarchal dominance. Their bias against women wasn't always open or spoken. Sometimes it was a hushed whisper that floated over conversations. I desperately wanted to expose it, to call people out on the veiled prejudice that surfaced from time to time. As I became frustrated with the world around me, I retreated back to Sikhi, falling in love with its message of equality. My Gurus empowered me as a woman, and I clung to Sikhi because it inspired me to demand that Sikh women, all women, have a voice in the twenty-first century around the world. I used Sikhi as my shield against the world silencing me.

I didn't know the meaning of the shabads Mumma would sing at night; I just remember how beautifully the words rolled off her tongue.

kahu naanak ho nirabho hoee so prabh maeraa oulhaa ||
Says Nanak, I am fearless; God has become my Shelter and Shield.

I soon found that the bias I was experiencing in my life was nothing compared to what was happening in India. It pained me to read about and understand how female infanticide, domestic violence, and rape were spreading like plagues in Punjab. I knew that being a Kaur meant that my Gurus had placed responsibility on my shoulders to fight for women, Sikhism, and equality throughout the world. And I knew I had to carry out that responsibility with the grace and fire of the Kaurs before me. All my life, I was drowning, suffocating in a sea of silence, discrimination, and female expectations. When I decided to pursue law and dedicate my life to advocating for human rights, I finally came up for air.

My passion for human rights led me to Chandigarh, India, where I accepted an offer to intern with a human rights attorney. I had begun what I thought was the most exciting experience of my life, and I was unbelievably terrified. I cried before getting on the plane, waving good-bye to my parents, leaving the sanctuary of my home for the first time in twenty-one years to go out on my own into the world.

I'm not sure exactly what I went looking for in India, but once I was there I was overcome with emotion. The bias I had experienced back home was nothing compared to the horrors of what I read in case files at the legal office. Never had I felt more blessed to be a Sikh, to be a Kaur, than I did in that moment. Looking out at the injustices India is facing now, I can only imagine how incredibly revolutionary Guru Nanak was to claim that women were equal to men in the sixteenth century.

The case files I read outlined details of horrific acts of violence against women. I heard a firsthand testimony from a newly married young woman about how her husband had abandoned her, returned to beat her, and let his parents abuse her and kick her out of her home. I read about girls who were hunted down and killed by their own parents because they'd made the mistake of falling in love and marrying a man of their own free will. I read reports about the biased judiciary that set rapists free. While I was in India, a woman was gang-raped and brutally killed on a bus in Delhi. Learning of all of this made me sick. My disgust with the state of the world, with the brutality of what was happening to my own people, with my utter powerlessness—all of this merged into a burning knot that lodged itself in my chest. I'd come to India with the hope of finding something that would empower me to make a difference, but instead what I'd found made me feel small. I didn't know why I was there.

On my last day as an intern, as I left the office, I passed the walls covered with shelves on which rested volumes of legal books such as *Judgments Today* and *Indian Law Reports* placed in chronological order. Next to the shelves of books, I noticed some images framed on the walls. When I realized who the paintings were of, my heart jumped and I froze in my tracks. There she was in my life again, just as beautiful and courageous as I remembered her. As I gazed upon the image of Mai Bhago—a *dastaar* on her head, fearlessly raising a sword, majestically riding her horse into battle, light radiating from her silhouette—the knot in my chest melted away. I remembered why I was there. There was also a battle ahead of me, and like this valiant Kaur, there was only love for my Guru in my heart. In that moment, I knew my Guru was asking me to fight this war against injustice for as I long as I lived.

> *jaa ko har rang laago eis jug mehi so keheeath hai sooraa ||*
> *He alone is called a warrior, who is attached to the Lord's Love in this age.*
>
> (Guru Granth Sahib, page 94)

Moving ~~On~~ Forward

Harleen Kaur

Any life is made up of a single moment, the moment in which a man finds out,
once and for all, who he truly is.
—Jorge Luis Borges

We all have that one moment. Sometimes it comes through a short interaction with a stranger, other times it is an event that we immediately know will change the direction of our lives. Either way, we never know until later how much impact that moment had. Looking back, a lot of little things have had an impact on me: going to a Sikh camp for the first time, moving from Wisconsin to Michigan, receiving *amrit* (the initiation ceremony into the Sikh faith), graduating from high school, and coming to the University of Michigan. And yet none of these sparked my big realization or my discovery of my inner self. For me, that moment came in the form of a shooting.

August 5, 2012. It was a relatively normal, albeit busy summer day. The *gurudwara* in Plymouth, Michigan, was wrapping up a weekend of hosting an international speech competition for Sikh youth. I was a volunteer and was enjoying the end of a fun, Sikh-filled weekend. The gurudwara was packed with more than seven hundred people as the *sangat* started to trickle in and attempt to find room among visitors from all over the world.

After the awards ceremony, my friend and I ducked out to go

eat before the rest of the crowd. We found space in the back corner and started to eat our *roti* and *mattar paneer*. We talked with our other friends, discussing what a great time we'd had that weekend and how sad we would be for the visitors to go. It was nice to see a different crowd around the gurudwara—even if most of them were complete strangers.

As we finished eating, my phone buzzed with a notification from Twitter. I glanced at it and noticed that a friend had tweeted something to me, so I opened it to read, "8 to 20 people have been injured in a shooting at a Sikh temple in Wisconsin." Then another notification: "BREAKING: Multiple victims reported at shooting at Sikh Temple in #OakCreek." With this one, a link was included, so I clicked on it, mindlessly reading without fully grasping what was going on.

"What's up?" my friend asked.

"I-uh-there-um-there was a shooting at a *gurudwara* in Wisconsin. The one I went to."

"What? Are you serious?"

"Sorry, I need to find my parents."

Ignoring her confused, probably concerned, look, I jumped up and ran into the hallway. Searching throughout the lobby, I didn't my parents in the crowd, so I pulled out my phone and called my mom.

"Yes?" she answered.

Frantically, I shouted, "Mom, where are you?"

"In the main hall. Your dad and I are counting the money from donations."

"Okay, I'm coming, I have to tell you something."

I immediately hung up and ran to the other side of the gurudwara, where the main hall was located. I slowed to a quick walk and collapsed onto my knees next to my parents, who were sitting in front of a pile of money with a few other sangat members.

"What happened?" my mom said, turning to look at me, her face slightly puzzled.

"There'sashooterintheOakCreekgurudwara—andpeoplearein there—andIdon'tknowwhat'sgoingon," I blurted, and then immediately started sobbing.

My parents' faces changed from shock to alarm to disbelief. I remember my dad grabbed my arm and forced me to get up, and we all left to go in the hallway. As I calmed down a bit, I started to form words and tried to explain the little information I knew to my parents. As soon as my mom understood, she pulled out her phone and started calling number after number from her phone book.

I wish I could say the rest of the day was a blur and move on. But, the reality is, I still remember every excruciating detail.

I remember my mom crying as she talked to our friends, closer than any family, back in Wisconsin. I remember my dad looking out the window, completely silent. I remember locating my younger brother in the lobby of the gurudwara, rushing home, and spending the rest of the day watching CNN while our phone rang off the hook. I remember how people called, pestering for information, without asking how I was doing, even though my sobs were audible through the phone. I remember praying that I wouldn't recognize any of the deceased, even though this was asking for a miracle.

The day went by painfully slowly as we waited for any news. When we received a list of the six victims, one stood out to me: Satwant Singh Kaleka. I immediately remembered a single moment, as if it had been a prerecorded video paused and ready to play at any time:

I started to learn classical Indian music and kirtan, the singing of Sikh hymns, at the age of seven and quickly became attached. I loved the sound that my voice made as it left my throat, the thrill I received every time I touched the cool, smooth keys of a vaajaa (harmonium), and the way my heart started to beat with the rhythm of the accompanying tabla (drum).

As with any mode of art, though, there is always a bit of hesitation before sharing your talent with others. Whether it is a fear of judgment or failure, most people do not jump at the chance to perform for the first time. Yet for each musician, there is something, or someone, that keeps them going. For me, it was the encouragement of an uncle from my gurudwara, Satwant Singh Kaleka.

As the years went on, I made sure to prepare a shabad (Sikh hymn) for every Sunday at the gurudwara. Without fail, as soon as I entered the main hall, Satwant Uncle would grab me by the arm and take me to the stage to do kirtan. My mom tells me that he and his wife always had the same conversation. They argued about how his speeches would embarrass me and that continually telling the other children to learn from my example would do no good. His response was the same every time: "If we don't recognize our kids, then who will?"

The rest of that day—and the following weeks and months—I went through a full spectrum of emotions. At first, I was in complete shock. The fact that something like this could happen in my childhood safe-haven was beyond my worst nightmares. Other times I was furious, especially when others tried to explain to me that they "understood" what I was going through, that they were Sikhs just like me, and that this could have been their gurudwara. In fact, I realized that it was the people in a gurudwara, not the building, that made it important. I never actually attended the physical gurudwara that the Oak Creek shooting occurred in, as it was built when I moved away to Michigan. However, it was the same community that I had grown up with in the Milwaukee location—the people, my sangat, they were my gurudwara. They were my pillars and my foundation, and when they were violated, it shook me from the core. I felt hopeless, and, that night, my family struggled to finish our prayers, because even *Waheguru*, our Creator, could not comfort us. That day, we had seen a new world.

Those next few days were, easily, some of the most influential in my life. I heard stories from my brother, my dad, and other Sikh men of strangers approaching them and offering their condolences. Sometimes it was just a handshake, other times a hug, before the two strangers parted ways, each a little more at peace. Yet these experiences never happened to me. *Well, I'm a Sikh. Why doesn't anyone talk to me?* That's when it hit me: I didn't *look* like a Sikh. I'd spent years trying to explain to my friends and community members that a turban was the most visible identifier of a Sikh. So how could I expect others to identify me as a Sikh when I wasn't accepting the Sikh identity?

The next couple of days, I continued to contemplate these thoughts, particularly when my family returned to Oak Creek the following weekend. As I heard more details of that horrid Sunday morning from my uncles and aunties (and sat in the sangat the week after), I was completely broken. I listened to the *Bhai Sahib* (sangat leader) read *Salok Mahala 9*, one of the last prayers in the Sikh holy book, but my mind drifted in and out throughout the program. I suddenly snapped into focus at the end of the program when I heard the following:

People become anxious when something unexpected happens. This is the way of the world, O Nanak; nothing is stable or permanent. ||51||

Whatever has been created shall be destroyed; everyone shall perish, today or tomorrow. O Nanak, sing the Glorious Praises of the Lord, and give up all other entanglements. ||52||

Immediately, I was struck by the message that Waheguru had been trying to send me: *nothing is permanent.* The brutality and suddenness of the shooting had made me realize the truth behind those fairly obvious words. My sangat was, and still is, important. But nothing compares to remembering Waheguru and realizing His presence within us.

This realization helped me as I tried to heal over the next few months. There are still after-effects, though. I have a hard time trusting people, especially society as a whole. My belief in the ability of non-Sikhs to understand the Sikh community is much more negative. I now wonder if my dream to work for Sikh civil rights and advocacy will have any impact, but I trust in one line:

jis dhaa saahib ddaadtaa hoe || this no maar n saakai koe ||
One who belongs to the All-powerful Lord and Master, no one can destroy him.

This was the main line of the theme shabad for a camp I went to several years ago, and it still sticks with me wherever I go. I am comforted that we all have a protector, and that the six lives that we lost on August 5 were not lost in vain. But as I move forward, I am still learning and still mending. I have been wearing a *dastaar* (turban) for over a year now, but every day is a struggle. I am starting to reconnect with my identity after losing so much faith two summers ago, and I am still working to understand my purpose. I know that I am greatly impacted by Satwant Uncle Ji's absence, but I have a harder time understanding why. On the day of the shooting, it had been five years since my family had moved away from Wisconsin, and I hadn't seen or talked to Uncle Ji in quite some time. And yet, to this day, I cannot talk about the shooting or those who were lost without losing my composure.

In many ways, I think the greatest impact Satwant Uncle Ji had on me was through his death. By embodying compassion throughout his life, Uncle Ji made me realize how important it is to truly care for and serve each person you meet. Although the world lost six beautiful souls on that day, their lives imprinted a message on each person that they had met. This understanding has continued to keep me, and the other sangat members of Oak Creek, strong. I will continue to question and work on myself in the coming days, weeks, and years, but I will never question my progress. Because no matter how difficult or frustrating it seems, it is all truly that. Progress.

A Lesson in Love

Sheba Remy Kharbanda

Burn worldly love,
rub the ashes and make ink of it,
make the heart the pen,
the intellect the writer,
write that which has no end or limit.
—Guru Granth Sahib, Raag Siree Raag, First Mehl, First House

My story begins the day I learned a lesson in love.

That day, an early August one, atypically wet and overcast, I made the one-hour-plus subway commute from my home in Brooklyn to the Queens Museum located in the outer reaches of the five boroughs. The event that had inspired me to cross half of New York City, alone and on a Sunday, was a film screening and discussion based on the life and work of the late great Punjabi Sufi mystic Baba Bulleh Shah.

I don't go to Queens very often and when I do, it's to eat *desi* food and stock up on dried *masalas* and *dhaals* at Patel Brothers on Seventy-Fourth Street. As I exited the subway at the second-to-last stop on the rickety number 7 line, I was bowled over by a diverse sea of humanity, in groupings of young and old, making their way to the adjoining Flushing Meadows Corona Park. To reach the museum I wound my way through the park via wide concrete pathways covered with umbrella-like trees, occasionally taking shortcuts through freshly mown grass. My ears picked up French Creole, Hindi, Punjabi, Bangla, Urdu, three different versions of Spanish, and half a dozen other languages I couldn't recognize.

The stroll through the park took me back to my childhood in Southall, West London. There, extended families like mine of first-, second-, and third-generation immigrants squeezed into houses intended for nuclear ones, all the while harboring memories of "back home," where the living spaces—the streets, the *sabzi* or fabric wallahs' shops, the parks, and the temples—are communal. As children, we wiled away many hours in the spacious and green expanse of the probably once very English—but in my childhood, very Punjabi—Southall Park. It's where those of us with one foot in the mythic Punjab and one in multi-culti West London kicked around a football or set up wickets and reenacted the ludicrousness of Pakistan–India rivalry, only sometimes observing the strange rules of cricket.

Ten minutes into my trip down memory lane, I found myself at the entrance to the Queens Museum, where I was greeted by the *Unisphere*, a massive globe made of stainless steel and surrounded by a circular water fountain dotted with lines demarcating the seven continents, the oceans, the seas, and dozens of nation states. The timing of this moment was, for me, quite poetic: just weeks before, and after making home in these lands for more than ten years, I had applied to become a US citizen.

I arrived at the museum to find the screening room at capacity and quickly made my way to one of the few empty seats. My usual ambivalence about long commutes notwithstanding, I was excited to be at this event. Like others raised in the mystical traditions of Sikhi, I have a fondness for the Sufi poets. Baba Bulleh Shah's work precisely echoes the core values of Sikhi—the value of unity and a most personal relationship to the divine. Even more so, the essence of Sufi mysticism, funneled through poetic Punjabi voices, speaks deeply to those like me who exist in that strange in-between state of spiritual/material no-man's land.

Sheba Remy Kharbanda

In happiness nor in sorrow, am I
Neither clean, nor a filthy mire
Not from water, nor from earth
Neither fire, nor from air, is my birth
Bulleh! to me, I am not known

Gathered in the screening room were Punjabis from across the demographic spectrum. For more than three hours I listened to the lyrical, singsong intonations of "proper Punjabi," the kind my elders would speak when in the company of their own. This did not seem to deter those not conversant in the language, for when folk singer Tahira Syed sang a well-known *ghazal*, the words of which I cannot remember, the audience responded with a collective sigh. When one of the guest speakers invited us to transcend the ethnic differences that had come to confine us, concluding his comments in English with the words "God is Love, Love is God," the audience responded in unison. Moments after, I became aware of one of the elders seated to my right—a balding man with a paunch. He had begun to weep. These were not wails of sadness; rather, they were a release from deep within. I knew because I felt the same. At first he was hushed, discreetly wiping his eyes with a rolled-up handkerchief, the kind my father carries to wipe his beard. With this rending of the heart, it is hard to hold back floods of feeling.

My own tears started early, almost upon entering and seating myself in front of an elder *Sardarji* and his son, next to the only other handful of folks in my age group. Definitely Punjabi—but who knows if they were Sikh, Muslim, Hindu, agnostic, or atheist? Having been born in London I am usually more buttoned up in public spaces. My mother's family, displaced from West Punjab in the wake of Partition, left India in the 1950s for stiff-lipped England to remake home. There is, however, an inexplicable solidarity and familiarity in such spaces, one that begins with then stretches beyond common language, history, and heritage. It has to do with a shared heart space, a shared willingness to attune to the divine, to all that is without us—the proof of which we find in openness and a love that the Greeks called *agape*. There is, for me, the rediscovery of soul in these spaces. It is like coming home.

238

I departed the event with a lighter heart, feeling embraced by a global family and glad I had made the trek halfway across the city on a Sunday, when most of the subway seems to be under repair. Upon checking my cell phone, as is the habit of we 24-hour people, I learned of the shootings at the *gurudwara* in Oak Creek, Wisconsin. Perplexed and more than a little fearful, I wondered if this was a case of a disgruntled worshiper going "postal." In the absence of details, and with my mood now unsettled, I sent prayers to the devotees and the shooter and made my way back to Brooklyn.

During that anxious train ride, I reflected on coming to the United States as an adult. As a child, I had briefly lived on the West Coast. The fates had decided it would this time be the East Coast, and on the heels of September 11, 2001. Arriving here at a time when the heart of the city and the entire nation was lost to itself—and, on the other hand, ripe for rediscovery—seemed jarring. There's nothing like the split soul of another—even a nation—to awaken feelings of discordance within one's own soul. Most disturbing was witnessing the sometimes-direct attacks by both government and citizenry on the American Sikh community, not to mention our Muslim brothers and sisters.

Had I made a mistake coming to this country? Those first few months in the United States triggered wounds and memories of my own as well as of my forbears. I recalled the paintings and reliefs that decorated the *langar* hall of our local gurudwara in Southall of Guru Gobind Singh, whose enduring challenge is to uphold the *Khalsa* at all costs. I remembered the stories my mother had raised us on, of the enduring strength of spirit of our Sikh ancestors, of an unswerving commitment to *Chardi Kala*, and of the courageousness of my kin. And yet I felt so far away from it all in those first few years in New York. Instead, my conscious awareness was filled with visions of the American flags positioned very prominently, almost deliberately prominently, in Sikh businesses, in taxis driven by Punjabis, and at the annual Sikh day parade, the flag worn and adorned not with pride but with fear, and as if for protection.

What I had left behind, where I had come from, contrasted in my psyche. Southall, the West London town in which I was raised, had become a home-away-from-home to many displaced Punjabis in the 1960s. Those early days of my family's departure from the subcontinent were difficult ones. My mother cringes over the sacrifices her father was forced to make: "When we arrived in London, we almost didn't recognize him. He did not tell us he had been forced to cut his hair. I think if he had, my mother would have insisted that he return to India immediately." *Papaji* eventually grew his hair back, and he and his generation are in no small part responsible for making it possible to be British and Sikh. My father, a senior member of the Indian Police Service and in active duty during the 1984 pogroms, refused to remove his *dastaar* or go into hiding. He would talk about the lessons his father had taught him about pride in oneself and of unity, of growing up in Peshawar alongside the largely Muslim population who, to him, were family—until Partition came, forcing them to leave for India, never realizing it would be forever.

Much of what Sikhi teaches in the way of honor and duty I have learned from these Singhs. In the days following Oak Creek, when hearts were breaking across a nation reeling from a spate of mass shootings, it occurred to me that it was the women in my family who had taught me about the love that breathes life into Sikhi. As I rode the subway home, these memories and reflections on who I am, where I come from, and where I found myself ran through my mind faster than the F train traversing the tracks between Queens and Brooklyn.

From her, kings are born. From woman, woman is born;
without woman, there would be no one at all.
O Nanak, only the True Lord is without a woman.
—Guru Nanak Dev Ji, Raag Aasaa Mehal 1

When I was three, my mother was my world. We lived in Papaji's suburban West London brick house. Like all the others on the street, the house was painted white, the wooden eaves stained a dark brown or black. Unlike the others on Portland Road, however, Papaji's house was bordered by a beautiful rose garden to which he tended more lovingly than he did his children. That rose garden was perhaps the one redeeming feature in an otherwise uninviting place, home only to those lost in time and space.

I was maybe three when my mother sat me on the ledge that separated my grandfather's rose-garden-bordered home from that of the neighbor and my caretaker, Aunty Carol. Simon, Carol's only son, a man much beloved to me and with whom I loved to play "Simon Says," was holding in his hands a pair of pliers. My mother had one hand wrapped around my right wrist and her index finger—the same one she would point at me in reprimand—wedged under the gold *kara* that had been placed on my wrist when I was a baby and had remained there until that day when Simon took his pliers to them. Three decades on and I can still recall the sound of the metal snapping into two. It would be many years before I'd receive a replacement, this time a simple steel kara purchased by my father at the Manikaran Gurudwara, which is situated between the Beas and Parvati Rivers beneath the majesty of the Himalayan peaks. Though now rusted in places, more gray than silver, it rarely leaves my wrist.

Kabeer, the paper is the prison, and the ink of rituals are the bars on the windows. The stone idols have drowned the world, and the Pandits, the religious scholars, have plundered it on the way . . . Kabeer, I have seen a person, who is as shiny as washed wax. He seems very clever and very virtuous, but in reality, he is without understanding, and corrupt. (Shaloks of Kabeer Ji, Shri Guru Granth Sahib)

My mother would habitually say to us, my brother and I, "God, faith—they reside in the heart. We can practice all the rituals, but if we do not truly believe, if we are not willing to rend the heart, then it is for nothing." She was the family rebel. From a young age, the third daughter and fourth child in a family of seven routinely challenged the authority of my Papaji. My Baby Massi, the eldest of the four daughters and the woman who taught me the *Japji Sahib* and insisted that my cousin Rajan and I recite it with her daily ("Because it is important! It is your culture!"), would say that my mom was

Papaji's favorite. I have heard a hundred times the story of how she snuck off to Paris at age sixteen, under the pretense of staying with a friend, returning the following day with expensive and lavish gifts for everyone. I learned only recently that she was a Rolling Stones fan and that Papaji, believing such music to be the devil's work, prohibited my mother and her siblings from attending concerts. Not one to be swayed by Papaji's word, my mother surreptitiously rented a television with the money she earned doing secretarial work. Every Saturday, from the privacy of her shared bedroom, she'd flick on the rented television and rock out to the Stones and their contemporaries on *Top of the Pops.*

My mother, named Harbinder Kaur Sodhi, according to the traditional birth and naming rituals, opted not to give me the name Kaur. My younger brother was given the name of Jai Singh Kharbanda on his birth certificate and passport. My father, only sometimes present, is Amrik Singh. But I was never made a Kaur. Not officially. With time, I came to understand why. My mother, though already firmly rooted in her heritage when I came along, had not always been secure in the path of Sikhi. When her mother died at the age of fifty, just eight years after leaving her beloved India, my mother lost her faith in *Waheguru.* She felt abandoned by a god that would allow her mother to suffer. It is the only time I have known my mother to be so angry, though I recognize in myself this kind of anger. It is really a wounding, a deep hurt. By the time I was born, faith had been restored, but my mother found herself distanced from the rituals in which she had been raised. For my mother, Waheguru resides in the heart. Chardi Kala is a way to walk in the world. From the way she raised me to be so utterly self-sufficient, I know my mother wants me to know these things principally in my heart.

My mother was twenty when *Biji* died. While I never met her, I know her because she is inside me. I was raised on the milk of her stories and on the fruit of her struggles. I know that my grandmother's was a life bookended by tragedy, from the loss of her own mother in childbirth to the loss of home during Partition and the neglect of a husband too damaged to love her. A talented musician, seamstress, and homeopath, often stifled in her creative expressions by the dictates of the times, she has nevertheless left behind a legacy of beauty, inner strength, and service. I feel her unexpressed words and life-giving energy come through my own art-making. It is as if she breathes life into my moments of truth.

I have come to understand that in her rebelliousness, my mother was expressing the pent-up energies of at least two generations of Kaurs in the bloodline: Biji's and that of Biji's mother. I have inherited this streak of rebellion and devil-may-care. I, too, love rock and roll. I, too, have had my faith in Waheguru tested.

> *This body is softened with the Word of the Guru's Bani; you*
> *shall find peace, doing seva.*
> (Guru Granth Sahib, Siree Raag, First Mehl, Fifth House)

The enduring myth of my grandmother seems to be that she walked a path of giving. When the sister-in-law who had always tormented her was abandoned and left on the street to die, my grandmother took her in, nursed her, cleaned her, and fed her like a defenseless child until she passed. Upon arriving on England's gray shores, well into her forties and reeling from the shock of leaving the motherland, Biji conceded the familiarity of homemaking to take up menial paid work with the rest of the newly migrated workforce. As if a mantra, I can affirm that despite her very scant means in the years following Partition and the move to England, my grandmother insisted on feeding and dressing her children with the best she could afford and make with her own hands. When she could, she would put away small amounts of money to buy gifts for her children such that when she passed, each was left something, though small, to remember her love for them. Remnants of her needlework and black-and-white photos fill boxes in my mother's home. Almost like a ritual practice, I have taken to wearing a pair of gold-and-pearl earrings bought by my mother with Biji's bequeathment.

My mother inherited this way of being in the world. Within the rebel is a humble servant. When Biji died, my mother stepped in as surrogate parent to her fourteen-year-old sister. Though Papaji was still alive, events had instilled a corrosive bitterness in his blood, and he as much as abandoned his children in favor of his roses. My mother would tell us—with more relief and astonishment at the miracles of her Waheguru than regret—that many dinners were eaten at the gurudwara because "money was too short to buy food." She would tell us of how she sold her much-prized Cliff Richard memorabilia collection to buy a winter coat for her youngest sister that first winter after Biji was no more. It was this same kind of selflessness that brought into our home the lost children of friends, family, and strangers . . . sometimes with not-so-benevolent results. What I learned from these women is that you do good not for the promise of a positive return but because you are called from a space deep within your heart, which sometimes does not know human reason. I will ask my mother sometimes if she would have done things differently. "It was as it was meant to be, Rem. We must do what we can," is her usual response.

I carry this awareness, these teachings, in my own practice as an energy worker and intuitive. I have learned, sometimes painfully and with resistance and doubt, that though the dictates of our time negate the value of "we," relegating us to a "me" versus "you" binary, for us to truly know love, our work in the world must be in service of something greater than the individual *I*.

For the sake of it, you journey to sacred shrines and holy rivers,
but this priceless jewel is within your own heart.
—Guru Granth Sahib, Raag Gauree Gwaarayree, First Mehl

The teachings of these women flooded my mind in the wake of the shootings and that continued to gird me through my seeking, questioning, and withholding. I remember hearing those same teachings echoed by elders and young folk alike, in Oak Creek, Wisconsin, as well as across this nation, urging us to keep the heart open, to remember the abiding principles of peace, love, and service. Instead of pointing the finger outward, toward a society that had perhaps not fully embraced us, the challenge was to wake up to how we, as a collective, might have failed the shooter, failed to respond adequately to the desperation and anger with which he was living. The tone was of fortitude, duty, and grace, a reminder of our promise to accept trials like these with Chardi Kala. To remember that there are deeper laws by which we all live.

Yet in those first few days, I found it almost impossible to utter the phrase *nanak naam chardi kala, tere bhane sarbat da bhala.* Just as my mother once shook her fist at Waheguru, I wondered what kind of a god would allow such tragedies. *Still, friends of all stripes were reciting it. I was reading it everywhere, hearing it on network news and even in my sleep. Eventually, beneath the loss, rage, and dislocation, I would see the firm but love-filled faces of my grandmother, mother, and aunt. "Hold peace in your heart" is what I intuited them to say.*

More than once I noted the synchronicity of this tragedy happening within hours of my heart-opening experience with the larger Punjabi family and indeed the world family in Queens. I would feel a calling, emanating from within my chest, to embrace the spoken and unspoken call to live all that I had been taught, and wonder how in Waheguru's name I was going to be able to fulfill it. I would cry tears much less for those lost and more for my own lost self.

In the months that followed, I came to realize that all I know about who I am I have learned from the women in my family, who claimed Sikhi for and in themselves by walking a true path. I recalled all that was lost and sacrificed by these women, ordinary women, immigrant women, ants in an army numbering tens of millions of dispossessed. Women with an abiding faith in something that did not bend to the demands of earthly proof. Women who gave all of themselves, because to not do so was a kind of spiritual death.

I became aware of how I had, until then, taken it for granted that my destiny was to live a life lost at sea, searching for the elusive home. All the while, home had been with me, inside of me, in that inner place that is imperceptible to the outer eye, found only through living in soul and claiming all of who I am.

The lesson I learned from that fateful August day as I was confronted with my Self is that we are not always able to choose the challenges placed before us. By the same coin, the legacies of the women in my family have shown me that we do have a choice in how we respond to the fate handed to us. I learned on that day in August that the choice of all those who walk the path of Sikhi, whether visibly or not, is to choose to with the knowledge that there is a greater rhyme and reason to our lives, even if we cannot always perceive the *why*. The lesson I learned is that to live the spirit of Chardi Kala is to thrive in a life that walks with love as a guiding force.

> *We have only to follow the thread of the hero path.*
> *And where we had thought to find an abomination,*
> *we shall find a God.*
> *And where we had thought to slay another,*
> *we shall slay ourselves.*
> *And where we had thought to travel outward,*
> *we shall come to the center of our own existence.*
> *And where we had thought to be alone,*
> *we shall be with all the world.*
> (Joseph Campbell)

Appendix A
Brief Summary of Sikhism

In the sixteenth century in Punjab, India, Guru Nanak Dev Ji, the founder of Sikhism, laid the framework for Sikhism with one simple message: "*Ek Ong Kar.*" We, everyone here on Earth (including humans, animals, and plants), are created by one Divine Power.

At the time, India was plagued by the caste system, ongoing religious conflicts, and religious persecutions, so Guru Nanak's presence and message were both powerful for his seekers and threatening to the status quo. Through his own actions, Guru Nanak Dev Ji demonstrated how to experience *Waheguru* (God) within one's self. By experiencing Waheguru within, Sikhs became protectors of justice, truth, and human rights for those who cannot advocate for themselves. Sikhs throughout the world continue to uphold this social and civic duty.

Guru Nanak Dev Ji's three golden rules include:

nam japna: *To meditate on God's Name and continuously remember God's Name with every breath throughout the day.*

dharam di kirat karni: *To work and earn an honest living through honest efforts and relationships, and to live a full family life.*

vand ki chakna: *To share the fruits of one's labor with others before considering oneself; to live as an inspiration and a support to the entire community.*

Guru Nanak Dev Ji's teachings were reiterated and reinforced through the teachings of the ten Sikh Gurus that followed him. The final Guru, the Guru Granth Sahib, embodies the *joth* (light) of love, truth, and knowledge. This light lives on as the guide for Sikhs in the world today.

Appendix B
Explanation of the Name *Kaur*

Women experienced severe hardship in India during the sixteenth century. Stripped of civil and human rights, they were held hostage to the decision-making of others. They were subject to *sati*, a custom that forced a married woman to burn herself to death in the funeral pyre of her husband; *purda*, another custom that required women to wear a veil; and to the caste system, which assigned socioeconomic status and worth to an individual according to family lineage. In addition, they were denied any status as spiritual seekers, thinkers, or decision-makers in all realms of life. The Sikh Gurus erased these chokeholds on women and granted them equal status to men.

The name *Kaur* was given to Sikh women by Guru Gobind Singh, the tenth Sikh Guru, when he created the *Khalsa* in 1699. The Khalsa is a community of people with pure consciousness. Guru Gobind Singh derived *Kaur* from the Sanskrit word *Kumgra*, which means "Prince." He then took the Punjabi word *Kuwari*, which means unmarried or single girl, combined the two words, and came up with *Kaur*, a term meaning "spiritual princess," which applies to both unmarried and married Sikh women today.

By designating them as Kaurs, Guru Gobind Singh empowered Sikh women and provided them an eternal connection to the Khalsa lineage, the spiritual line of the Sikh Gurus. *Kaur* also signals that a Sikh woman is equal to a man according to the Sikh principle.

of equality. Kaurs are imbued with all rights that are accorded to men as spiritual seekers, readers of Sikh scriptures, and pursuers of knowledge and education and leadership in domestic and public spaces. *Kaur* ensures that a woman is not judged according to the caste system or typecast according to her family name. Sikhs as a community, like the rest of the world, are still working towards the Gurus' vision of humane and just treatment of women.

The Kaur legacy brings a poise and wisdom to Sikh women, empowering them to live in the world as spiritual royalty, understanding they are equals with all women and men across communities and cultures. Some Sikh women today choose to take *Kaur* as their name and legacy. It is a choice they can make. *Kaur* means they are neither superior nor inferior to anyone, and they have a duty to contribute to the world in meaningful and purposeful ways.

Sikh American women are positively engaged in society today. Balancing work and personal commitments, demolishing stereotypes, and bringing awareness, they have created their own space in the social fabric while making a difference in the world. In *Her Name Is Kaur* they speak out as wives, mothers, daughters, daughters-in-law, sisters, friends, professionals, and community members, and provide a glimpse into their struggles and triumphs. Their spirit is strong. Their stories are inspirational.

Glossary

akal—Means "timeless."

Akal Takhat—Means "Throne of the Immortal," and is the highest political institution of the Sikhs. The Akal Takhat is an impressive building that sits directly in front of the causeway leading to the Golden Temple in Amritsar, Punjab, India. The Akal Takhat was founded by Guru Hargobind on June 15, 1606, and was established as the place from which the spiritual and temporal concerns of the Sikh community could be acted upon.

amrit—Means "nectar." Amrit is composed of water and sugar and is stirred with a double-edged sword (see *khanda*, below) while prayers are said. Initiation into the Khalsa domain involves the drinking amrit, holy water, used in Sikh initiation ceremonies.

Amrit Vela—The "ambrosial" period, 3 a.m.–6 a.m., when prayers can be recited. Guru Nanak urged his disciples to get up at this auspicious time and chant and meditate on God.

Amritdhari—Refers to a Sikh who has been initiated as a Khalsa by taking amrit. "Dhari" means "practitioner" or "endowed with." So an Amritdhari is one who has received baptismal vows of the Khalsa, initiated by Guru Gobind Singh on March 30, 1699. He or she abides by these vows and follows the *panj kakari rahit* (rules of wearing the Five kakkars), which are: *kesh* (long, unshorn hair, and for men, also an uncut beard), *kangha* (a comb to keep the hair tidy), *kirpan* (a sword), *kara* (a steel bracelet worn about the wrist), and *kaccha* (a short undergarment).

Amritsar—The spiritual center for the Sikh religion and the administrative headquarters of the Amritsar district in the state of Punjab. It is home to the Harmandir Sahib (referred to as the "Golden Temple" in the Western media), the spiritual and cultural center for the Sikh religion. This important Sikh shrine attracts more visitors than the Taj Mahal—more than 100,000 visitors on weekdays alone—and is the most popular destination for Non-resident Indians (NRI) in the whole of India.

Anandpur Sahib—The City of Bliss; one of the holiest places of the Sikhs, second only to Amritsar. Anandpur is framed between the Shivalik Hills to the east and the Sutlej River farther away to the west, with vast green expanses and profound tranquility all around.

Ardas—A humble request or supplicatory prayer.

Asa Di Var—Song of Hope; a set of hymns sung in early morning.

Bani—Refers to the utterances and writings of the Sikh Gurus.

Babaji—God.

Bari Nani—Maternal grandmother.

Baytay—Means "beloved child."

Bhai Sahib—Means "brother."

Bhaktas—Also known as Bhagats. Refers to a holy person who leads a life of spirituality and dedication to God.

bhangra—A dance that celebrates the harvest and is associated with the festival of Baisakhi (April 13), when the sight of tall heaps of golden wheat fill the farmer's heart with joy. Bhangra music is based around the catchy sound of large drums called *dhols*. The farmer and his fellow villagers circle round and round in a leaping, laughing caper. It's a dance that cuts across all divisions of class and education. To *pao* the bhangra is to dance to this music, which is traditionally performed during harvest festivals and weddings.

Bhattan di Bani—Verses written in honor of the Gurus by bards known as the Bhatts.

Glossary

bhua—Paternal aunt.

Biji—Grandmother.

boliyan—Usually a boli is sung and introduced by one woman and then the other girls form a chorus. Boliyan are usually passed down orally, generation by generation.

cha—Tea. Tea vendors are *cha-valas*.

chaat masala—A masala used in Indian and Pakistani cuisine. It typically consists of amchoor (dried mango powder), cumin, kala namak (black salt), coriander, dried ginger, salt, black pepper, asafoetida (*hing*), and chili powder.

Chacha—An uncle, specifically the father's little brother.

Chachi—An aunt, specifically the father's youngest brother's wife.

Chardi Kala—An important expression used in Sikhism for a frame of mind that a Sikh has to accept and practice. It loosely means a "positive, buoyant, and optimistic" attitude toward life and the future. It calls for Sikhs to always be in "high spirits," "ever progressive," and "always cheerful." It reflects the eternally evergreen and blissful mental state of a Sikh.

Charni Lagna—A coming-of-age ceremony where either a young Sikh man or woman (12–18) reads publicly from the Guru Granth Sahib, the Sikh scriptures.

chhap—Imprint. Stamp.

Chhote Sahibzade—Means "Younger Princes," and refers to the two younger sons of Guru Gobind Singh, the tenth Sikh Guru.

chola—A long robe.

chonkri marke—Refers to sitting in the lotus position, cross-legged.

chunni—A multipurpose scarf that is essential to many South Asian women's suits and matches the woman's garments.

Daadi Ji—Paternal grandmother.

Darbar Sahib—Also known as the Darbar Hall. Refers to the Main Hall within a Sikh gurudwara. It also refers to the central building at Harmandir Sahib, Amritsar. "Darbar" means "court"; the terms together refer to the Guru's Court.

Darji—A term of endearment for a grandfather. It can also refer to a tailor or a carpenter.

Darshani Deori—Means "the doors where you meet Waheguru." Darshani Deori is the entrance that leads to the pathway into Harmandir Sahib, the Golden Temple, in Amritsar.

dastaar—Turban or headdress worn by both men and women.

desi—Indian from South Asia.

dhaari—Beard.

Dhadi Ji—Paternal grandmother.

dharma—Spirituality or morality.

dhobis—Washerman or woman.

dholki—A two-headed hand drum.

diwan—A religious event or gathering. This word was mostly used by the ancient kings.

dumala—Turban.

garhi—Small fortress or fortified house.

gathra—A strap, usually made from cloth, used to wear the *kirpan*, one of the Sikh articles of faith, around the neck and shoulder. The gathra allows the kirpan to be suspended near one's waist or tucked inside one's belt.

ghazal—A poetic form consisting of rhyming couplets and a refrain. Each line must share the same meter.

giddha—A popular folk dance performed by women in Punjab, which exhibits teasing, fun, and the exuberance of Punjabi life. The dance is derived from the ancient ring dance and is just as energetic as bhangra; at the same time, it manages to creatively display feminine grace, elegance, and elasticity.

Glossary

granthi—A ceremonial reader of the Guru Granth Sahib. Duties include arranging daily religious services, reading from the Sikh scripture, maintaining the gurudwara premises, and teaching and advising community members. A granthi is not equivalent to a minister, as there are no such religious intermediaries in the Sikh religious tradition.

gur—A traditional unprocessed or raw sugar, also known as jaggery, used in many delicacies.

gurbani—The revealed wisdom of the Sikh Gurus in their own words, found in the Guru Granth Sahib; the devotional songs of the Gurus.

Gurmantar—Religious chant or mantra where "Waheguru" is repeated.

Gurmat—Liberation from the cycles of birth and death.

Gurmukhi—The script used in writing primarily the Punjabi (and, secondarily, the Sindhi) language. It is used in the Sikh scripture and in contemporary India.

Gurpurab—A Sikh religious festival; literally, Day of the Guru.

Guru—Teacher; one who takes you from darkness to light.

Guru Arjan Dev Ji—The fifth Sikh Guru, who among many achievements compiled hymns into the Guru Granth Sahib and authored *Sukhmani Sahib*, the prayer of peace.

Guru Gobind Singh—The tenth Sikh Guru, born Gobind Rai. He infused the spirit of both saint and soldier in the minds and hearts of his followers in order to fight oppression; restore justice, peace, and righteousness; and uplift the downtrodden people of the world. It is said that after the martyrdom of his father, Guru Tegh Bahadur, the tenth Master declared that he would create a *panth* (community/ society) that would challenge the tyrant rulers in every walk of life to restore justice, equality, and peace for all of mankind. Unlike many other prophets, he never called himself God or "the only son of God." Instead he referred to all people as the sons of God, sharing His Kingdom equally. For himself, he used "slave" or "servant of God."

Guru Granth Sahib—Sikh holy text, which spans 1,430 pages and contains the words spoken by the founders of the Sikh religion (the

Ten Gurus of Sikhism), as well as the words of various other saints from other religions, including Hinduism and Islam.

Guru Nanak Dev Ji—The founder of the religion of Sikhism and the first of the Sikh Gurus. Guru Nanak traveled far and wide teaching people the message of one God who dwells in every one of God's creations and constitutes the eternal Truth. He set up a unique spiritual, social, and political platform based on equality, fraternity love, goodness, and virtue. It is part of Sikh religious belief that the spirit of Guru Nanak's sanctity, divinity, and religious authority descended upon each of the nine subsequent Gurus when the Guruship was devolved onto them.

gurudwara/gurdwara—Literally "Home of the Guru." Any building or room dedicated to housing the devotional songs of the Guru for the purpose of spiritual practice; a Khalsa training institution, open to anyone, which provides communication, food, and shelter to travelers and the needy.

Guruji—God.

gutka/gootka—A small missal or breviary containing chosen hymns or prayers from Sikh scriptures.

haldi—Turmeric.

Hukam—Divine will or a decree by a high authority. Hukam can also refer to a passage from the Guru Granth Sahib, selected by randomly opening the Sikh scripture during a daily ceremony. The passage is considered by Sikhs to be the divine "command of the Guru" for the day.

ishnaan seva—A community service act of washing

Japji Sahib—Morning prayer or the first composition in the Guru Granth Sahib.

jugnu—Fireflies.

kakkars—The five articles of faith worn by all baptized Sikhs. Many non-baptized Sikhs also begin on the path of Sikhi by wearing some or all of these Sikh symbols. The baptized Sikhs both male and female are required to wear a uniform to unify and bind them to their commitment to the true, universal, social, and temporal principles defined and amplified by the ten Sikh Gurus and laid down in the Guru Granth Sahib. This commitment was publicly announced, made prominent, and confirmed by Guru Gobind Singh in 1699 at the Vaisakhi gathering.

kannat—Tent wall.

kara—A steel slave bangle is one of five articles of faith, collectively called *kakkars*, that form the external symbols of one's commitment and dedication to the order (Hukam) of the tenth master and to becoming a member of the Khalsa. The kara is to constantly remind Sikhs that whatever they do with their hands, those actions must be in keeping with the advice given by the Guru.

katha—Religious story or discourse.

keralae—Bitter melon cooked into a dish for dinner.

kesari kapra—Saffron-colored cloth.

kesh—Long, uncut hair; one of the five articles of faith for Sikhs.

keths—Farms.

Khalsa—Belonging only to the divine. The collective body of all initiated Sikhs, who drink the amrit instituted by Guru Gobind Singh, and agree to live by the highest ideals of Sikh principles. Committed to one's own purity of consciousness and actions.

Khalsa Panth—Belonging to the community that is committed to purity of consciousness and actions.

khanda—A double-edged sword; the Sikh nation's symbol.

kirpan—A four-inch, curved, ceremonial dagger that Sikh men and women are obliged to wear at all times.

kirtan—Sikh devotional music that originated in the Hindu tradition as loving songs sung to God. Kirtan also refers to the singing of the Sacred Hymns from the Guru Granth Sahib accompanied by music. The Sikhs place huge value on this type of singing, and a Sikh is expected to listen to and/or sing Guru-Kirtan as frequently as possible.

Kirtan Sohila—The nighttime prayer said by all Sikhs before they go to sleep.

kuri/kuriye—Girl/girls.

kurta—A loose, collarless shirt worn by people from South Asia.

langar—A community kitchen; also refers to the devotional meal eaten by the congregation as part of the religious service. Langar is free and open to all, regardless of religious background. It is an illustration of putting into practice the Sikh belief in the equality of all humanity, and the rejection of the Hindu caste system, which forbade people of different castes from eating together. The community kitchen is located in the Langar Hall.

lengha—A long skirt with a top and coordinating shawl.

maasi—Maternal aunt.

Maharani Jindan Kaur—The youngest wife of the first Maharaja of the Sikh Empire, Ranjit Singh, and the mother of the last Maharaja, Duleep Singh. She was renowned for her beauty, energy and strength of purpose and was popularly known as Rani Jindan, but her fame is derived chiefly from the fear she engendered in the British in India, who described her as "the Messalina of the Punjab."

Mai Bhago—A Sikh woman who led forty Sikh soldiers against the Mughals in 1705. She killed several enemy soldiers on the battlefield, and has been considered a saint-warrior by the Sikh Nation for more than three hundred years.

Mala—Rosary beads, made out of various materials: steel, iron, glass, etc.

Mamaji—Maternal uncle.

Manji—Religious leadership organized by Guru Amar Dasii, the third Guru.

maryada—Tradition.

Ma Shakti—Shakti is the concept, or personification, of divine feminine creative power, sometimes referred to as "The Great Divine Mother" in Hinduism.

massard—Maternal brother-in-law.

Mata Gujri—The wife of the ninth Sikh Guru, Guru Tegh Bahadur; the mother of the tenth and last human Sikh Guru, Guru Gobind Singh; and the grandmother of the four Sahibzade.

Mata Ji—Mother

matha tayk—Refers to bowing down and touching the floor with one's forehead; bowing to the Guru.

Matter paneer—Peas and cheese.

Maya—A veil or curtain concealing reality; illusion.

mehndi—Henna that is typically applied to women's hands and feet for weddings.

Moh—An illusion of worldly love and attachment.

Mool Mantar—A brief composition encompassing the entire universally complex theology of the Sikh faith. It has religious, social, political, logical, martial, and spiritual implications for human existence, and is a truly humanitarian and global concept of the Supreme power for all to understand and appreciate.

Naam—Conveys the message of the need to remember God (the Creator) by repeating and focusing the mind on His Name and Identity. The names given to God primarily refer to the attributes of the Almighty and His various qualities.

Nan—Term of endearment for a mother's friend.

Naniji—Maternal grandmother.

nitnem—Daily prayers.

paath—From the Sanskrit *patha*, which means "reading" or "recitation," this term, in the religious context, means reading or recitation of the holy texts and refers to the recitation of gurbani. Recitation may be done alone (with others listening) or as a group; it can include just one Bani, or section, of the Guru Granth Sahib, or the complete Holy Granth.

pagh—Turban.

pakhi—Fan.

palki—Altar upon which the Guru Granth Sahib is placed.

Panj Pyare—The Five Beloved Ones; the five who answered Guru Gobind Singh Ji's call for five Sikhs who were willing to give "their heads" for the faith.

papaji—Father.

Paramatma—Absolute Soul; another way to describe God.

Parkarma—Means both "circumambulatory," as in the act of circumambulation, and to circumambulate by walking clockwise around a sacred altar, holy shrine, or other place of pilgrimage while turning in a circular manner.

parsad—A sacred sweet porridge that delivers Waheguru's blessing by eating it—similar to the wafer in Catholic church.

patka—A man's head covering consisting of a small piece of cloth wrapped around the head; worn especially by Sikh boys or young men.

phere—This is in reference to the wedding ceremony, where a Sikh couple circles around the Guru Granth Sahib four times for the marriage union. The *phere* is the round taken around the scriptures.

phuphards—In a brother and sister relationship, the sister's husband is a phupard.

pinds—Villages.

prakaash—A ceremony that involves installation of the Guru Granth Sahib, the holy book for Sikhs, onto a religious platform for the day.

parshad—A sweet vegetarian pudding that is offered to all visitors to the Darbar Sahib in a gurudwara. Kara parshad is made from equal parts, by weight, of flour, ghee (clarified butter), water, and gur (raw sugar); it is understood to be a blessing from the Guru and should not be refused.

prontay—Special Indian bread made from stone-ground, wholemeal flour that is layered like a croissant and can be stuffed with cheese, vegetables, or meats.

purdah—Ancient Hindu and Islamic custom of covering a woman's face.

qawalis—A form of Sufi devotional music.

ragi—Performer of Sikh religious hymns.

rakha—In care of Waheguru.

rarak—Irritation (like that caused by grit in the eye).

rehat—Code of conduct and rules for practicing Sikhs.

Rehras Sahib—The evening prayer of the Sikhs, which speaks of the greatness of Waheguru.

rickshaw-valas—Rickshaw drivers.

roti—Indian bread made of stone-ground, whole-meal flour.

saakhis—Stories of the Sikh Gurus.

salvar kameez—Traditional style of dress worn by both women and men in India and other South Asian countries. It is also known as a "Punjabi suit" because it is believed to have originated in the Punjab state in India and Pakistan. The garment is made up of two separate parts. *Salvar* refers to the trouser-like lower garment, and *kameez* refers to the shirt or tunic-like top garment.

salwaar kameezes—A long tunic and tailored pants with a matching head scarf. Worn for social functions and to gurudwara and comes in various color and fashion trends.

samskara—The imprints left on the subconscious mind by experience in this or previous lives, which then color all of life, one's nature, responses, states of mind, etc.

sangat—The Gurus taught that living in the company of the "holy" is a way to be closer to God or Waheguru. Sangat is the idea that a group offers spiritual support to its members; Sadh Sangat is the company of Holy people who are completely dedicated to Waheguru and who all aspire to the concept of dharam (the elevation of the person to a higher and better level of understanding of righteousness and Gurmat).

Sangeet—a Punjabi term used to refer to any type of classical or traditional singing.

sardar—Respectful title for a Sikh male; literally, "Chieftain."

saroop—Refers to the outward appearance of the Sikhs, especially their tenet of leaving their hair unshorn.

sarovar—Sacred pool of water. The most prominent Sikh Temple is the Harimander Sahib in Amritsar. A very large pool, or sarovar, surrounds the central temple building. The devotees who visit these shrines will bathe in these pools, as the Sikhs believe that spiritual and worldly benefits are gained by immersion in these holy waters.

Sat Naam—Means "true name."

sati—Refers to an ancient Hindu practice, prevalent during the time of Guru Nanak, when the widow(s) of a deceased Hindu would throw themselves, voluntarily or forcibly, onto their husband's funeral pyre. Along with force, social pressure and drugs were also used to assure the continuance of this practice, as a Hindu widow's life in old India was nothing for a woman to look forward to. A widow who survived had to do all the worst tasks in the household, and was not allowed to wear colored clothes or participate in festivities. Remarriage was banned, and the widow's *karma* (evil done by her in a past life) was presented by the rest of the family as the reason why her husband had died.

Sat Sri Akal—A common Sikh greeting, meaning, "God is True and Timeless."

sawari—Processional.

Sehaj—State of equipoise; goal of how Sikhs should live their lives.

seva—Community service, a central aspect of Sikh theology; selfless service, which is believed to bring one closer to God.

sevadar—A volunteer who offers his/her services to a gurudwara or to the community. It refers to a person who performs *seva* (work, service, or assistance of any kind) purely because of his/her dedication to Guru and God, and as part of his/her duty to the Sikh community.

shabad—A sacred Sikh hymn from the Sikh scriptures. *Shabad-kirtan*—hymn-singing—was the earliest form of devotion for the Sikhs.

shaheed—Person who suffers and endures death on behalf of a belief or faith. One who engages in *shaheedi* (martyrdom).

Sikhi—Sikhism.

simarna—Rosary or prayer beads.

simran—Refers to the remembrance of God by repetition or recital of His Name.

sindhoor—A red, powder-like substance that Hindu women typically put on their foreheads close to the hairline to proclaim their marital status.

Sohni Mahiwal—A tragic love story that subverts the classical motif of Hero and Leader. Here, the heroine Sohni, unhappily married to a man whom she despises, swims every night across the river to where her beloved Mehar herds buffalo. One night her sister-in-law replaces the earthenware pot that Sohni uses to keep afloat with a vessel of unbaked clay, which dissolves in the water. Sohni dies in the whirling currents of the river.

Soniye—Pretty girl.

Sphere—The physical rounds the bride and groom take around the Sikh scriptures to solidify the spiritual marriage of two people.

Suhi—An India musical *raga* (composition) that appears in the Sikh tradition from northern India and is part of the Sikh holy scripture.

sukh—Peace or bliss.

Sukhmani Sahib—Song of Peace, written by Guru Arjan Dev Ji, the fifth Guru.

Surya Namaskara—Sun salutations.

tabiya—The seating space behind the altar that displays the Guru Granth Sahib.

tablas—Indian drums.

tanpura—Indian string instrument.

tonga—A light, two-wheeled, horse-drawn vehicle used in India.

Tosha Khana—Treasury.

Waheguru—God.

Acknowledgments

These stories are released into the world to celebrate our greatest human and spiritual capacity: *daya*, our limitless compassion, and *pyaar*, the love we have for ourselves, our families, our communities, and the world. Many thanks for the collaboration and support of the following:

Waheguru, the Sikh Gurus, Sikh history, Banjot S. Chanana, Benanti Kaur, Sidak Singh, Xoitsal Villaneuva, Dhanna S. Malhi, Harsha Malhi, Ripan Malhi, Alison Bell, Aksha Bedi, Charan Chanana, Rajinder Chanana, Jasmin Chanana, Dipika Chanana, and Parminder Dhillon.

The Sikh Love Stories Editorial Board: Sangeeta K. Luthra, Jessi Kaur, and Simran Kaur.

Cover artist Rupy Cheema Tut, editorial intern Tanveer Bhaurla, foreword author Nikky-Guninder Kaur Singh, poet Preeti Kaur, Sikh Love Stories Men's Collection Editor Winty Singh, The Sikh Love Stories Women's Collection writers, She Writes Press Publisher Brooke Warner, Hedgebrook, Sikh Lens Director Bicky Singh, InshAllah co-editors Ayesha Mattu and Nura Maznavi, The Bay Area Sikh Community, SAFAR, The Sikh Family Center, The Sikh Coalition, The Sikh Advocates Academy, *Hyphen* Magazine, The Sikh Spirit Foundation, Simranjeet Singh, Erika Martinez,

Gurpreet Bindra, Jalmeen Arora, Anu Kaur, Harrup Kaur, Deepa Sethi, Reshma Kaur, Naheed Hasnat, Simran Kaur Dang, Sarah Zacharias, Sargun Kaur, Gurleen Kaur, Jasleen Kaur, Jennifer Soloway, Sara Campos, Harmeet K. Dhillon, Melanie Hilario, Sam Sattin, Elmaz Abinader, Victor LaValle, Kirsten Saxton, Ruth Saxton, Minal Hajratwala, Daisy Hernandez, Kirpa Kaur, Rahuldeep Singh, Pashaura Singh, Harpreet Kaur, Sapreet Kaur, Valarie Kaur, Neha Singh Gohil, Anisha Mishra, Deepika Shah Malu Trehan, Meghan Ward, and Amy Kessel.

Special thanks to SikhiWikhi (www.sikhiwikhi.org) for providing precise explanations of all customs related to Sikhism.

About the Contributors

A. Kaur grew up watching the same classic Disney movies you did, thinking Prince Charming was an inevitable simplicity that comes with the future. She went through an awkward middle school phase with restless thoughts of why periods and boys always seemed to dampen her confidence. Some time after that, she let Sikhi into her life as a concept bigger and more significant than the begrudging Sunday Punjabi school routine. At age twenty-two, with the whirlwind of childhood and college barely settling down, and the future of "career" and grad school setting in, the only thing she's sure of in life is her love of chocolate soufflés and her thick thighs.

Anu Kaur is a Registered Dietitian Nutritionist, Certified Wellness Coach, and Registered Yoga Teacher. She is a nationally selected Diversity Leader and past recipient of the Emerging Dietetic Leadership Award from the Academy of Nutrition and Dietetics. Anu has served on several professional boards and has a private practice. Anu counsels and coaches individuals for optimal nutrition and wellness while integrating a mind-body-spirit approach. She lives with her family in the greater Washington, DC, Metropolitan area close to a local farm, and she enjoys gardening.

Anu also loves to sculpt, write, and jog, and she thrives when she is part of a community.

Gunisha Kaur is a physician and human rights activist. She earned her BS from Cornell University and her MD from Cornell University Medical College, and is now a part of the New York-Presbyterian/ Columbia University Medical Center and New York-Presbyterian/ Weill Cornell Medical Center in the Department of Anesthesiology. She will be pursuing a degree in medical anthropology from Harvard University with the goal of applying medicine to human rights work. Gunisha has written extensively on social justice issues in Punjab; her first book detailing and documenting human rights violations is titled *Lost in History: 1984 Reconstructed.*

Gurleen Kaur is a third-year student at UC Berkeley studying Society and Environment for a career in city planning and public health. She wants to design the physical spaces that we can live and enjoy our lives in. In her journey of life, she pursues a critical thought framework that also recognizes love in all humans and things. She recognizes the imperfectness of her own being and continues to strive towards humility.

Gurpreet Kaur is a Family Medicine physician who specializes in Hospice & Palliative Medicine. She furthered her postdoctoral education with a mini-fellowship in Ethno Geriatrics from the Stanford Geriatric Education Center. She lives in the Bay Area with her husband and her twin children and is passionate about being involved in local professional, school, and community events. She serves on the local domestic violence and wellness committees. She is a cofounder and serves on the board of directors of the Sikh Family Center, a nonprofit organization that aims to promote healthy families in the Sikh American community by closing current gaps in access to resources and increasing community awareness and activism.

Harbani Ahuja is a student at the Benjamin N. Cardozo School of Law in New York City, where she is pursuing her passions for international human rights, public service, and law. She has been involved in multiple legal and advocacy NGO efforts in the United States and abroad, with a focus on human rights, Sikh rights, and gender discrimination. Harbani is an avid blogger, graphic designer, and cake decorator. As an aspiring attorney, writer, and educator, she hopes to advocate for Guru Nanak's social vision of equality. Harbani holds a Bachelor of Business Administration in Economics from Macaulay Honors College at Baruch College.

Harleen Kaur is a junior at the University of Michigan in Ann Arbor. She is concentrating in English with a minor in Community Action and Social Change. Her goal is to eventually work in the nonprofit sector to advocate for the civil rights minority groups in the United States through community outreach. Harleen is the president of her Sikh Student Association, works as a Volunteer Advocate with the Sikh Coalition, and spends the majority of her free time as a counselor and teacher at Sikh camps around the United States.

Harsohena Kaur is a Sikh by birth, belief, and practice. She grew up in India and moved to the United States in her twenties when she married her husband, Jasjit Singh Ahluwalia. She has a thirteen-year-old son, Ikbal, and an eleven-year-old daughter, Jaitsiri, both of whom she is raising as Sikhs. Harsohena is a pediatrician. She has been writing poems and essays off and on since she was in her teens. She also loves to read and garden.

Jalmeen Arora PhD is a Licensed Clinical Psychologist who resides in Northern California with her husband and two children. She has been practicing for more than fifteen years; she specializes in women's issues, and has expertise in treating eating disorders and trauma. Jalmeen feels passionately about helping others find their inner wisdom to transform and create deeply fulfilling lives. Jalmeen graduated cum laude with a BA in Psychology from Washington University in St. Louis, Missouri, and earned her PhD in Clinical Psychology from George Mason University in Alexandria, Virginia. Presently, she works part time in her private practice in Lafayette, California. With the remainder of her time, Jalmeen is actively involved in her school community, the local Sikh community, and her professional community, hoping to positively impact her environment.

Jasminder Kaur originally hails from Singapore. She completed a BS in Sociology & Women's Studies at the University of Manchester, United Kingdom. Thereafter she returned to Singapore and worked as a Written & Language Arts Teacher, where, among other things, she taught five-year-olds Shakespeare through visual arts and drama. She relocated to the United States in 2002. Jasminder is currently completing the fifth year of the PhD in African Diaspora Studies program at UC Berkeley. Her dissertation focuses on unraveling the crossings between the fields of visual culture, diaspora, and queer theory. She currently resides in Miami with her partner and their beloved furry feline, where she is completing her doctorate while also teaching at Florida International University.

Jessi Kaur is the author of *The Enchanted Garden of Talwandi*, *Dear Takuya . . . Letters of a Sikh Boy*, and *The Royal Falcon*, three highly acclaimed children's books. She is the editor of Sikhpoint (www. sikhpoint.com), a Sikh-centric Web magazine. A theater aficionado, Jessi produced *The Royal Falcon Musical*, a show that won accolades as the first ever Sikh musical of its kind. She has traveled extensively to deliver workshops and seminars, speak at Sikh youth camps, and represent the Sikh tradition and culture in several interfaith and multicultural festivals, including the Parliament of the World's Religions in Barcelona and Melbourne and the Smithsonian Folklife festival in Washington, DC. She is serving her second term as Fine Arts Commissioner for the city of Cupertino, California, and is on the Sikh Love Stories Project editorial board.

Manbeena Kaur was born in San Francisco, California, but has lived most of her life in Fort Worth, Texas. She joined the Sikh Coalition team as Operations Manager in 2006. Since then she has been promoted to Education Director, a new position at the coalition. The education program seeks to create a positive image and foster appreciation for Sikhs around the country by engaging in nationwide and community-based educational initiatives. With a BS in Elementary Education from the University of Texas at Austin, Manbeena has taught in Texas and New York. Manbeena has also worked at the American Embassy School in New Delhi. She has previously served in various leadership roles, including serving on the planning committee for the Surat Sikh Conference for three years and organizing various youth focused projects in Texas and New York.

Mandeep Kaur and Neesha Kaur. Mandeep grew up in a small town in California. A recent college graduate, Mandeep is pursuing a graduate degree in environmental health and is passionate about addressing health inequity. She enjoys discussions about social justice and writing in her spare time. Neesha was also born and raised in a small town in California. Upon graduating college, Neesha began working in the field of health research and wants to address women's health in underserved communities. Neesha also enjoys cooking, and she hopes to one day run her own fusion cuisine restaurant.

Manpreet Singh earned her MD at Michigan State University and her MS at University of Michigan. She completed a combined residency in Pediatrics, Psychiatry, and Child and Adolescent Psychiatry at Cincinnati Children's Hospital Medical Center. After two years of neuroimaging training at the Center for Interdisciplinary Brain Sciences Research at Stanford University, she joined the faculty at Stanford in 2009; she currently serves as Assistant Professor in the Department of Psychiatry and Behavioral Sciences and as the Director of the Pediatric Mood Disorders Program at Stanford University School of Medicine.

Prabhjot K. Ahluwalia was born in India, and has lived in the United States since age six. She attended the University of Maryland and has degrees in Chemistry and Secondary Education. She is currently working part time as a math and science substitute teacher for middle and high schools in California. Sikhi has always played a major role in Prabhjot's life, and she uses Sikhi as a guiding light or compass. She and her husband try to instill that same Sikh pride and strength in their two daughters. Prabhjot loves to read, hike, bike with her family, and travel. She currently lives with her family in Danville, California.

Puneet Kaur Sahota is a Sikh American anthropologist, physician, wife, and mother. Puneet grew up in St. Louis, Missouri, and has also spent time living and working in the Southwestern United States, where she has conducted research in partnership with Native American communities. She currently lives in Philadelphia, Pennsylvania, with her husband and son.

Sangeeta K. Luthra is an anthropologist and educator. She has taught classes in cultural anthropology, gender studies, and cultural studies, and has written about women's empowerment, workplace literacy, microlending, and sustainable development with a special focus on nongovernmental organizations in urban northern India. Sangeeta's current research seeks to understand the cultural and social experiences of Sikh Americans through an analysis of community spaces, institution building, and transnationalism. In addition to teaching and research, Sangeeta is a member of the editorial board of the Sikh Love Stories Project and an advisor to the Kaur Foundation. Currently Sangeeta is teaching at Santa Clara University as an adjunct faculty member in the Anthropology Department.

Sargun Kaur is a fresh UC Berkeley graduate who is hoping to get around to saving the world with a Computer Science degree in hand. She attributes her great wit in a large part to Lorelai and Rory Gilmore. She is a lover of good food, but her staple diet largely consists of bread, cheese, and cookie dough. You can call her an "artist," if using the word in loose terms, as she enjoys to create and work in many different mediums including charcoal, watercolor pencil, java and python code, photography, and now words. If you ever run into her on the streets of Berkeley, please approach her and say something more substantial than hello, as she is horribly averse to and incapable of small talk. Some helpful topics include women's empowerment, Karl Marx, and Harry Potter.

SatJot Kaur was born and raised in Los Angeles, where she lives now with her husband and daughter. She has a BA in Spanish from the University of San Diego and an MA in Science in Teaching from Pace University. She works part time at a langar charity called Khalsa Peace Corps, feeding the local community and needy around LA. She plays kirtan regularly at Guru Ram Das Ashram. In her spare time she enjoys spending time with her family and sangat members, going to the beach, exploring different parts of LA and its surrounding areas, and having spontaneous dance parties with her daughter everywhere and anywhere.

Sheba Remy Kharbanda is a metaphysician, filmmaker, and storyteller born in London and now residing in Brooklyn, New York. Kharbanda first discovered the power of storytelling and oral testimony during her time as a human rights researcher with Amnesty International, where she monitored the human fallout of the United States government's War on Terror. She later cofounded a research collaborative dedicated to working with grassroots groups in New York and beyond on shifting policy and practices related to immigration, law enforcement, and violence against women. In 2005, she launched the Vilayati Tarti/Foreign Land Project, a documentary film and online oral history archive that chronicles the stories of elder women from the Punjab, who, in the decades following the Partition of India, left the subcontinent for England. On the heels of this work, Kharbanda began her journey into metaphysics and currently maintains a practice in Brooklyn. She is also cofounder of Callejero Films Inc, a boutique video production company dedicated to narrative filmmaking.

Simran Kaur currently works for the Sikh Coalition, the nation's largest Sikh civil rights organization. Prior to this, Simran managed a health program in Central California. Simran travels regularly for global health projects and has worked to improve access to health for immigrant and refugee communities. She is an active member of the Sikh community in California—volunteering with Jakara Movement, cofounding The Langar Hall, a progressive Sikh blog, and acting as a liaison for Saffron Press, an independent publishing house focused on multicultural literature. She is on the editorial board of the Sikh Love Stories Project and the board of directors for The Women's Building, a women-led community space that advocates self-determination, gender equality, and social justice; additionally, she has served as the Affirmative Action Officer on the board of directors for the American Civil Liberties Union (ACLU) of Northern California.

Sonam Bhimbra graduated from the College of Charleston with a double major in English and biology, and a minor in neuroscience. Sonam writes for a hip-hop blog, is the Queen of cha-making (non-debatable), and is overly zealous about good food and holding babies. In addition, she is a kung fu enthusiast, apocalyptic dystopia theory generator, and has a curious obsession with giving away all belongings and settling down on a farm in Norway. Her favorite authors include Toni Morrison and Junot Diaz.

Subrina Singh is currently a master's candidate of South Asian Studies at the South Asian Institute of Columbia University. She graduated from Stony Brook University in 2013, receiving her BA in Asian and Asian American Studies with a focus on South Asian philosophy and religion. Born and raised in New York, Subrina grew up in a small town on Long Island and currently resides in Riverdale, New York.

Surinder Singh is a Nurse Practitioner (NP) residing in Northern California with her husband and two young children. She enjoyed the adrenaline rush of working as a critical care nurse for eight years prior to becoming an NP. She completed her graduate degree in Michigan and joined her husband's medical practice and practiced

Family Medicine with him for eight years. She has served as a clinical preceptor and lecturer for various Michigan universities. She recently returned to her home state of California and has been caring for veterans in the fields of Orthopedic Surgery and Podiatry. She devotes much of her time giving back to her community by volunteering at her children's schools and The Sikh Family Center, and by teaching bhangra classes. She is extremely passionate about arts and crafts and is an avid foodie who looks forward to opening up her confectionary shop, Singh and Dance Sweets Shop.

About the Editor

© Blake Richards

Meeta Kaur is a writer and the managing editor of the Sikh Love Stories Project. Kaur is committed to the literary arts and the power storytelling has to transform lives. Meeta has written several essays, op-eds, and articles for NPR, *Hyphen* magazine, *Asian Week*, *India West*, and *SikhChic*. As an online *Hyphen* magazine blogger and a Sikh Coalition advocate, she explores civil rights, gender rights, and community issues through essays. Kaur was awarded the Hedgebrook Residency for fiction in 2006 and The Elizabeth George award for fiction in 2008. She graduated with an MFA in creative writing from Mills College, and has taught several students in literature, fiction and nonfiction writing. She has also presented discussions on writing at Mills College, the SAFAR Feminist Conference, and Sikh Lens Film Festival. She looks forward to her next full-length book project in fiction and expanding her world as a writer, speaker, and teacher. She loves spending time with her family, cooking, swimming, traveling, and exploring her spirituality through family and community.

SELECTED TITLES FROM SHE WRITES PRESS

She Writes Press is an independent publishing company
founded to serve women writers everywhere.
Visit us at www.shewritespress.com.

Seeing Red: A Woman's Quest for Truth, Power, and the Sacred
by Lone Morch $16.95, 978-1-938314-12-4
One woman's journey over inner and outer mountains—a quest that
takes her to the holy Mt. Kailas in Tibet, through a seven-year marriage, and into the arms of the fierce goddess Kali, where she discov-
ers her powerful, feminine self.

Daring to Date Again: A Picaresque Memoir by Ann Anderson Evans
$16.95, 978-1-63152-909-2
A hilarious, no-holds-barred memoir about a legal secretary turned
professor who dives back into the dating pool headfirst after twelve
years of celibacy.

*Flip-Flops After Fifty: And Other Thoughts on Aging I Remembered
to Write Down* by Cindy Eastman. $16.95, 978-1-938314-68-1
A collection of frank and funny essays about turning fifty—and all
the emotional ups and downs that come with it.

Tasting Home: Coming of Age in the Kitchen by Judith Newton
$16.95, 978-1-938314-03-2
An extraordinary journey through the cuisines, cultures, and politics of the 1940s through 2011, complete with recipes.

Times They Were A-Changing: Women Remember the '60s & '70s
edited by Kate Farrell, Amber Lea Starfire, and Linda Joy Myers
$16.95, 978-1-938314-04-9
Forty-eight powerful stories and poems detailing the breakthrough
moments experienced by women during the '60s and '70s.

Three Minus One: Parents' Stories of Love & Loss edited by Sean
Hanish and Brooke Warner $17.95, 978-1-938314-80-3
A collection of stories and artwork by parents who have suffered
child loss that offers insight into this unique and devastating
experience.